About The Authors

Dr. George Manning

Dr. Kent Curtis

George Manning is a professor of psychology and business at Northern Kentucky University. He is a consultant to business, industry, and government; his clients include AT&T, Sun Oil, IBM, Marriott Corporation, United Auto Workers, the Internal Revenue Service, and the National Institutes of Health. He lectures on economic and social issues including quality of work life, work force values, and business ethics. He serves as advisor to such diverse industries and professions as energy, transportation, justice, health, finance, labor, commerce, and the military.

He received graduation honors from George Williams College, the University of Cincinnati, and the University of Vienna. He was selected Professor of the Year at Northern Kentucky University, where his teaching areas include management and organization, organizational psychology, and personal adjustment. He maintains an active program of research and study in organizational psychology. His current studies and interests include the changing meaning of work, leadership development, and coping skills for personal and social change.

Kent Curtis has served as an administrator and faculty member at Northern Kentucky University since its inception in 1970. He is a professor in the departments of industrial technology and education. His teaching areas include supervisory development, human relations in business and industry, techniques of research design, counseling, and group dynamics.

He received a baccalaureate degree in biology from Centre College, a master's in counseling from Xavier University, and a doctorate in adult technical education from the University of Cincinnati. He has designed numerous employee and management training and development programs, which are presented to Fortune 500 companies, small businesses, and federal, state, and local government agencies.

Kent also presents open seminars and on-site programs for the Office Productivity Institute and VistaSystems in the areas of time and stress management, communication skills, and team building. His current studies and interests include developing effective "executive pairs" (secretary/manager teams); the manager as an effective teacher; and improving the quality of work life in organizations using employee involvement groups.

HUMAN BEHAVIOR

Why People Do What They Do

GEORGE MANNING

Professor of Psychology
Northern Kentucky University

KENT CURTIS

Professor of Industrial Technology and Education
Northern Kentucky University

U253

VistaSystems

DEVELOPING HUMAN POTENTIAL
A Division of South-Western Publishing Co.

ISBN: 0-538-21253-5
Library of Congress Catalog Card Number: 86-62745

1 2 3 4 5 6 7 8 E 2 1 0 9 8 7

Printed in the United States of America

PREFACE

Each book in *The Human Side of Work* is special in its own way. Many consider *Human Behavior* to be the most interesting. What could be more fascinating than learning why people do what they do? Each section — Motivation, Values, and Personality — rests on solid theoretical footing. But foremost, this is an "applied" book.

Our goal is for you to use the concepts and tools presented in the book to improve your understanding of people and to improve your skills in dealing with others. The result should be a better understanding of why people do what they do and better relationships at work and at home.

Specific topics, questions, and activities include:

- Why do people do what they do? Explore *motivation* on pages 7–17.

- How does employee motivation affect *job performance?* Find out what companies should do to meet employee needs. See pages 17–39.

- Examine *social values* and the role of culture — are you a twenties, thirties, forties, fifties, sixties, seventies, or eighties person? See pages 52–75.

- What type of person are you? Find your *personality traits* on pages 104–125.

- Learn personal adjustment and *coping techniques.* See pages 125–136.

- There are specific stages in life, each with unique developmental tasks. Where do you stand regarding life's *transitions?* See pages 136–146.

HOW TO USE THIS BOOK

This is a desk book for ready reference, a handbook for teaching others, and a workbook for personal development in the areas of motivation, values, and personality. The material is arranged in a logical sequence for learning.

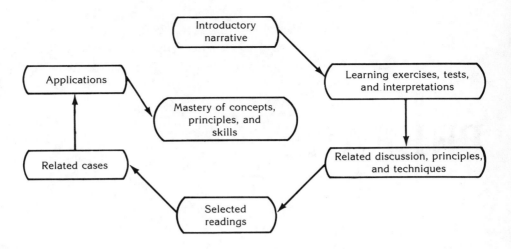

The best approach is to *interact* with the material. Read the narrative, take the tests and exercises, examine the interpretations, and review the principles and techniques — then ask: "How does this apply to me? How can I use this concept or information to improve?" Then take action. Also, use the related readings, cases, and applications to improve your knowledge and skills.

To increase interest and to improve your overall learning, try the following:

1. Use the learning objectives, discussion questions, and study quizzes included in each part of the book. This will focus your reading, improve comprehension, and increase retention of the material.

2. Share the results of your tests and exercises with family, friends, and co-workers. In this way, you can make tangible use of what you learn and may even help others.

3. Write in the book. Use the margins; underline; write your own ideas and personalize the material.

Good luck in your learning!

HOW TO TEACH FROM THIS BOOK

Personalize *Human Behavior* for yourself and for the learner. Use the information, exercises, questions, activities, and tests to complement your own teaching style and resources; use any or all of the materials provided to suit the needs and goals of the group.

Steps

First, scan the material for topics and exercises. Second, outline a curriculum and lesson plan based on time frames and learning goals. Third, arrange learning aids, media, and other resources for smooth instruction.

For assistance in this area, refer to the suggested readings, cases, applications, and films that accompany each part of the text. Also, see Appendix A for suggestions on teaching, testing, and grading as well as for information about other books in *The Human Side of Work* series.

Instruction

Multimedia, multimethod instruction usually works best. Each class period ideally would include a lecture to set the stage, learning exercises to personalize the subject, a discussion to interpret results, and use of related activities such as cases and readings to increase knowledge and skills. A film, followed by group discussion and panel debate, is an ideal learning enhancer. See Appendix C for an annotated list of excellent films.

Final Note

Because this book is easy to read and covers the factual information needed by the learner, class periods should be used primarily for group involvement. Learning activities and group discussion will personalize the subject and promote maximum enjoyment and learning.

Human Behavior: Why People Do What They Do is a popular book. Students relate positively to the topics of motivation, values, and personality. But they won't learn the material unless they get involved with it. As the instructor, the more practical you can make it for them, the better; the more personalized it is, the better. In this spirit, we conclude with a favorite proverb:

> I listen and I hear;
> I see and I remember;
> I do and I understand.
>
> *Confucius* (551–479 B.C.)

Good luck in your teaching!

Request: We want your suggestions. If you have questions or see a way to improve this book, please write. Thank you.

George Manning
Kent Curtis
Northern Kentucky University
Highland Heights, Ky. 41076

ACKNOWLEDGMENTS

The Human Side of Work is written by many people. It is the result of countless hours and endless effort from colleagues, students, and others who have helped in some important way. From initial draft to final form, many hands bring these books to life. To each we are grateful.

For this book, recognition is given to the following scientists and authors whose ideas and findings provide theoretical framework and important factual data:

Gordon Allport
Bernard Berelson
Benjamin Bloom
James Coleman
Erik Erikson
Peter Farb
Viktor Frankl
Sigmund Freud

Erich Fromm
Jay Hall
Harry Harlow
Robert Havighurst
William James
Abraham Maslow
Morris Massey

Douglas McGregor
Karl Menninger
Jean Piaget
Carl Rogers
B. F. Skinner
Gary Steiner
Daniel Yankelovich

Appreciation goes to the following colleagues and supporters for substantive help in research, manuscript review, preparation, and advice:

Angie Boh
Paula Brewer
Robert Caplon
Jerry Carpenter
Ken Carter
Lucien Cohen
B. J. Cummings

Pat Donoghue
Jane Dotson
George Jana Foltz
Charlotte Galloway
Mary Gray
JoAnn Hamilton
Janet Krebs

Julia Malott
Steve McMillen
Amini Mehrdad
George Rogers
Robert Schehr
Vince Schulte
Anna Stegman

Bill Stewart   Sam Vinci   Don Welti
Ralph Tesseneer   Art Walsh   Allison Whaley
James Thomas   Ray Wash   Bonnie Winters
Jerri Thomas   Susan Wehrmeyer

We want to thank J. Ellen Gerken for many of the figures, illustra-tions, and photographs.

George Manning
Kent Curtis

CONTENTS

Behavior

be • hav • ior   (bi-hāv′ yēr), noun, [<behave by analogy with ME. havior, property<OFr. aveir<avoir, to have],1. manner of behaving or acting; actions; conduct. 2. Psychology a) the total of responses of an organism to internal and external stimuli. b) any activity taken as the subject matter of psychology, the study of human and animal behavior. 3. the actions or reactions of persons or things under given circumstances.

A *friend asked Michelangelo:*

"How's the work going at the Sistine Chapel?"

Michelangelo answered:

"About the same. You know, I really never should have started this thing. Four years, on and off, I've been at it. What I really wanted to do was a tomb for Julius II. But they made a decision, and I'm stuck with it. The worst thing is that I had to start at the entrance of the chapel first, which I thought was a stupid idea. But they wanted to keep the chapel open as long as possible while I was working."

His friend inquired:

"What's the difference?"

Michelangelo replied:

"What's the difference? Here I am trying to do a ceiling mural on the creation of man, right? But I have to start with the end of the whole scheme, and then finish with the beginning. Besides, I never painted a ceiling before, and I'm not very experienced at murals either."

The friend sympathized:

"Boy, that's tough."

Michelangelo went on:

"And on top of that, the scaffolding material I have to use is dangerous. The whole thing shakes and wiggles every time I climb up there. One day it's boiling hot, and the next day it's freezing. It's dark most of the time. Working on my back, I swallow as much paint as I put on the ceiling. I can't get any decent help. The long climb up and down the ladders will kill me yet. And to top everything, they are going to let the public in and show the thing off before it's even finished. It won't be finished for another year at least. And that's another thing, they are always nagging me to finish. And when I'm finished, what then? I've got no security. And if they don't like it, I may be out of work permanently."

The friend responded:

"Gee, Michelangelo, that's tough. With no job security, such poor working conditions, irritating company policies, and inadequate subordinates, you must really be dissatisfied with your job. Are you ready to quit?"

Michelangelo replied:

"What? Quit? Are you crazy? It's a fascinating challenge. And I'm learning more and more every day about murals and ceilings. I've been experimenting and changing my style for these last few years, and I'm starting to get a lot of recognition from some very important people. You can see for yourself that it's going to be one of the finest achievements of all time. I'm the only one responsible for the design, and I'm making all of the basic decisions. It may bring me other opportunities to do even more difficult things. Quit? Never. This is a terrific job."

Source: B.J. Cummings, Organizational Psychology, Northern Kentucky University, 1978

PART ONE

Motivation

Learning Objectives

After completing Part One, you will better understand:

1. how biological factors and psychological forces influence human behavior;

2. the normal needs all people have;

3. the programs and activities an organization should offer to meet employee needs;

4. the relationship between employee needs and job performance;

5. the importance of matching the needs of the person with the demands of the job;

6. your own motivation — physical, security, affiliation, social esteem, and self-fulfillment needs.

INTRODUCTION

"I wonder why she acts that way?"
"People! I'll never understand them."
"We've met the enemy, and he is us."

If you have ever had such thoughts as these, this book will be of interest to you. Motivation, values, and personality are subjects that touch everyone, both on the job and in the home. Understanding why people do what they do is important for employee morale and job performance. When the work is done, this understanding is important in dealing with family and friends.

Psalm 8 asks, "What is man that thou art mindful of him?" The scientist answers, "Man is a product of internal and external forces." Each person is the result of interaction between biological heritage and cultural history. The kind of person you are and what you do depend on both raw material (heredity) and what is done with this raw material (how it is shaped and grown). You must eat to live; but whether you eat rice or meat, and whether you use fingers or utensils, are influenced by culture and experience.[1]

The following is a discussion of the world within the person.

THE WORLD WITHIN

Two primary determinants of behavior are within the person — biological factors and psychological forces.

Biological Factors

From the moment of conception, biology plays a major role in your development. Inherited makeup determines such important distinctions as whether you are male, female, black, white, nearsighted, or bald. Each person is born as a unique biological entity. This uniqueness is so fundamental that it influences all of a person's experiences throughout life.[2] It expresses itself in the following ways.

Intelligence. Differences in problem-solving ability are important in determining a person's learning rate and the complexity of problems he or she can solve. Intellectually gifted people have an advantage in nearly all that they attempt. Research shows that they are usually healthier, happier, more emotionally mature, and more likely to achieve in both educational and social activities than are their less advantaged counterparts.[3]

Sensitivity. Even during the first few weeks of life, children differ significantly in their sensitivity to stimulation. Some are startled by even minor sounds and cry if sunlight hits their faces. Others are seemingly insensitive to such stimulation.[4]

Vitality. Observation of any group of babies reveals that they vary considerably in energy and activity levels. This is reflected in differences in exploratory activity and in the tendency of highly vigorous infants to deal with life in a more active, aggressive manner than less vigorous babies. Similar differences in vitality level can be seen in the adult world.[5]

Temperament. Temperament refers to a person's emotional makeup and prevailing moods. From early childhood, some people tend to be unemotional and do not easily become fearful, angry, joyful, or anxious. Others tend to become emotional in the face of even minor events and conditions.[6]

Resistance. From birth through adulthood, people show distinct differences in their vulnerability to both physical and psychological setbacks and in their ability to recuperate from such disturbances.[7]

Appearance. General physical appearance greatly influences the way people are treated, which, in turn, influences feelings of self-confidence, self-worth, and other important aspects of development from an early age onward. As a rule, a pleasing personal appearance results in favorable treatment, and this results in a positive self-image.[8]

Sex Identity. Although whether a person is male or female makes little difference in inherent capacity for most types of achievement, it contributes significantly to individuality because of differing cultural expectations for men and women. In all cultures, there are fairly consistent differences between the sexes in such characteristics as personal interests, athletic ability, intellectual achievement, and emotional response.[9]

To understand the importance of biology in your own life, think of your physical appearance, vitality level, temperament, and gender. How have these factors affected you? These few examples show the important role biology plays in determining what you do and why and how you do it.

Psychological Forces

In addition to biological factors, psychological forces are major determinants of behavior. Dominant among these forces are physical and emotional needs. Sometimes you are conscious of your needs, and sometimes not. In any case, the drive to satisfy needs constitutes the motivation behind all purposeful human behavior, helping to explain why people work, why they have certain personal goals, and what they want in their relationships with others. Psychologist Abraham Maslow divides human needs into five categories.[10]

Survival. Survival is a basic and natural need. Taking a breath of air and acting in self-defense are normal expressions of the need for survival. If asked, "What is important to you?", most people will say, "Life." If asked, "How long do you want to live?", most people will answer, "Forever." Survival needs that motivate behavior include:

- *Health.* Anyone who has ever been sick or felt pain knows the overwhelming desire to get well and feel better.

- *Nutrition.* When you are hungry, you seek food, and it is natural for this need to influence your actions.

- *Exercise.* Who has not felt the normal urge to stretch limbs, tense muscles, and breathe deeply?

- *Rest.* Can you recall a time when the primary thing you wanted to do was to sleep? You needed rest, and your behavior was influenced by this need.

- *Shelter.* Without protection from climate and weather, people become uncomfortable and may even die; the need for shelter can be a powerful motivator.

Survival needs are basic, strong, and natural forces within the person. Psychologist Viktor Frankl tells of his experiences in a Nazi concentration camp during World War II: "What did the prisoner dream about most frequently? Of bread, cake, cigarettes, and nice warm baths."[11] During waking hours prisoners were concerned, above all else, with what they would get for their evening meal and how much would be available. When they received food, they were torn between whether they should consume all of it immediately, or save a part of it for that later time when their stomachs would hurt from hunger. In short, whether awake or asleep, their greatest concern was for the most basic physical needs — food and physical comfort.[12]

Using the space below, cite an instance when your own actions were motivated by survival needs.

_____

_____

_____

_____

_____

Security. Once survival needs are satisfied, security becomes important. Freedom from threat and protection from loss are major security goals, helping to explain our interest in savings accounts, medical insurance, seniority rights, and burglar alarms. People do not want to lose what they have gained.

All ages and types of people experience the need for security. Both the child who is afraid of the dark and the worker who fears unemploy-

ILLUS. 1.1

The need for food is basic and, in some situations, can dominate one's life.

UPI/THE BETTMANN NEWSPHOTOS

ment feel the need for security, and the drive to satisfy this need influences their actions.

Security needs can motivate the behavior of societies as well as individuals. In the United States during the 1950s, fallout shelters were common, and an elaborate civil defense program was in place because of fear of nuclear war. Justifiably or not, people believed that the danger of nuclear war decreased during the 1970s. Consequently, fallout shelters lapsed into ill repair and often went unstocked, and civil defense readiness was reduced during that period. Only in recent years have large numbers of Americans again felt vulnerable, thus motivating a renewed interest in civil defense.[13]

Typically, when people feel they have fair and reasonable protection, such as when they have an early warning system in the case of national security or a financial nest egg in the case of material security, they can tolerate quite a bit of uncertainty. However, if conditions are dangerous or events appear out of control, the need for security can become a powerful motivator.

Can you remember a time when your own behavior was influenced by fear of loss or by the desire to keep something you had acquired?

_____

_____

_____

_____

Love. When survival and security needs are satisfied, the need for affiliation (love) emerges. The need for love is an emotion that people share with other species. Researcher Harry Harlow's classic studies on rhesus monkeys show that the normal growth and development of these animal cousins of ours depends on the satisfaction of affiliation needs.[14]

In the case of people, each person strives to secure a place as an accepted member in a social milieu. This is true for people in all cultures, whether aggressive or peaceful, primitive or advanced. Every individual makes a distinct effort to belong to some aspired social group.[15] If you have ever felt a need for love or a need to express love, you have experienced a natural need for affiliation, and this has influenced your behavior.

The need to give love can be as powerful a motivator as the need to receive love. Consider the following:

> Martha was eleven years old when it was learned that her father was dying of kidney disease. There was only one way to save his life. The situation was explained to everyone—mother, father, and Martha—and the little girl's answer was yes, she would give her kidney to her father.
> On the day of the operation, Martha was placed on one table, her father was placed on the table next to her, and anesthesia was administered. Eight hours later, the little girl opened her eyes, looked at her mother, and asked, "Mommy, am I dead yet?" . . . Martha had misunderstood. She thought that in order to save her daddy's life, she must give up her own. What motivated Martha to do this? Martha was motivated by the need to give love to her daddy.[16]

The need for love is a normal human need. People are psychologically built so that they require this interaction. Studies of children in institutions

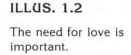

ILLUS. 1.2

The need for love is important.

in which they do not receive affection show that they do not develop normally, in spite of the fact that all of their physical needs are met.[17] The following shows the life-and-death importance of the need for love:

> The evidence is now compelling that emotionally deprived animals, including humans, are less resistant to stress effects and to disease than emotionally satisfied animals; that they have higher morbidity and mortality rates, and that they tend to be less developed physically and behaviorally.
>
> Death is but an extreme consequence of general physical and psychological decline that affects children completely starved of emotional interchange. They die from deprivation of love, just as if they had been deprived of food and died from hunger — for what they indeed die from is an unsatisfied hunger for love.
>
> In the late 1920's, several hospital pediatricians began to introduce a regular regimen of "mothering" in their wards. Dr. J. Brennemann, who for a time had attended an old-fashioned foundling home where the mortality rate was nearer 100 percent than 50 percent, established the rule in his hospital that every baby should be picked up, carried around, and "mothered" several times a day. At Bellevue Hospital in New York, following the institution of "mothering" on the pediatric wards, the mortality rate for infants fell from 55 percent to less than 10 percent.
>
> In short, it was discovered that infants need something more than the satisfaction of basic, physical needs if they are to make any progress — that is, to survive and grow and develop in physical and mental health. That something came to be recognized as what was later called "Tender Loving Care."[18]

More recent evidence of the importance of human interaction comes from studies of children who have been deliberately isolated from human contact by their own families. Usually, they have been locked in an attic room or cellar. In all of these cases, the children are underdeveloped in the areas of motor skills, speech, and socialization. Attempts to socialize them usually result in extremely slow progress, and death often occurs at a very early age. Consider the case of Anna:

> Anna was discovered at the age of six. She had been born illegitimate, and her grandfather had insisted that she be hidden from the world in an attic room. Anna received a bare minimum of physical care and attention and had virtually no opportunities for social interaction. When she was found, she could not talk, walk, keep herself clean, or feed herself; she was totally apathetic, expressionless, and indifferent to human beings. In fact, those who worked with her believed at first that she was deaf and possibly blind as well.
>
> Attempts to socialize Anna had only limited success. The girl died 4 1/2 years later, but during that time, she was able to learn some words and phrases, although she could never speak complete sentences. She also learned to use building blocks, string beads, wash her hands, brush her teeth, follow directions, and treat a doll with affection. She learned to walk, but could run only clumsily. By the time of her death at almost eleven, Anna had reached the level of socialization of a child of two or three.
>
> Kingsley Davis (1948) comments: "Here was a human organism who had missed nearly six years of socialization. Her condition shows how little her purely biological resources, when acting alone, could contribute to making her a complete person."[19]

People need more than the basic biological and physical necessities. Human contact, affection, and love are essential for normal growth and development. Indeed life itself depends on it. The words of social psychologist Erich Fromm summarize our need for love:

> Man is torn away from the primary union with nature that characterizes animal existence. Having at the same time reason and imagination, he is aware of his aloneness and separateness, of his powerlessness and ignorance, of the accidentalness of his birth, and of his death. He could not face this state of being for a second if he could not find new ties with his fellow man that replace the old ones, regulated by instincts. . . . The necessity to unite with other living beings, to be related to them, is an imperative need on the fulfillment of which man's sanity depends. This need is behind all phenomena that constitute the whole gamut of intimate relations, of all passions that are called love in the broadest sense of the word.[20]

Use the space below to describe a time or situation in your life when you needed to give or to receive love. _____

_____

_____

_____

_____

Respect. Once survival, security, and affiliation needs are satisfied, people are motivated by the need for social esteem (respect) — the need to be considered favorably by others. The pursuit of fame, regardless of the field — business, government, the arts — can only be explained by this powerful need. It is natural to want the recognition and respect of others; when this need is not satisfied, an individual feels inferior, weak, and discouraged. William James, the father of American psychology, writes:

> We are not only gregarious animals, liking to be in sight of our fellows, but we have an innate propensity to get ourselves noticed, and noticed favorably, by our kind. No more fiendish punishment could be devised, were such a thing physically possible, than that one should be turned loose in society and remain absolutely unnoticed by all the members thereof.[21]

The need for recognition is a major determinant of behavior from youth through adulthood:

- a youngster may excel in school to win the praise of parents;
- a teenager may diet or exercise to be considered attractive by the opposite sex;
- a young adult may choose a certain career or mate to achieve the respect and admiration of others;
- an older adult may build a business or become a community leader to be considered successful.

The need for social esteem is the motivating force behind each of these behaviors. To evaluate this motive in your own life, consider the following questions: Do you dress up when you go out? Do you clean house when you expect company? Do you "put your best foot forward" on the job? What have you done, or what are you doing now, that is an expression of your need for respect? _____

_____

_____

_____

_____

Fulfillment. After physical and social needs are satisfied, people are motivated by the need for self-fulfillment. Self-fulfilled people may or may not please others by what they do, and their efforts may or may not result in the attainment of intended goals. Regardless of consequences, if a person does something because it is valued personally, then the act itself is fulfilling.

In studying the characteristics of the self-fulfilled person, Maslow identified people he believed were living rich, fulfilled lives. Included were Albert Einstein, Eleanor Roosevelt, Ludwig van Beethoven, and Albert Schweitzer.[22] Maslow found that these people shared 15 characteristics:

- *Acceptance of self and others.* Self-fulfilled people accept themselves and others as they are. They place a high value on every person as a unique individual and accept individual differences as normal and even desirable.

- *Accurate perception of reality.* Self-fulfilled people have the ability to see events and conditions as they actually are, without denying painful or unpleasant information. Their assessments and judgments are realistic.

- *Intimacy.* Self-fulfilled people are able to have close, intimate friendships in which they reveal themselves fully. They are easily able to express and receive affection.

- *Personal autonomy.* Self-fulfilled people are self-sufficient, with the strength to stand alone when necessary. They will stick by their personal convictions, even when others disagree. This strength helps them to survive crises and losses.

- *Goal-directedness.* Self-fulfilled people have a sense of purpose in life. They make decisions based on life goals, even if this means temporary sacrifice and frustration.

- *Spontaneity.* Self-fulfilled people are spontaneous and natural. They respond to life in an effortless way and are not bound by social convention.

The nine remaining characteristics of the self-fulfilled person are as follows: a need for privacy; an appreciation for new experiences; a sense of unity with nature; a sense of brotherhood with all people; the ability to relate to others without consideration of race, religion, or creed; distinct ideas of what is right and wrong; a sense of humor; creativity; and the ability to resist cultural influences that run counter to personal principles.[23]

In summary, Maslow writes about the self-fulfilled person:

> I have found none of my subjects to be chronically unsure about the difference between right and wrong in his actual living. Whether or not they could verbalize the matter, they rarely showed in their day-to-day living the chaos, confusion, inconsistency, or conflict that are so common in the average person's ethical dealings. Further, the self-fulfilled person practically never allows convention to hamper him or inhibit him from doing anything that he considers very important or basic.[24]

To evaluate your development as a self-fulfilled person, complete the following exercise.

CHARACTERISTICS OF THE SELF-FULFILLED PERSON

Directions

Rate yourself on the following characteristics. Circle the number that best represents your current status (1 is low; 10 is high).

Acceptance of self and others

1   2   3   4   5   6   7   8   9   10

Accurate perception of reality

1   2   3   4   5   6   7   8   9   10

Close relationships

1   2   3   4   5   6   7   8   9   10

Personal autonomy (independence)

1   2   3   4   5   6   7   8   9   10

Goal-directedness; achievement orientation

1   2   3   4   5   6   7   8   9   10

Naturalness (spontaneity)

1   2   3   4   5   6   7   8   9   10

Need for privacy

1   2   3   4   5   6   7   8   9   10

Orientation toward growth and new experience

1   2   3   4   5   6   7   8   9   10

Sense of unity with nature

1   2   3   4   5   6   7   8   9   10

Sense of brotherhood with all people

1   2   3   4   5   6   7   8   9   10

Democratic character

1   2   3   4   5   6   7   8   9   10

Sense of justice

1   2   3   4   5   6   7   8   9   10

Sense of humor

1   2   3   4   5   6   7   8   9   10

Creativity

1   2   3   4   5   6   7   8   9   10

Personal integrity (high principles)

1   2   3   4   5   6   7   8   9   10

SCORING AND INTERPRETATION

How did you do on the Characteristics of a Self-fulfilled Person test? The following scale will help you to assess your progress toward becoming a self-fulfilled person. Add up the numbers you circled to find your total, then compare it with the following scale:

If Your Score Is:	Your Progress Is:
15– 45	Not great — Should definitely improve
46–120	Just OK — Needs work
121–150	Very good — Keep going!

The three characteristics I want to improve are: _____

_____

_____

_____

_____

_____

_____

_____

Before an individual can experience the need for self-fulfillment, certain cognitive structures of the brain must be developed. Only with maturation of the higher centers of the nervous system is a person capable of abstract reasoning and independent value judgments. Psychologist Jean Piaget, in his cognitive theory of human development, refers to this as the "formal operations stage," which covers the period from adolescence to adulthood.

In the early teens (approximately age twelve), the potential to think as an adult usually develops and continues to mature for several years. During this period, individuals are able to think abstractly about such things as creativity, achievement, and fulfillment. From this time onward, the young person may be motivated to satisfy self-fulfillment needs.[25]

> The essential difference is that adolescents and adults are no longer tied to concrete and specific objects in their logical thought. They can perform all of the operations entirely in their heads. During this period, children's cognitive structures become mature. They acquire all of the cognitive capability and mental powers of an adult. This does not mean that their thinking is equivalent to that of an adult; rather, it means that they have developed the potential to think as adults do. The content, function and use to which they may apply their intellectual powers will be enriched throughout adulthood, but all of the structures of intelligence have emerged.[26]

Although an individual may appear to behave independently prior to adolescence, only the maturely functioning human brain can discover, define, and express independent views on what is good, bad, right, and wrong.[27]

Once self-fulfillment is experienced, the need for it can become a dominant determinant of behavior, overriding all other motives, including needs for survival, security, love, and respect. Further, if a person seeks self-fulfillment but is unfulfilled, discontent and mental anguish can be expected. In Maslow's words, at this level of motivation, "a musician must make music, an artist must paint, and a poet must write, if he is to be at peace with himself."[28]

The English author-philosopher Julian Huxley summarizes the need for self-fulfillment with the following:

Human life is a struggle—against frustration, ignorance, suffering, evil, the maddening inertia of things in general; but it is also a struggle for something. Fulfillment seems to describe better than any other single word the positive side of human development and human evolution—the realization of inherent capacities by the individual and of new possibilities by the race; the satisfaction of needs, spiritual as well as material; the emergence of new qualities of experience to be enjoyed; the building of personalities.[29]

Is there something that you do, or have done, that is the result of your own need for fulfillment? Explain briefly.

_____

_____

_____

_____

_____

MOTIVATION IN THE WORK SETTING

The following exercise evaluates motivation in the work setting. By completing this test, you will better understand the role of needs in the world of work.

MOTIVATION AT WORK— WHAT ARE YOUR NEEDS?

Directions

Rank your responses for each of the following questions. The response that is most important or most true for you should receive a 5; the next should receive a 4; the next a 3; the next a 2; and the least important or least true should receive a 1.

Example

The work I like best involves:

A   _4_   Working alone.

B   _3_   A mixture of time spent with people and time spent alone.

> *Source:* *This questionnaire is based on the concepts presented by Abraham Maslow in* Motivation and Personality *(New York: Harper & Brothers, 1954); interpretation is based on Jay Hall,* Understanding Motivation at Work According to Types of Needs.

C   1   Giving speeches.

D   2   Discussion with others.

E   5   Working outdoors.

1. Overall, the most important thing to me about a job is whether or not:

A _____ The pay is sufficient to meet my needs.

B _____ It provides the opportunity for fellowship and good human relations.

C _____ It is a secure job with good employee benefits.

D _____ It allows me freedom and the chance to express myself.

E _____ There is opportunity for advancement, based on my achievements.

2. If I were to quit a job, it would probably be because:

A _____ It was a dangerous job, such as working with inadequate equipment or poor safety procedures.

B _____ Continued employment was questionable because of uncertainties in business conditions or funding sources.

C _____ It was a job people looked down on.

D _____ It was a one-person job, allowing little opportunity for discussion and interaction with others.

E _____ The work lacked personal meaning to me.

3. For me, the most important rewards in working are those that:

A _____ Come from the work itself—important and challenging assignments.

B _____ Satisfy the basic reasons why people work—good pay, a good home, and other economic needs.

C _____ Are provided by fringe benefits—such as hospitalization insurance, time off for vacations, security for retirement, etc.

D _____ Reflect my ability—such as being recognized for the work I do and knowing I am one of the best in my company or profession.

E _____ Come from the human aspects of working—that is, the opportunity to make friends and to be a valued member of a team.

4. My morale would suffer most in a job in which:

A _____ The future was unpredictable.

B _____ Other employees received recognition, when I didn't, for doing the same quality of work.

C _____ My co-workers were unfriendly or held grudges.

D _____ I felt stifled and unable to grow.

E _____ The job environment was poor—no air conditioning; inconvenient parking; insufficient space and lighting; primitive toilet facilities.

5. In deciding whether or not to accept a promotion, I would be most concerned with whether:

A _____ The job was a source of pride and would be viewed with respect by others.

B _____ Taking the job would constitute a gamble on my part, and I could lose more than I gained.

C _____ The economic rewards would be favorable.

D _____ I would like the new people I would be working with, and whether or not we would get along.

E _____ I would be able to explore new areas and do more creative work.

6. The kind of job that brings out my best is one in which:

A _____ There is a family spirit among employees and we all share good times.

B _____ The working conditions—equipment, materials, and basic surroundings—are physically safe.

C _____ Management is understanding and there is little chance of losing my job.

D _____ I can see the returns on my work from the standpoint of personal values.

E _____ There is recognition for achievement.

7. I would consider changing jobs if my present position:

A _____ Did not offer security and fringe benefits.

B _____ Did not provide a chance to learn and grow.

C _____ Did not provide recognition for my performance.

D _____ Did not allow close personal contacts.

E _____ Did not provide economic rewards.

8. The job situation that would cause the most stress for me is:

A _____ Having a serious disagreement with my co-workers.

B _____ Working in an unsafe environment.

C _____ Having an unpredictable supervisor.

D _____ Not being able to express myself.

E _____ Not being appreciated for the quality of my work.

9. I would accept a new position if:

A _____ The position would be a test of my potential.

B _____ The new job would offer better pay and physical surroundings.

C _____ The new job would be secure and offer long-term fringe benefits.

D _____ The position would be respected by others in my organization.

E _____ Good relationships with co-workers and business associates were probable.

10. I would work overtime if:

A _____ The work is challenging.

B _____ I need the extra income.

C _____ My co-workers are also working overtime.

D _____ I must do it to keep my job.

E _____ The company recognizes my contribution.

SCORING

How did you do on the Motivation at Work test? First, place the values you gave A, B, C, D, and E for each question in the spaces provided in the score key in Figure 1.1. Notice that the letters are not always in the same place for each question. Then, add up each column and obtain a total score for each of the motivation levels.

The five motivation levels are as follows (each will be discussed in the Interpretation section):

Level I   Physical needs

Level II   Security needs

Level III   Affiliation needs

Level IV   Social esteem needs

Level V   Self-fulfillment needs

FIGURE 1.1

Score Key

	I	II	III	IV	V
Question 1	A	C	B	E	D
Question 2	A	B	D	C	E
Question 3	B	C	E	D	A
Question 4	E	A	C	B	D
Question 5	C	B	D	A	E
Question 6	B	C	A	E	D
Question 7	E	A	D	C	B
Question 8	B	C	A	E	D
Question 9	B	C	E	D	A
Question 10	B	D	C	E	A
TOTAL SCORE					
	I	II	III	IV	V
	MOTIVATION LEVELS				

Next, make a picture of your motivation at work on the "Motivation Graph" in Figure 1.2. Find the number on the scale that corresponds to each motivation level, and draw a line across that point in the column. Then fill in the area creating a bar chart of your needs at work (see Figure 1.3).

The highest points of your motivation graph indicate the most important needs identified by you in your work. The lowest points show those needs that have been relatively well satisfied or de-emphasized by you at this time.

FIGURE 1.2

Motivation Graph

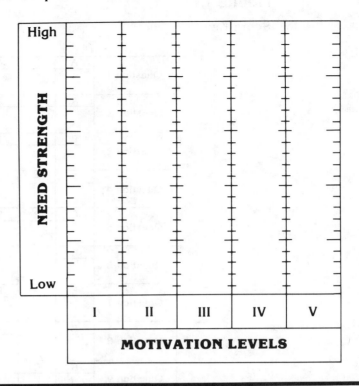

FIGURE 1.3

Sample Motivation Graph

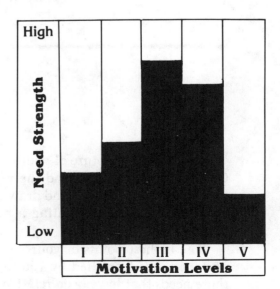

INTERPRETATION

The following is a description of the five motivation levels. Also included are policies and practices an organization should consider to help satisfy employee needs at each motivation level.

First Motivation Level — Physical Needs

People motivated at the first level are concerned with physical and economic survival. If they do not presently have a job, they feel the need to find one. If they do have a job, their goal is to keep it and to have a safe work environment. There is also concern for comfort and the avoidance of physical irritations such as inadequate space, inefficient equipment, and inconvenient parking, rest room, and eating facilities.

A worker motivated at the first motivation level is concerned primarily with issues that are secondary to the job being done. Any job that meets physical and economic needs is acceptable, and the nature of the work itself is relatively unimportant.

Physical needs may dominate the behavior of a person who has no job or who is in economic difficulty. Consider the plight of millions of people during the Great Depression, or that of an individual today who has lost a job, whose children need clothing, and whose dependent parents are ill; or consider Ma's words in John Steinbeck's *The Grapes of Wrath:*

> But I like to think how nice it's gonna be, maybe, in California. Never cold. An' fruit ever'place, an' people just bein' in the nicest places, little white houses in among the orange trees. I wonder — that is, if we all get jobs an' all work — maybe we can get one of them little white houses. An' the little fellas go out an' pick oranges right off the tree. They ain't gonna be able to stand it, they'll get to yellin' so.[30]

An organization can meet the physical needs of its employees by providing sufficient pay and safe working conditions. A living wage and a safe working environment are basic employee concerns. Also, a supportive physical environment, with good lighting, heat, air conditioning, and rest rooms, is necessary to meet needs of the first motivation level.

Does your organization meet the physical needs of its employees? Evaluate on a scale of 1 to 10 (1 is low; 10 is high). _____

Second Motivation Level — Security Needs

People motivated at the second level feel the need for security and predictability in their lives. They want assurance that their jobs are not subject to loss or change. As such, there is a concern for benefits of a protective nature, such as health insurance, retirement income, and seniority rights. There is also a need for signs of stability from upper management.

The second motivation level, like the first, involves issues that are peripheral to the work itself; therefore, any job that provides economic protection and a dependable work environment will be valued by the person motivated at this level.

Security needs may erupt at all levels of responsibility and in all lines of work if business conditions are poor or if managers act in a threatening way. Think of how you would feel if you sensed that your job was in jeopardy; or imagine the concern you would feel if the equipment, supplies, and other resources required to perform your job were taken away.

An organization can meet the security needs of its employees by providing:

- proper tools, equipment, and materials to do the job;
- job aids, such as training manuals and technical assistance;
- economic protection through insurance and retirement programs;
- job security through career counseling, in-service training, and seniority systems;
- confidence in management through stable and dependable actions of managers.

How well does your organization meet its employees' security needs? Evaluate on a 1 to 10 scale. _____

Third Motivation Level — Affiliation Needs

People motivated at the third level are concerned with being an accepted member of the work group or organizational family. A sense of belonging and the giving and receiving of support are important incentives at this level.

When affiliation needs are the primary source of motivation, employees value work as an opportunity for establishing warm and satisfying human relationships. Jobs that allow them the opportunity to interact with people and to create friendships are likely to be valued, regardless of the nature of the work itself. A person motivated at this level may be more interested in human relations than job duties when considering which career to pursue or which company to join.

Employee needs for affiliation are normal. How these needs are met (whether by counterproductive cliques and gripe sessions or by constructive work groups and employee meetings) can influence the success of an organization.

An organization can meet the affiliation needs of its employees by providing the following:

- communication sessions between employees and management (these are most effective when conducted in small groups);
- celebration of holidays, birthdays, and special events;
- expressions of consideration, such as notes of appreciation, hospital visits, and sympathetic understanding when employees have personal problems;

Some jobs provide warm and satisfying human relationships.

- job participation vehicles, such as regular staff meetings, annual employee meetings, employee task forces, committees, and quality circles;

- communication outlets, such as employee newsletters, notices from management, bulletin boards, and annual reports; and, most important,

- an open-door policy in which every employee feels free to share concerns and suggestions with every other employee, regardless of level of responsibility.

How well does your organization support the affiliation needs of its employees? Rate conditions on a 1 to 10 scale. _____

Fourth Motivation Level — Social Esteem Needs

The fourth motivation level reflects a person's need for recognition. The respect of others for one's special traits or competencies is important. Based on social esteem, the individual develops a sense of self-worth.

This is the first motivation level that is closely related to the nature of the work and depends on aspects of the job itself for satisfaction. Work that provides the opportunity to display skills that one feels others respect will be valued and will have motivation strength. The person who is primarily interested in self-image or reputation is motivated at the fourth motivation level.

An organization can meet its employees' needs for recognition by providing:

- individual incentives for high performance, such as achievement awards, worker-of-the-month honors, attendance awards, and recognition for suggestions;

- public acclaim for outstanding contributions at award banquets, retirement dinners, and annual meetings;

- opportunities to improve job status through training programs, job titles, and promotions;

- tangible rewards like increased pay, commemorative plaques, letters of recognition, gifts, and privileges; and most important,

- day-to-day recognition and praise for a job well done.

Does your organization provide recognition for employees' achievements? Evaluate on a scale of 1 to 10. _____

Fifth Motivation Level — Self-Fulfillment Needs

When a person is motivated at the fifth level, his or her primary concern is to express personal values and to experience growth. There is an interest in mental and emotional challenges and a desire to demonstrate life values on the job. Writer Studs Terkel explains the motivation of employees at the fifth level:

> It's about a search, too, for daily meaning as well as for daily bread, for recognition as well as cash, for astonishment rather than torpor; in short, for a sort of life rather than a Monday through Friday sort of dying.[31]
>
> There are, of course, the happy few who find a savor in their daily job: The Indiana stonemason who looks upon his work and sees it is good; the Chicago piano tuner who seeks and finds a sound that delights; the bookbinder who saves a piece of history; the Brooklyn fireman who saves a piece of life.
>
> But don't these satisfactions, like Jude's hunger for knowledge, tell us more about the person than about the task? Perhaps. Nonetheless, there is a common attribute here: a meaning to their task well over and beyond the reward of the paycheck.[32]

The nature of one's work is particularly critical for satisfying self-fulfillment needs, because the job itself must allow a good deal of freedom of expression and opportunity for experimentation. When the fifth motivation level is dominant, the individual channels more creative and constructive energy into the work activity than he or she would if motivated solely by the need for social esteem, social acceptance, economic security, or physical safety.

An organization can meet the self-fulfillment needs of its employees by:

- discussing organization values and goals in light of individual values and goals, and tailoring job duties to accomplish both;

- providing the opportunity for personal growth, through both on-the-job assignments and after-hours activities. For example, an organization may support an employee's involvement in community service activities or may support his or her continuing education efforts.

How well does your organization meet its employees' needs for self-fulfillment? Evaluate on a 1 to 10 scale. _____

MOTIVATION — 14 POINTS TO REMEMBER

There are 14 points to remember about human motivation. With these in mind, you will be able to understand why people do what they do, both on the job and in their lives away from work. These points can also explain the complicated relationship between personal goals and work behavior.

The welfare worker studied the involved questionnaire on the table before her, and then regarded the work-worn mother of four. "I just don't understand why you work so hard while your husband simply refuses to get a job. You not only work outside during the day, but when you come home in the evening, you have to cook and take care of your children and your home. Why do you insist on making a living for your whole family, while that trifling husband of yours does nothing?" The woman listened to the scolding in silence, and then answered simply, "I make the livin' 'cause my man makes the livin' worthwhile."[33]

- *Personal needs motivate behavior.* People are motivated by the needs they personally feel; they do what they do for their own reasons. Consider the following:

  Do you know why your co-workers, family, and friends behave as they do? What personal need is each trying to satisfy? Explain briefly. _____

  _____

  _____

  _____

  _____

  _____

- *A satisfied need is not a motivator.* It is not what people have that motivates behavior; it is what they do not have, or what they have done without. One person may be motivated never to be hungry again; another, never to be dependent again; another, by a need for love; another, to be somebody someday; and yet another, by a need for self-expression. Each is motivated by a need that is not fully satisfied.

  Understanding people involves gaining insight into their unsatisfied needs. The principle is that a satisfied need is not a motivator; only unsatisfied needs motivate behavior. Think of the people with whom you live and work. The minute one need is satisfied, up comes another. Try as you may, it seems you can never completely fill a person's motivational cup. This fact can be exasperating until you realize that you yourself are this way as well. It is human nature to want what you do not presently have.

  With this in mind, look at your own motivation graph. Your highest motivation levels represent unsatisfied needs, and your work must allow the satisfaction of these needs if you are to be both happy and productive. If your employer were to provide more satisfaction of lower level needs, you would probably appreciate it, but this would not cause you to do anything differently. It would not motivate you, because these needs are already filled and therefore are not as important to you as those that are not. Again, only unsatisfied needs motivate behavior.

  What needs have you satisfied? What unsatisfied needs are important to you? What motivates you on the job? Discuss briefly.

  _____

  _____

  _____

  _____

  _____

  _____

- *Motivation levels explain work force behavior.* To show how the principle "a satisfied need is not a motivator" applies in the work setting, imagine a group of employees with the motivation graph in Figure 1.4. In this case, providing higher wages (motivation level I) and increasing security (motivation level II) would not satisfy the true needs of the work group. Employees may ask for these benefits because they are tangible and traditional, and they would probably appreciate them. But more money and increased security will not significantly change the employees' job satisfaction or job performance because these are not the primary needs that concern them.

FIGURE 1.4

Employee Needs

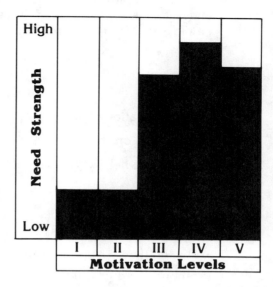

For this group of employees, a family or team spirit and a sense of belonging should be fostered in order to satisfy needs at the third motivation level; pride in workmanship and pride in the company should be created to meet needs at the fourth motivation level; and opportunities for growth and self-expression should be provided to satisfy needs at the fifth motivation level.

Managers should be sensitive to employee needs and should provide programs and activities to motivate people at every level. In this way, employee morale and job performance will be maximized. Note that different workers experience different needs at different times. As much as possible, each person should be considered individually. Figure 1.5 shows the importance of understanding employee needs.

The turnover rate for American industry in 1981 was 48 percent; 4 percent of the work force changed jobs every month.[34] How much turnover do you think was caused by discrepancies between what employees wanted and what managers provided? Discuss briefly. _____

_____

_____

_____

FIGURE 1.5

How Managers and Employees Rate Ten Job Factors

When employees were asked to rate what was important to them and managers were asked what they thought was important to employees, the differences were dramatic.*

Job Factors	Average Worker Rating	Average Supervisor Rating
Full appreciation of work done	1	8
Feeling "in" on things	2	9
Sympathetic help with personal problems	3	10
Job security	4	2
Good wages	5	1
Work that keeps you interested	6	5
Promotion and growth in the organization	7	3
Personal loyalty to workers	8	6
Good working conditions	9	4
Tactful disciplining	10	7

*What workers rated as 1, 2, and 3, their managers rated as 8, 9, and 10. Also, while managers thought that good wages would be the primary concern of their employees, the workers themselves rate it a mere 5.

Source: William C. Menninger and Harry Levinson, Human Understanding in Industry *(Chicago: Science Research Associates, 1956). Reprinted by permission.*

- *Self-actualization is the normal goal for people.* In the process of self-actualization, each lower level need must be satisfied before a person can experience the next higher level need. An individual must achieve firm footing on the first rung before proceeding to the next, and so on to the top of the ladder. The sequence is as follows: The satisfaction of survival needs leads to the experience of security needs; when security needs are satisfied, the individual feels the need for love. When this need is met, respect becomes important; when this need is satisfied, the individual experiences the need for fulfillment, the highest possible motivation level. The higher a person is able to progress on this ladder of needs, the greater the degree of self-actualization that he or she will experience as a human being.[35]

The oracle of Delphi said, "Know thyself"; Ralph Waldo Emerson said, "Trust thyself"; Søren Kierkegaard said, "Choose thyself"; and Albert Camus said, "Be thyself." These, then, are the challenges for the self-actualized person: You must know who you are; you must have confidence in your ability to cope with life; you must make choices and take responsibility for your life; and you must be true to your nature.[36]

How high have you progressed on the ladder of motivational needs? Discuss briefly. _____

_____

_____

_____

_____

• *People experience needs on all five motivation levels.* A chimpanzee will perform an arbitrary task, such as playing poker, in order to receive food and thus physically survive. A chimp will also play poker in order to maintain comfort and thus satisfy security needs, or in order to be an accepted member of the group, thus meeting affiliation needs. Finally, a chimp will play poker with the goal of being respected and admired by the other chimps, thus meeting the need for social esteem. But, other than from idle curiosity, a chimpanzee will not play poker — or do anything else — apart from survival, security, affiliation, and social esteem needs. A chimpanzee will not do something because the act itself is valued as a means of self-fulfillment; and neither will children prior to adolescence. Neither the chimp nor the young child has the cognitive skills of the maturely functioning human brain, the seat of abstract reasoning and independent value judgments.[37]

Both chimps and young children respond best to training by example, prescription, and reinforcement. Models and guidelines for behavior reduce confusion for them and facilitate their growth. However, after puberty, some people behave primarily to satisfy self-fulfillment needs. If work and social relationships are to be satisfying and productive for these people, there must be ample opportunity for freedom of expression and personal growth.

What can an organization do to meet employee needs at each motivation level? Discuss. _____

_____

_____

_____

- *Psychological needs and social values are not the same.* Both Adolf Hitler and Mahatma Gandhi may have been motivated by the need for respect (the fourth motivation level), but their actions reflected different social values. One believed in totalitarianism and war, and the other struggled for democratic ideals through nonviolent demonstration. Similarly, two employees may be motivated by self-fulfillment needs — both behaving for self-discovered, self-defined reasons. Yet the actions of one may harm other people, while the actions of the other may help others. The psychological forces are the same, but the values are not. Psychological needs explain human motivation; social values are the concern of ethics.

  Can you think of people whose motivation levels are the same, but whose values are different? Describe them briefly. _____

  _____

  _____

  _____

- *Different needs influence behavior at different times during a person's day and life.* Within a 24 hour period, you may eat breakfast because you are hungry (physical needs), go to work in order to keep your job (security needs), interact with co-workers in a friendly manner (affiliation needs), go out with an attractive person to impress other people (social esteem needs), and write poetry as a means of self-expression (self-fulfillment needs).

  To understand how different needs can dominate your behavior at different periods of your life, consider the case of Abram, a young employee who takes his first job with a large accounting firm. The initial interview and the young accountant's successful efforts to locate housing remove his concerns about base salary and shelter [see physical needs — Figure 1.6(a)]. Because the new accountant has a wife and a small child, he seeks information about job stability and medical coverage and other fringe benefits. This information, coupled with a long discussion with his supervisor about job security, satisfies his concerns about these factors, and he takes the job [see security needs — Figure 1.6(b)]. Once on the job, frequent social interactions with his supervisor, fellow workers, and clients prove to be most satisfying, and he becomes an accepted member of the firm [see affiliation needs — Figure 1.6(c)]. As time passes, the accountant concentrates more and more effort on doing his job as effectively as possible. Within three years, Abram receives a promotion to the position of senior staff accountant [see social esteem needs — Figure 1.6(d)]. Subsequent years find the accountant in the newly created position of Director of Administrative Services, the external consulting arm of the accounting firm. His outside activities include participation in civic, school board, and charitable affairs, plus a revitalized interest in building furniture in his garage workshop [see self-fulfillment needs—Figure 1.6(e)].

At what motivation level are you in your career? Are you experiencing the same or different needs in your work and home life? Explain. _____

FIGURE 1.6

The Career of an Accounting Graduate

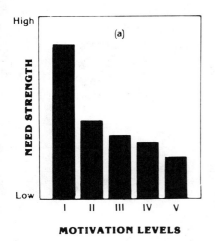
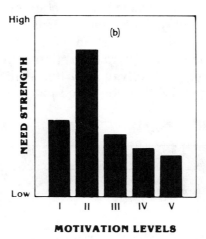
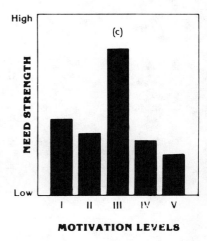
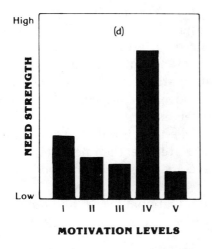
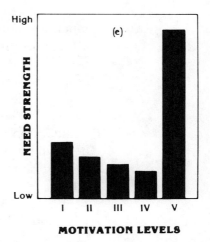

Source: From Management and Performance *by Andrew D. Szilagyi, Jr. Copyright © 1981 by Scott, Foresman & Company. Reprinted with permission.*

_____

_____

_____

_____

_____

• *The same act can satisfy any of the five motivation levels.* Consider that a person may work for any of the following reasons: (1) because there is no food to eat, thus meeting survival needs; (2) because job stability is in danger, thus meeting security needs; (3) to be an accepted member of a work group, trade, or profession, thereby meeting affiliation needs; (4) to be recognized as important, skillful, or otherwise worthy of admiration, thus meeting social esteem needs; (5) for the personal satisfaction experienced doing the job, thereby meeting self-fulfillment needs.

   At what motivation level is your organization operating? Why do people put extra effort into their jobs? What is the organizational norm — survival, security, affiliation, social esteem, or self-fulfillment? Why would you put forth extra effort at work? Explain.

_____

_____

_____

_____

• *All people have the same needs, but to different degrees and accompanied by different wants.* Although all people have the same psychological needs, what it takes to satisfy these needs and how much is required are unique to each person. To illustrate: (1) Sue's affection satisfies Bill's need for affiliation, while Jim's affiliation needs are satisfied by acceptance into his work group. Bill and Jim require different amounts of affiliation to satisfy their needs because some people require more love than others; (2) Jill's need for social esteem will be satisfied when she is recognized as a successful actress, while Karen's need for social esteem is reflected in her goal of owning her own business. Jill and Karen feel their needs to different degrees because some people have a greater need for ego satisfaction than others.

   What satisfies your motivational needs, and how much of it do you require? Discuss briefly. _____

_____

_____

_____

- *A person can be deficiency motivated, bringing harm to self or others.* It is possible to have an extreme fixation on a natural need, so strong that it can lead to neurotic and even destructive behavior. To illustrate, a person can be so hungry for love that the need becomes destructive. Gustave Flaubert, for example, describes Madame Bovary's relationship with her husband as follows:

> She had to have her chocolate every morning, attentions without end. She constantly complained of her nerves, her chest, her liver. The noise of footsteps made her ill. When people went away, solitude became odious to her; if they came back, it was doubtless to see her die.
>
> When Charles returned in the evening, she stretched forth two long thin arms from beneath the sheets, put them around his neck, and having him sit down on the edge of the bed, began to talk to him of her troubles: he was neglecting her; he loved another; she had been warned she would be unhappy; and she ended by asking him for a dose of medicine and a little more love.[38]

No matter how much Charles showed his wife that he loved her, she was never satisfied, and in the end, her need for proof that she was loved ended in tragedy. Similarly, the need for respect and social esteem can be so consuming that it becomes harmful. Jett Rink, in the novel *Giant*, is an example of this type of person. At one point, Rink says:

> Look, someday I'm going to have more money than any Benedict ever laid hands on. Everybody in Texas is going to hear about me. I ain't sitting here sleeping with my eyes open. I'm going to be a millionaire and I ain't kidding. I'm going to have a million dollars. I'm going to have a billion. I'm going to have a zillion.[39]

However successful Rink became, his ego demanded more, and in the end, an insatiable need for recognition ended in destruction.

In contrast, the healthy individual is growth motivated and reasons, "I have satisfied this need; now I am ready to satisfy other needs." This point is important in interpersonal relations, especially superior-subordinate relationships such as teaching and counseling. For example, when someone is deficiency motivated and psychologically "stuck" at one of the need levels (except the fifth), direction from others is needed. In this case, help and advice from the wise would be appropriate. On the other hand, when someone is growth motivated, the primary need is for understanding and nonpossessive caring. Those who want to help should listen in a nonjudgmental and nondirective way as the person talks and discovers his or her own answers.[40]

Are you psychologically stuck, or are you growth motivated? Which people in your life require intervention and advice, and which ones require nonjudgmental listening and nonpossessive caring? Explain. _____

_____

_____

_____

_____

- *Unsatisfied needs can make you ill, as surely as if you were physically stricken.* If you feel the need for recognition, but no one respects you; if you feel the need for love, but no one cares; if you feel the need for self-expression, but have no outlets, you can develop motivation malaise, an emotional condition as harmful as physical illness. Frustration can result in depression. Therefore, a person's environment should be supportive and should allow for the satisfaction of psychological needs.[41]

  To understand the importance of satisfying one's psychological needs, consider the following:

  > Tim went to Greenwich Village to paint. He felt the need to express himself, and art was to be the means. The fact that no one else liked his work, and that he could not sell his paintings, mattered little to Tim; he was happy. Then Tim met Sarah. They fell in love and were married.
  >
  > A year later, twins were born to Tim and Sarah. With this change in his life, Tim's mind turned to food, clothing, and other needs for the children. Soon he went to work in an automobile factory as a production worker. Tim loved his family, and he was proud of himself for sacrificing his need for self-expression — his desire to paint — in the interest of his family.
  >
  > By the time four years had passed, Tim was experiencing poor physical health and recurrent mental depression. His inner need to paint, sidetracked because of the need to earn a living, would not be quieted. He felt incomplete and unhappy. Tim developed problems at work and became increasingly irritable.
  >
  > Tim's health, job, and family problems were the result of motivation malaise — the needs of the individual and the demands of his world were out of step.

  Tim's situation is not unusual in America today. Increasingly, our culture and economy are on opposite courses: while the culture calls for freedom, the economy calls for constraint. While the individual seeks fulfillment, life demands economic survival and security.[42]

  Is your world allowing you to satisfy the needs you personally feel? Are your personal needs and work life compatible? Discuss.

  _____

  _____

  _____

- *Leadership is important in meeting employee needs and preventing motivation problems.* Leaders have enormous power to help satisfy employee needs. The question is, will they? Whether or not a leader does depends almost entirely on the individual. No law requires it, and there is little social pressure to do so.

Leaders are rare who ask, "What are the needs of my subordinates?", then actively try to satisfy them. Yet, think of how their employees appreciate them, and think of how effective they are as managers. Such leadership is unusual because it requires extra sensitivity, effort, and unselfishness, especially when the leader knows that as soon as one employee need is satisfied, another will follow; a person's motivational cup is never completely filled.

The leader who cares about employee needs should use the following questions to evaluate each subordinate:

"What type of need is this person experiencing—physical, security, affiliation, social esteem, or self-fulfillment?"

"What specific action will satisfy this need?"

"Is it possible to satisfy the employee's needs on the job? If not, can I refer this person to others?"

"If the employee's needs are work related, what can I do to help?"

"Will I help?"

"I will."

Exactly what a leader does to meet employee needs varies with the circumstances. Typical actions include clarifying job assignments (security needs), offering a word of encouragement (affiliation

ILLUS. 1.4

Effective managers care about employees' needs.

needs), and providing praise for a job well done (recognition needs). In any case, such leadership motivates employees and brings out their best in job performance. It is an example of enlightened leadership. It would be good if all leaders in all work settings were so wise and caring.

Have you ever had a supervisor who cared about employee needs? Are you now, or would you be, an enlightened leader? Discuss.

_____

_____

_____

_____

- *The ideal is to integrate the needs of the individual with the goals of the organization.* If the needs of the individual can be satisfied while advancing the mission of the organization, the ultimate in employee morale and organization effectiveness will be achieved. Too many people are dissatisfied and perform below their potential because their jobs do not motivate them. Many employees care more about and work harder on off-the-job projects than on-the-job duties because these outside activities satisfy their psychological needs. This can represent a significant loss or "brain drain" for the organization.

Does your organization make the effort to satisfy employee needs while meeting organizational goals? Explain. _____

_____

_____

_____

- *Motives are powerful determinants of human behavior, allowing people to perform nearly impossible feats . . . if they want to.* A humorous and instructive story makes the point:

There once was a young man visiting a cemetery. It became late in the day, and it started to rain, so he decided to leave. As he was walking toward the gate, he tripped over a headstone, and fell six feet into an open grave.

The young man clawed desperately at the sides of the grave. But the walls were steep, the rain was heavy, and it was dark, so he could not get out. Realizing he was trapped, he knelt in a corner, pulled his jacket over his head, and waited for the rain to subside.

After a while, the young man heard a noise at the other end of the grave. He looked out from under his jacket and saw that another man had fallen into the same open grave. He saw that he too was frightened and was frantically trying to climb the wall of the grave.

The first young man felt sorry for the second. He could understand his fear, and from his own experience, he knew there was no way out of the grave. So he decided to help.

Slowly, the young man stood up, walked over to the other man, reached out, and put his hand on his shoulder. He said, "You can't get out of here." *But he did!* He got out of there . . . *because he was motivated.*

Can you recall a time when you were able to accomplish the seemingly impossible—because you were motivated? Explain.

_____

_____

_____

_____

_____

To review, the fourteen points to remember about motivation are:

• personal needs motivate behavior;

• a satisfied need is not a motivator;

• motivation levels explain work force behavior;

• self-actualization is the normal goal for people;

• people experience needs on all five motivation levels;

• psychological needs and social values are not the same;

• different needs influence behavior at different times during a person's day and life;

• the same act can satisfy any of the five motivation levels;

• all people have the same needs but to different degrees and accompanied by different wants;

• a person can be deficiency motivated, bringing harm to self or others;

• unsatisfied needs can make you ill, as surely as if you were physically stricken;

• leadership is important in meeting employee needs and preventing motivation problems;

• the ideal is to integrate the needs of the individual with the goals of the organization;

• motives are powerful determinants of human behavior, allowing people to perform nearly impossible feats.

RECOMMENDED RESOURCES

The following readings, cases, application, and films are suggested for further insight into the material in Part One:

Readings	— Abraham Maslow and the New Self
	The Human Side of Enterprise
	Demotivation: Its Cause and Cure
	On the Folly of Rewarding A, While Hoping for B
	What Job Attitudes Tell About Motivation
Cases	— Making Eight Is a Hassle
	The EZ Cleaners' Bonus Plan
Application	— Money as a Motivator
Films	— Maslow's Hierarchy of Needs
	The Self-Motivated Achiever
	Motivation Through Job Enrichment

REFERENCE NOTES

1   William C. Menninger and Harry Levinson, *Human Understanding in Industry* (Chicago: Science Research Associates, 1956), 21.

2   Arnold Gesell and Catherine Amatruda, *The Embryology of Behavior* (New York: Harper & Brothers, 1945), 248.

3   James C. Coleman, *Personality Dynamics and Effective Behavior* (Glenview, Ill.: Scott, Foresman & Company, 1960), 50, and Harrison G. Gough, "Factors Relating to Differential Achievement Among Gifted Persons" (Paper presented at the annual meeting of the American Psychological Association, San Francisco, 1 September, 1955).

4   Coleman, *Personality Dynamics and Effective Behavior*, 50–51.

5   Coleman, *Personality Dynamics and Effective Behavior*, 51.

6   Coleman, *Personality Dynamics and Effective Behavior*, 51.

7   Coleman, *Personality Dynamics and Effective Behavior*, 51.

8   Coleman, *Personality Dynamics and Effective Behavior*, 51–52.

9   Coleman, *Personality Dynamics and Effective Behavior*, 52.

10   Abraham Maslow, *Motivation and Personality* (New York: Harper & Brothers, 1954).

11   Viktor Frankl, *Man's Search for Meaning* (New York: Pocket Books, 1963), 44.

12   Frankl, *Man's Search for Meaning*, 44–45.

13 Michael Armine, "How to Build a Better Foxhole," *Popular Science* (March 1951): 113–19.

14 H. F. Harlow, M. K. Harlow, and S. J. Suomi, "From Thought to Therapy: Lessons from a Primate Laboratory," *American Scientist* 59 (September–October 1971): 538–49.

15 Muzafer Sherif and Hadley Cantril, *The Psychology of Ego-Involvements* (New York: John Wiley & Sons, Inc., 1947), 5.

16 Source unknown.

17 R. A. Spitz, "The Psychoanalytic Diseases in Infancy: An Attempt at Etiologic Classification," *Psychoanalytic Study of the Child* 6 (1951): 255–75.

18 Ashley Montagu and Floyd Matson, *The Human Connection* (New York: McGraw-Hill, Inc., 1979), 114, 116, 118.

19 Kingsley Davis, *Human Society* (New York: Macmillan, Inc., 1947), 204–6.

20 Erich Fromm, "Values, Psychology, and Human Existence," in Abraham Maslow, ed., *New Knowledge in Human Values* (New York: Harper & Brothers, 1952), 151.

21 William James, *Principles of Psychology* (Henry Holt and Company, 1890 / New York: Dover Publications, Inc., 1950), 293–94.

22 Abraham Maslow, *Motivation and Personality*, 2d ed. (New York: Harper & Row Publishers, Inc., 1970), and adapted from James F. Calhoun and Joan Ross Acocella, *Psychology of Adjustment and Human Relationships* (New York: Random House, Inc., 1978), 35.

23 Maslow, *Motivation and Personality*, and Calhoun and Acocella, *Psychology of Adjustment and Human Relationships*, 35.

24 Maslow, *Motivation and Personality*, 220–21.

25 Engler, *Personality Theories: An Introduction*, 286–89, 337, and John R. Frank, "Disharmonies in Education with Laws of the Mind and Life," *Journal of the Indiana State Medical Association* 52, no. 10 (October 1959): 1741–45.

26 Engler, *Personality Theories: An Introduction*, 286–89, 337.

27 Engler, *Personality Theories: An Introduction*, 286–89, 337.

28 Engler, *Personality Theories: An Introduction*, 339.

29 Julian Huxley, *Evolution in Action* (New York: Harper & Row Publishers, Inc., 1953), 162–63.

30 John Steinbeck, *The Grapes of Wrath* (New York: The Viking Press, 1939), 124.

31 Studs Terkel, *Working* (New York: Pantheon Books, Inc., 1974), xi.

32 Terkel, *Working*, xi.

33 Henry D. Spaulding, *Encyclopaedia of Black Folklore and Humor*, in Will Forpe and John McCollister, *The Sunshine Book: Expressions of Love, Hope and Inspiration* (Middle Village, N. Y.: Jonathan David Publishers, Inc., 1979), 229.

34 Lester C. Thurow, "A Plague of Job Hoppers," *Time* (June 22, 1981): 66.

35 Engler, *Personality Theories: An Introduction*, 337.

36 Coleman, *Personality Dynamics and Effective Behavior*, 315.

37 Engler, *Personality Theories: An Introduction*, 286–89, 337; and Frank, "Disharmonies in Education,"1741–45.

38 Gustave Flaubert, *Madame Bovary*, ed. Paul DeMan (New York: W. W. Norton & Co., Inc., 1965), 8.

39 Edna Ferber, *Giant* (Garden City, N. Y.: Doubleday & Company, Inc., 1952), 216.

40 Engler, *Personality Theories: An Introduction*, 338–41; Sheldon B. Kopp, *If You Meet the Buddha on the Road, Kill Him*! (New York: Bantam Books, 1976).

41 Engler, *Personality Theories: An Introduction*, 338–41.

42 Daniel Yankelovich, "Who Gets Ahead in America?," *Psychology Today* 13 (July 1979): 43.

STUDY QUIZ

As a test of your understanding and the extent to which you have achieved the objectives in Part One, complete the following questions. See Appendix D for the answer key.

1. The kind of person you are is influenced by heredity and environment.

   a. True
   b. False

2. Low points on the "motivation graph" indicate that certain needs have not been satisfied and need more emphasis.

   a. True
   b. False

3. Satisfaction of needs progresses according to the following sequence:

   a. survival, social, security, belonging, self-actualization
   b. survival, belonging, security, self-fulfillment, social
   c. survival, acceptance, belonging, love, security
   d. survival, security, love, respect, fulfillment

4. The highest need possible is:

   a. psychological
   b. self-fulfillment
   c. self-esteem
   d. security

5. A company that promotes communication, employee relations, and the open-door policy would interest an applicant at the:

   a. third motivation level
   b. fifth motivation level
   c. fourth motivation level
   d. none of these levels

6. In order to understand why people do what they do, you must:

   a. motivate positive behavior
   b. gain insight into unsatisfied needs
   c. observe and categorize behavior
   d. satisfy basic needs

7. There are two primary determinants of human behavior that are inside the person — biological factors and _____.

   a. social forces
   b. environmental forces

c. psychological forces
d. cultural forces

8. All of the following are expressions of the uniqueness of a newborn baby except:

a. sensitivity
b. intelligence
c. temperament
d. hostility
e. vitality

9. Survival needs that motivate behavior include all of the following except:

a. sleep
b. exercise
c. shelter
d. security
e. food

10. When survival needs are satisfied and a person feels fairly secure, the need to give and receive _____ normally emerges.

a. praise
b. affection
c. money
d. food

11. Maslow identified all of the following as characteristics of a self-actualized person except:

a. superiority
b. intimacy
c. autonomy
d. spontaneity
e. creativity

12. Before an individual can experience the need for fulfillment, certain _____ of the brain must develop.

a. cognitive structures
b. biological substrates
c. biochemical structures
d. white areas

13. All of the following motivational levels and psychological needs are correctly matched except:

a. first level — physical needs
b. second level — security needs

c. third level — self-fulfillment needs
d. fourth level — social esteem needs

14. The _____ motivational level is closely related to the nature of the work and depends on aspects of the job itself for satisfaction.

a. first
b. second
c. third
d. fourth

15. The nature of one's work is particularly critical in satisfying _____ needs.

a. self-fulfillment
b. physical needs
c. affiliation needs
d. security needs

16. An employee concerned primarily with the seniority system, insurance plan, and retirement policy is motivated by:

a. security needs
b. affiliation needs
c. social esteem needs
d. self-fulfillment needs

17. An employee interested primarily in professional recognition and increased social status is motivated by:

a. physical needs
b. social esteem needs
c. affiliation needs
d. security needs

18. _____ needs are natural forces within all people, without respect to ethics.

a. psychological
b. cosmetic
c. material
d. aesthetic

19. The role of leadership is critical in meeting human needs and preventing _____.

a. motivation malaise
b. work force productivity
c. employee malnutrition
d. motivational excess

20. Maslow identified _____ characteristics of the self-actualized person.

   a. 11
   b. 8
   c. 15
   d. 21

DISCUSSION QUESTIONS AND ACTIVITIES

The following questions and activities help personalize the subject. They are appropriate for classroom exercises and homework assignments.

1. What role has biology played in your life? What biological factors have influenced your behavior?

   _____

   _____

   _____

2. How do you rate against Maslow's self-fulfilled person? Have you achieved the 15 qualities?

   _____

   _____

   _____

3. What needs do you feel on the job? What needs are satisfied or unimportant at this time? Does your work allow the satisfaction of your motivational needs?

   _____

   _____

   _____

4. Discuss in small groups what a company should do to meet employee needs for (a) survival; (b) security; (c) belonging; (d) recognition; (e) fulfillment. What policies and practices would you recommend?

5. Discuss the role of money as a motivator in the world of work. What pay plan would you recommend — salary; hourly; commission; fee by job; merit; seniority; free market determined; social value determined?

PART TWO

Values

Learning Objectives

After completing Part Two, you will better understand:

1. how environment influences behavior;

2. the importance of culture and values;

3. the four periods during which values are formed — imprinting, identification, socialization, and adult;

4. how significant emotional experiences can change one's values;

5. the seven forces that shape human behavior — family, social class, school, the media, music, religion, and institutions;

6. the values of different generations;

7. how your values compare with those of "older-than-average-age" Americans and "younger-than-average-age" Americans;

8. the conflicts between the generations — motivation to work, reaction to change, respect for authority, attitudes toward money, sex roles;

9. how to close communication gaps and improve understanding;

10. the relationship between internal and external forces as these interact to determine human behavior.

THE WORLD OUTSIDE

There are other elements in the human-behavior equation besides biological factors and psychological forces. These elements are present in the world outside the person. This world — the environment — includes all of the conditions, circumstances, and people that surround the individual. In 1925, psychologist John Watson believed that these outside forces were the sole determinants in the outcome of people's lives:

> Give me a dozen healthy infants, well formed, and my own specified world to bring them up in, and I'll guarantee to take any one at random and train him to become any type of specialist I might select — doctor, lawyer, artist, merchant, chief, and yes, even beggar-man, and thief, regardless of his talents, penchants, tendencies, abilities, vocations, and race of his ancestors.[1]

Studies of sensory deprivation support the importance of environment as a determinant of human behavior. In these studies, researchers deprive subjects of stimulation from the outside world. In the typical experiment, the individual is isolated in a chamber, translucent goggles are worn to eliminate visual variability, fingers are separated by cotton to prevent tactile sensation, and sounds are shut out to avoid auditory stimulation. Under these environment-poor conditions, the deterioration of purposeful, meaningful behavior is dramatic. Such experiments show the critical role of environment in determining behavior.[2]

Environment has physical, social, and psychological effects on human behavior.

Physical Effects

To understand how environment can influence even the physical makeup of a person, consider that the circulatory system of the Eskimo lies deep within a protective fatty layer of flesh, allowing the preservation of body heat, so needed in the arctic habitat;[3] and consider that native Indians who work in the tin mines of Bolivia, in an oxygen-rare atmosphere as high as 18,000 feet above sea level, have an extraordinary number of red corpuscles in their blood and a lung capacity about twice as efficient as most Americans'.[4] Both of these physical effects are the product of environment.

Social Effects

To understand how environment can influence social habits, consider the following:

The Sirono Indians of eastern Bolivia, who live in thick, tropical rain forests where food is very scarce, provide an extreme example. This nomadic group lives in an almost perpetual state of semi-starvation. Food and the quest for food — game, fish, nuts, berries, fruit — have assumed prime significance.

Sirono customs, values, and general personality makeup reflect the effects of centering existence around food. Women do not marry for love, but are wooed by promises of fat meat and wild-bee honey. Wives usually do not resent their husbands for making love to another woman, unless he gives her food.[5]

Psychological Effects

To show how environment can influence even what a person sees, consider that in Western societies most objects are rectangular in shape. Doorways, television screens, and the shapes of houses are examples. On the other hand, South African Zulus build circular houses that are formed into circular compounds, and they keep their cattle in circular pens. An optical illusion known as the Sander parallelogram shows that human perception can be affected by the traditional physical shapes found in these two cultures. See Figure 2.1.

People in Western cultures who look at this parallelogram usually believe that the diagonal *AC* is longer than the diagonal *CB*. Measurement with a ruler, however, shows that *AC* is actually about 15 percent shorter than *CB*. Westerners are likely to make this error because the carpentered world in which they live exposes them to many rectangular surfaces, but these are rarely seen as right angles. They almost never see rectangular figures from directly overhead. Rather, they view them from one side and at an acute angle, which distorts them into the form of a parallelogram. Everyday experience shows that the diagonal *AC* on a table (or any other three-dimensional rectangular object) would be longer than

---

FIGURE 2.1

Sander Parallelogram

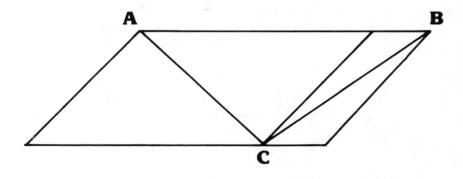

Source: Melville J. Herskovits et al., A Cross-Cultural Study of Perception *(Indianapolis: The Bobbs-Merrill Co., Inc., 1969), in Peter Farb,* Humankind *(New York: Bantam/Houghton Mifflin, 1978), 285–86.*

the diagonal *CB*. Therefore, in a two-dimensional parallelogram, *AC* is automatically perceived as though it were longer.

In contrast, people in rural Africa, who live in a circular world, are not hampered by preconceptions concerning rectangular forms. To them, it is obvious that *CB* is longer than *AC*. On the other hand, people in rural Africa are much more likely to be susceptible to various optical illusions involving circles.[6]

HUMAN AND NONHUMAN ELEMENTS

The world outside the person includes both human and nonhuman elements. Nonhuman elements may be natural events, such as a tidal wave, or technological advancements, such as a television or computer. Nonhuman elements can have an enormous effect on human behavior. Consider just two examples—climate and electricity.

Human elements in the environment are summarized by one word—culture. Each person is the product of other people—family, community, and society. Culture explains how so many creatures of one species (more than 5 billion people are alive at present) can be so dissimilar in appearance and behavior.[7] Culture explains why some people wear clothing and others do not, why some people live in permanent communities and others are nomadic, why some people honor children and others abuse them, why some people are industrious and others are not, and why some people love peace and others make war.[8]

CULTURE, VALUES, AND HUMAN BEHAVIOR

The young human being is like a book, and what will be written for four score and ten will be determined largely by culture. This is because man is nature's most flexible creature and the one most capable of growth. Human drives are less rigid and the brain less developed at birth than in any other species, and the human childhood is the longest.[9] Anthropologist Margaret Mead summarizes the importance of culture in shaping our lives:

> The functioning of every part of the human body is molded by the culture within which the individual has been reared—not only in terms of diet, sunlight, exposure to contagious and infectious diseases, overstrain, occupational hazards, catastrophes, and traumatic experiences, but also by the way he, born into society with a definite culture, has been fed and disciplined, fondled and put to sleep, punished and rewarded.
>
> Culture is seen as a principal element in the development of the individual that will result in his having a structure, a type of functioning, and a pattern of irritability different in kind from that of individuals who have been socialized within another culture. . . . [10]

The most important elements of culture are values, because they affect everything a person does or is. Values are those things we hold dear. They are the stars by which we navigate. Before we fully value something, certain criteria must be met. That which we value must be freely chosen, personally cherished, publicly affirmed, acted on, and worthy of sacrifice.

The more you understand your values, the clearer you can be in your ideas about life and the more confident you can be in your actions. Author-educator Maury Smith describes how values are developed:

> The process of acquiring values begins at birth. But it is not a static process. Our values change continually throughout our lives. For example, as children, our highest value might have been play; as adolescents, perhaps it was peer relationships; as young adults, our highest values may have been relationships with the opposite sex; and as adults, our highest value may be the care of our families or the work we do. For many older people, service to others is the highest value. We are formed largely by the experiences we have, and our values form, grow, and change accordingly.[11]

To understand the importance of values, consider how your own values influence you as you read this page. You are screening what you read and are continually judging, "this is right and that is wrong," and "this is good and that is bad."

CULTURAL PERIODS*

Values are formed during four periods of life. These periods are summarized in Figure 2.2.

Imprinting (Ages One Through Seven)

The family is the major cultural force during the first period of life, as children learn such skills as how to eat, talk, and walk. Habits are formed, and the right and wrong ways to do things are learned by example, direction, and reinforcement. To understand the importance of experiences during the imprinting period, consider that a child who is fed when hungry, held when frightened, and played with often will learn to behave differently from one who is fed according to a rigid schedule, left to cry it out when frightened, and rarely held just for fun.[12]

Early conditioning influences our behavior for the rest of our lives. Research shows that the less affection, approval, and encouragement a child receives, the less developed the subsequent personality is likely to be, and the less quickly the child will mature—that is, the more apathetic,

---

*Reference Note: This and the following sections (Cultural Periods; Cultural Forces—Then and Now; Forces in Your Life and Personal Values; How Generations Differ; and Values and Communication—Five Important Points) are based on *The People Puzzle: Understanding Yourself and Others* by Morris Massey (Reston, Va.: Reston Publishing Co., 1979). This excellent book provides the conceptual framework for these sections and gives many examples that help to explain why people do what they do.

FIGURE 2.2

Cultural Periods

Period	Ages	Source of Influence
Imprinting	1–7	Family
Identification	8–12	Heroes and villains
Socialization	13–20	Peer group members
Adult	21 onward	Value system firm unless there is a significant emotional experience

unresponsive, and incapable of independent action the child will be and the less strength of character and sense of self he or she will be likely to develop.[13]

The following summarizes the powerful and long-lasting influence of the family during the imprinting period:

> In interactions with father, mother, and siblings, the young child begins differentiations of self as liked or unliked, wanted or unwanted, acceptable or unacceptable, able or unable, worthy or unworthy, adequate or inadequate. These are the kinds of perceptions through which individuals are able to symbolize their own degree of self-worth.
>
> The more positive the self-concept a child acquires, the greater is the feeling of adequacy and need satisfaction; conversely, the more negative the self-concept acquired, the more frustrated and unhappy the child becomes.
>
> Experience later in life may change the concepts developed as a product of family living, but never easily or quickly. The most basic of self-concepts may be so deeply rooted in the individual's organization that they cannot easily be changed, even by the most drastic of later experiences.[14]

The role of the family as it affects work experiences is especially interesting. For example, a highly mechanized or isolated work setting in which employees cannot talk to one another because of noise level or the distance between them will hardly meet the needs of people who are accustomed to warm family relationships or a high degree of contact with others.[15]

How has your childhood influenced your life? How were you treated by your family? What people and experiences made an imprint on you? Explain briefly. _____

_____

_____

_____

Identification (Ages Eight Through Twelve)

During the identification period, the young person identifies heroes and villains. These people may be family members or others outside the family. In any case, the young person is attracted by the behavior of heroes (association) and repelled by the behavior of villains (aversion). The theory is that the central characters and favorite fantasies of childhood become dominant themes of one's life. These identifications tend to solidify and are important determinants of adult behavior. Imagine your favorite stories and heroes of childhood, and think of the personal characteristics and life-styles they imply: Peter Pan (the boy who never grew up), Wendy (who looked after others); Tarzan (strong and silent); Jane (beautiful and loving toward animals); and the Lone Ranger (who did good works and always left a silver bullet).

Sports figures, movie celebrities, and music stars often play hero roles for young people in our society. Through the things they say and do, how they look and act, and the ideas they promote, they become models for the young person, who tries to be like them. It is important for society to have positive heroes for the young. If such heroes do not exist, or if bad heroes are rewarded, values will deteriorate.

Who were the heroes and villains of your identification period? Who did you want to talk like, walk like, and be like? Who served as a model for your behavior? Explain briefly.

_____

_____

_____

_____

_____

Socialization (Ages Thirteen Through Twenty)

Friends represent the major cultural force for teenagers. The peer group affects everything, from dress and hairstyle to study and dating habits, during the socialization period. What the group does is critical. If you ask teenagers why they are doing something, they are likely to say, "Because everyone is." Although basic religious and political values are shaped primarily by parental example, the things teenagers care about most — music, cars, dress — are usually influenced more by members of their own generation.[16]

The adolescent years are especially important because it is during this period that a person normally becomes capable of making independent value judgments. Although teenagers often do not think independently and usually rely heavily on the opinions of friends and others whom they

Teenagers are greatly
influenced by their
friends.

like or respect, they are capable of complex reasoning and independent thought, and in this sense, they are mature. It is only natural that they want to be treated as adults.

Whether it is formed independently or as a result of social influence, when a teenage point of view is reached, it is usually held with conviction. Therefore, the values teenagers develop are difficult to alter. Often, these values remain with them for the rest of their lives.

Who were the friends who influenced you during your socialization period? Did you influence others during your teenage years? What values do you have now that were formed at that time? Discuss briefly.

_____

_____

_____

_____

_____

Adult (About Age Twenty-One and Onward)

By the time a person has lived through imprinting, identification, and socialization, his or her value system is fairly firm. Ideas about what is right, wrong, good, and bad are well established and are unlikely to change — unless a significant emotional experience takes place, an event so emotional and so dramatic that it changes the person's entire life.

For most people in their adult years, few experiences are significant or emotional enough to disrupt the basic value system formed during the years of imprinting, identification, and socialization. Typically, values and beliefs solidify at about the age of twenty-one, and when you are thirty, fifty, seventy, and ninety years of age, you will be doing what you do largely because of the forces and events that occurred in your life between the ages of one and twenty-one. As a rule, if a person changes his or her basic values during the adult years, it is only because a problem is met that old world views cannot resolve.

If you are in your adult years, think of your own life, and consider: have you ever had a significant emotional experience that has changed your values and beliefs? It may have been a brush with death or a loss of something or someone important to you; it may have been a book you read or a film you saw; it may have been a person you met or an adventure you had. Any of these experiences can have an effect on you that is significant and emotional enough to change your values. Explain briefly. _____

_____

_____

_____

_____

_____

CULTURAL FORCES — THEN AND NOW

The following is a discussion of major cultural forces that help to shape our values. This review should explain why different age groups think and act the way they do. There are several points to keep in mind:

- Although cultural forces help to explain the behavior of groups of people, the behavior of individuals must be evaluated individually; each person is a unique human being.

- Culture has more influence on some people than others; some are more externally directed, while others are more internally directed.

- No one is culture free. From the moment of birth to the moment of death, each of us is influenced by our environment.

Family

The family is the first and most critical cultural force influencing human behavior. As the French author Marcel Proust writes, "After a certain age, the more one becomes oneself, the more obvious one's family traits become." Everything the family does affects the growing person. How the family earns and spends money, how it distributes and accomplishes household chores, and how it celebrates birthdays and holidays are all important determinants of the behavior of its members.

ILLUS. 2.2

Family work and value systems are important determinants of children's behavior.

USDA

Basic attitudes toward people of the same sex and those of the opposite sex are influenced to a large degree by a person's family experiences. The little girl who attracts her daddy's attention by acting cute and feminine is later likely to relate with her male age-mates in the same way; the little boy who grows up resenting his father's autocratic manner will probably always feel uncomfortable with strict or close supervision from other authority figures—teachers, employers, or military officers; and whoever has seen a male subordinate act as if his immediate supervisor were non-existent, or refuse to listen to advice, should know that this pattern of behavior is common among men who grew up fatherless.[17]

Birth order and whether or not one is an "only child" can be important factors in family life, since birth order and number of siblings tend to influence how an individual is treated. There is evidence that firstborn children are typically more serious, less carefree, and more anxious than later born children. Also, they are usually more easily swayed by group and authority pressures than are later born children. Further, in large families, there is a tendency for performance on IQ tests to decrease from firstborn to last born.[18]

Consider your own childhood: were you the oldest (responsible), the youngest (spoiled), or in between (confused about whether to be big or small)? _____

_____

_____

_____

As for only children, they tend to be viewed in extremes: some characterize them positively as self-starters, independent thinkers, and strong leaders, while others see them as spoiled, self-centered, and aloof.[19] In either case, only children usually develop verbal abilities earlier and to a greater degree than do children from larger families. They also have a tendency to prefer one best friend rather than move easily among many friends. Finally, having been the center of attention in their families, only children tend to be willful and demanding in their relationships, and they often have trouble taking orders.[20]

Birth order and number of siblings alone are not the major determinants of behavior; more important is the way parents and other family members treat and deal with firstborn, later born, and only children as they are growing up.

The structure of the family has been changing in American society. During World War II, the demands of war forced many women to work outside the home, and the number of traditional families with mothers at home and fathers working began to decline. Women have continued to work outside the home in increasing numbers—some by choice and some by necessity. Today there are approximately 43 million working mothers with 7.2 million children under six years of age and 14 million

ILLUS. 2.3

An increasing number of mothers are working outside the home.

children aged six through thirteen. These young people are learning social and economic roles from Mom and Dad that differ from those formerly taught.[21]

Families are also less permanent than they used to be. Divorce rates in America have risen so that at present, one out of every three marriages ends in family breakup. Children are often raised by single parents and stepparents, while siblings include his, hers, and theirs. In addition, many adults are choosing to remain single, thus reducing the number of families. Consider that in the late 1950s, 80 percent of all Americans believed that being single was unnatural for either a man or woman; to be normal was to be married. By the late 1970s, a mere generation later, almost the exact proportion (75 percent) had changed their normative preference.[22]

One of the most important changes in family life is the shift in attitudes toward the care of children and aging parents. Today's young people expect to make fewer sacrifices for their children than their parents did, and they don't expect to be as dependent on their children in their later years.[23]

The family unit today is very different from that portrayed in Currier and Ives paintings of the past, and this is particularly disturbing to older generations. Realizing that the society of tomorrow is shaped by what children are exposed to during their impressionable growing-up years, many older people are distressed to see younger adults destroying the family unit as the elders think it should be.

Social Class

Social class is a major cultural factor, affecting everything about a person, from occupational choice (lawyer or laborer) to entertainment preference (theater or baseball) to clothing worn (Brooks Brothers or Sears).

A person's social class can even have life-and-death consequences; studies have shown that the higher the class standing, the longer the life expectancy. This is largely because of nutritional, medical, and other advantages that money and position can provide. Consider the fate of the passengers of the luxury ship *Titanic*, which struck an iceberg in the North Atlantic in 1912 and sank, causing the loss of more than 1,500 lives. Not all social classes had an equal chance to survive. Only 3 percent of the female passengers traveling first class were drowned, whereas 16 percent in second class, and 45 percent in third class, lost their lives.[24]

Social class can also make a difference in the area of legal justice. Social status can influence whether a person is arrested, indicted, convicted, and sent to jail, and if jailed, how long the person will stay. White-collar criminals in America spend less time in jail than do lower class offenders. They can afford to post bond while they await trial, and if convicted, they receive lighter sentences than do members of the lower class.[25] Indeed, studies show that a person driving a prestigious car, such as a Mercedes-Benz, is much less likely to be stopped for speeding than is a person driving a low-prestige car.[26]

Social class influences living standards, educational attainment, and marital relations, three basic considerations in life:

Living Standards. The wealth of the upper class tends to be self-perpetuating; there is truth in the saying that it takes money to make money. Lack of wealth in the lower class tends to be self-perpetuating as well, as seen in the following downward spiral: low family income leads to early entry into the work force for children; leaving school early restricts later job opportunities and qualifications for job advancement; limited job opportunities and advancement lead to low family income; low family income leads to early entry into the work force for children, etc.[27]

Educational Level Attained. Educational opportunities available to members of the upper class provide advantages throughout their lives. One study showed that six years spent in a superior educational environment increased the IQ scores of the children involved by an average of 5.1 points.[28] The upward spiral is as follows: advantaged children benefit from better elementary and secondary educations; this makes it possible for them to enter more prestigious colleges; graduation from these colleges results in advantages in entering the labor market; this provides the means that enable them to afford superior educations for their children; this, in turn, allows the children to continue as members of the upper class.

Marital Relations. Marital stability rates differ among the classes in that divorce, separation, and abandonment are greater in the lower class than the upper and are lowest in the middle class. Also, marital adjustment tends to be easier when both partners are from the same class.[29]

Figure 2.3 summarizes the attitudes of people from various socioeconomic levels in five important areas: family, education, aggression and destruction, sex, and recreation.

Differences between classes have always existed. However, primarily because of federal assistance programs and the egalitarian philosophy of public schools, many young people do not feel the full impact of these differences. From subsidized school lunches to democracy in the classroom, young people today receive roughly equal treatment. It is usually not until they become adults, and must provide for themselves, that they learn that society treats some people as "less equal" than others.

School

Throughout the identification and socialization periods, the behavior of young people is heavily influenced by schools, as knowledge, skills, and attitudes are conveyed. This includes what is taught (the curriculum), how it is taught (the teacher), and with whom the child learns (other students).

FIGURE 2.3

**Differing Attitudes at Various
Socioeconomic Levels**

Attitudes Toward:	Upper Class	Middle Class	Lower Class
Family	Family tightly knit; emphasis on maintaining family name and prestige	Considerable emphasis on independence; family ties often less close and less permanent than at upper levels	Family less closely knit than average family in higher socioeconomic groups and homes more apt to be broken
Education	Emphasis on quality of education and prestige of schools; training for high-level administration rather than financial gain	Great emphasis on grades and concern about failure; education seen as the road to advancement and security	Family's needs often given priority over child's education; school usually regarded as unpleasant; low premium put on good grades
Aggression and destruction	Value of property stressed; destruction and fighting discouraged	Value of property stressed; guilt and anxiety over open expression of anger, but "fighting back" sometimes encouraged at school age	Children often permitted or encouraged to settle differences by fighting; physical prowess valued; less emphasis on value of property
Sex	Inhibition of sexual behavior during early years, but considerable freedom by later adolescence	Severe inhibition in early years, with accompanying anxiety over sexual impulses; adolescent sexual activity usually limited to petting and masturbation	Sex accepted as matter of course; tendency to early sexual experience, often regarded by boys as proof of masculinity; petting and masturbation often regarded as perversion
Recreation	Relatively exclusive sports common, like golf, sailing, horseback riding; strong tendency to participate in community activities; reading and TV viewing common	Considerable emphasis on social skills like dancing, ping-pong, tennis; tendency to join organized community activities; reading and TV viewing common	Basketball, softball, boxing popular; little reading; TV viewing common

Source: From Personality Dynamics and Effective Behavior *by James C. Coleman. Copyright © 1960 by Scott, Foresman & Company. Reprinted by permission.*

The Curriculum. The Bible and the *Origin of Species* teach two entirely different conceptions of the creation of man; one is theistic, and the other is based in science. A person's view about what is true, what is real, and what is valuable is influenced by what is learned in school.

The Teacher. Whether a person is taught that things are either black or white, or that reality exists in shades of gray, will influence beliefs and human relationships throughout the person's life.

Other Students. Whether a person goes to a school that is integrated or segregated has a lot to do with attitudes toward people who are different. Dealing with different types of people at an early age usually makes it easier to do so later in life.

Schools have changed over the years, and these changes have affected relations between the generations in the work setting. Differences in the older and younger generations' management practices, work habits, and social attitudes support this point:

- *Management practices.* In the past, students were taught to follow instructions without question, and teachers tended to be autocratic in their relations with students. Now, young people commonly challenge ideas to which they are exposed, and teachers are more democratic in their relationships. An increasing demand for democracy in the work setting and an increasing tendency to question rules and orders are the natural consequences of this shift.

- *Work habits.* In the past, students were not promoted to the next grade until they had mastered the material of their present grade. Now, young people often are graduated from high school without the knowledge and skill expected of eighth graders. As a result, many younger employees today expect pay raises and job advancement without a great deal of effort on their own part.

- *Social attitudes.* In recent years, new subjects have been added to the school curriculum in addition to reading, writing, and arithmetic. Children in many schools are learning about computers, human sexuality, and ecology. As a result, value gaps are common between younger workers, who think computers are as natural as light bulbs, who are sexually sophisticated, and who are deeply concerned about the relationship between business and the environment, and older workers, who have a basic distrust of computers, who do not agree with new sexual mores, and who see environmentalists as irrational people responsible for slowing economic growth and putting people out of work.

Media

The communication media are major determinants of human behavior. Books, newspapers and magazines, radio, film, and television shape your values and help to form your attitudes:

- *Books.* Books have tremendous influence. A few examples make the point — the Bible (Christianity), the Koran (Islamic religion), and the *Teachings of Mao* (Chinese communism).

- *Newspapers and magazines.* Newspapers and magazines can significantly influence human behavior. Consider the role of the press during the 1970s in reporting the Watergate political affair and publishing the government's Pentagon papers, detailing U.S. involvement in the Vietnam War.

- *Radio.* Literally every home has a radio, which transmits ideas and alters moods. Think of the impact of Orson Welles' historic radio show, "War of the Worlds," which terrified audiences and even drove some to suicide. Consider Franklin D. Roosevelt's radio intonation, "The only thing we have to fear is fear itself," which helped many Americans to gain confidence and recover from the Great Depression. Finally, think of how radio music and news broadcasts today can lift your spirits or depress you as you listen in your home or car.

- *Film.* Films can be important in shaping values. Your own ideas probably have been affected by films, particularly during your youth. Impressionable audiences have been influenced by "good guy" heroes (Roy Rogers, Gary Cooper, John Wayne, Luke Skywalker, and Indiana Jones) and "bad guy" heroes (the rascal who gets the girl) and have attempted to emulate the behavior portrayed as glamorous and successful. Whether a person identifies with forces of good or of evil can be influenced by films.

- *Television.* Television is the dominant communication medium in America today. Fully 99 percent of U.S. homes have television sets. Contrast this with the fact that only 96 percent have indoor toilets. In a period of just over 30 years, television has graduated from a fuzzy image on a small screen, which fascinated the viewer, to an electronic babysitter and adult pacifier that the average person watches nearly three hours a day, yet is bored with unless something spectacular is being shown.[30]

How has television helped to create a society that is bored unless it is intensely stimulated? The unknown stimulates curiosity. So once you have been to the moon with Neil Armstrong, watched the assassinations of John Kennedy, Robert Kennedy, and Martin Luther King, Jr., and seen thousands of people killed night after night during the evening news, where do you go for the unknown and unexperienced — Aldous Huxley's "feelies" in *Brave New World?* These are not available yet, leaving people who have a single-dimensional and vicarious approach to stimulation bored.

Television influences all Americans. To prove the point, answer this question: "Where were you on November 3, 1963?" If you were alive at that time, you can probably remember exactly what you were doing the day John Kennedy was assassinated in Dallas, Texas. You can remember because you saw it on television. You can remember the horrible scenes and the terrible feelings you had at that time because of television images. Psychologists treating patients with total amnesia regarding their own past can flash a scene of the Kennedy assassination, and these patients will recall that day with near-perfect detail. Again, television touches almost everyone, and it is a major determinant of American culture.[31]

The media have had a significant effect on relations between the generations. For example, where do children and many young adults get the idea that money is abundant and problem solving is easy? Probably from watching television, where week after week, over and over again, the most complex problems are identified and solved in just one hour, and where everyone they see has nice clothes, a nice home, and a nice car. People raised with such cultural images have learned to expect a high standard of living with quick solutions to every problem, and when this is not the case in their own lives, they become upset.

On the other hand, older people, who never believed television's promise of instant satisfaction and instant success because of their own firsthand experiences with economic depression, world wars, and hard work, believe there are few shortcuts and no substitutes for personal effort in order to accomplish goals.

The frustration of young people whose world of expectations and world of reality are out of step, and the frustration of older people who wish young people would appreciate what they have been given and would be more enterprising themselves, can lead to conflict between the generations both in the home and on the job.

Music

Music has always been an important cultural force. The rhythm, notes, and lyrics evoke moods and convey messages that affect the listener. The influence of music has been particularly great in recent years. Consider the impact of Elvis Presley, the Beatles, the Rolling Stones, and Michael Jackson on the dress and behavior of several generations of young people. It seems that every month, a new star emerges to be the pied piper for the young.

Different values are programmed into different generations through music. Think about the values represented in two popular songs of two different periods — "Bridge Over Troubled Waters" of the 1960s, dealing with human relations, and "How Much Is That Doggy in the Window" of the 1950s, dealing with economic conditions. Consider the values being programmed into young people today by such lyrics as "All in all, you're just another brick in the wall" and "If you want my body, and you think I'm sexy, come on sugar, let me know." New social values and new ways of expressing sexuality are being taught through music. Yet how many adults are conscious of this, and how many simply say: "Turn that thing off. Who could listen to such noise"?[32]

Religion

Religion is an important element of culture, having a significant influence on human behavior. It is most likely to be brought into play during major life events, such as birth, marriage, war, and death. The more uncertainty that surrounds an event, the more likely it is that religion will play a part. In a study of the Trobriand Islanders, Polish anthropologist Bronislaw Malinowski observed that the villagers did not extend their magical rituals to fishing the safe and reliable inner lagoon, but did use magical ceremonies in the case of open-sea fishing:

> It is most significant that in lagoon fishing, where man can rely completely upon knowledge and skill, magic does not exist; while in the open-sea fishing, full of danger and uncertainty, there is extensive magical ritual to secure safety and good results.[33]

Figure 2.4 demonstrates the different values and experiences that characterize members of various religious groups.

Religious preference can have a major effect on life in the work setting. At different times and locations in America, if you were not of a certain faith, you might even have been denied a job. Even today, in some situations and some work settings, there is a tendency to discriminate in favor of one religious group over another. Masons, Knights of Columbus, Mormons, or Jews may receive preferential treatment, depending on which group is dominant in a particular work environment. This phenomenon is more prevalent with older people than younger, but regardless of age, religious discrimination can be a point of misunderstanding and suffering in the world of work.

Institutions

The institutions of society are important cultural forces, as they preserve and shape human values. Some, such as schools, have their primary effect during the formative years of identification and socialization, while others affect people throughout their lives. In American society, the goals of the YMCA, Scouts, Junior Achievement, and 4-H are to influence the beliefs and skills of young people in the areas of physical fitness, outdoor life, commercial enterprise, and farming, respectively, and each attempts to teach such universal values as resourcefulness, honesty, and brotherhood. On the other hand, government, as an institution, exerts influence on people throughout their lives as laws are made and executed and transgressors are judged. The actions of government help determine everything about people's lives, from birth until death.

Conflict between the generations can occur within and about institutions, particularly if young people view them as self-serving, bureaucratic, and irrelevant entities. If alienation develops, young people will avoid society's institutions; either physically or mentally, they will drop out. The best way to prevent alienation is for leaders to manage institutions so that they are genuinely responsive, nonbureaucratic, and above all, relevant for the people they are designed to serve. All institutions—school

FIGURE 2.4

A Comparison of Four Religious Groups

Characteristic	Order of Groups on Each Item (Most to Least)
1. Enjoys occupation	(1) Jews, (2) white Protestants, (3) white Catholics, (4) black Protestants
2. Utilizes installment buying	(1) Black Protestants, (2) white Catholics, (3) white Protestants, (4) Jews
3. Saves to achieve objectives far in the future	(1) Jews, (2) others
4. Believes in the American Dream	(1) White Protestants, (2) Jews, (3) white Catholics, (4) black Protestants
5. Votes Republican	(1) White Protestants, (2) white Catholics, (3) black Protestants, (4) Jews
6. Favors the welfare state	(1) Jews, (2) black Protestants, (3) white Catholics, (4) white Protestants
7. Takes a liberal point of view on the issue of freedom of speech	(1) White Protestants, (2) white Catholics, (3) Jews, (4) black Protestants
8. Opposes racial integration in the schools	(1) White Protestants, (2) white Catholics, (3) Jews, (4) black Protestants
9. Migrates to another community	(1) Black Protestants, (2) white Protestants, (3) white Catholics, (4) Jews
10. Maintains close ties with family	(1) Jews, (2) white Catholics, (3) black Protestants, (4) white Protestants
11. Develops a commitment to the principle of intellectual autonomy	(1) Jews, (2) white Protestants, (3) white Catholics, (4) black Protestants
12. Has a large family	(1) Black Protestants, (2) white Catholics, (3) Jews, (4) white Protestants
13. Completes a given unit of education (rather than drop out)	(1) Jews, (2) white Protestants, (3) white Catholics, (4) black Protestants
14. Rises in the class system	(1) Jews, (2) white Protestants, (3) white Catholics (4) black Protestants

Source: *Figure from* The Religious Factor *by Gerhard Lenski. Copyright* © *1961 by Gerhard Lenski. Reprinted by permission of Doubleday & Company, Inc.*

systems, churches, businesses, social groups, and political parties—face this problem, and each must solve it in order to meet its mission.

FORCES IN YOUR LIFE AND PERSONAL VALUES

As a review of cultural forces, and in order to personalize this important subject, complete the following questionnaire.

NAVIGATION AIDS—PEOPLE AND EXPERIENCES

Directions

Consider the people and experiences that have helped to shape your values in each of the following areas. Write these in the spaces provided.

Family

People: _____

_____

Significant experiences: _____

_____

_____

_____

Social Class

People: _____

_____

Significant experiences: _____

_____

_____

_____

School

People: _____

_____

Significant experiences: _____

_____

Media
(Books, Newspapers and Magazines, Radio, Film, and Television)

People: _____

_____

Significant experiences: _____

_____

_____

_____

Music

People: _____

_____

Significant experiences: _____

_____

_____

_____

Religion

People: _____

_____

Significant experiences: _____

_____

_____

_____

Institutions

People: _____

_____

Significant experiences: _____

_____

_____

_____

As a result of the people and experiences in your life, are your values more aligned with "older-than-average-age" Americans or "younger-than-average-age" Americans, or do your values lie somewhere in between? Use Figure 2.5 to evaluate your values. Simply circle the statements you agree with, then count the total circled in each column.

HOW GENERATIONS DIFFER

Different age groups form basic values while living through different experiences. Imagine a person raised during the Great Depression of the thirties and another raised during the social reform movements of the sixties or the Vietnam War of the seventies. If these people live or work together, they will need to put forth extra effort to understand and appreciate each other's views.

Life experiences can help to explain differences between older and younger people on a variety of important subjects, such as money, dress, work habits, and drugs. Consider the following examples.

FIGURE 2.5

A Comparison of Values

Views of Younger-Than-Average-Age Americans	Views of Older-Than-Average-Age Americans
I spend a great deal of time thinking about myself	I spend a lot of time working on other people's problems and needs
I receive more personal satisfaction from developing myself than from developing others	A woman's primary responsibility is to her home and family
I feel a strong need for excitement, new experiences, and new sensations	Taking care of the wife and family is a man's primary duty
I want something meaningful to work toward	I believe in close-knit families and life-long relationships between parents and children, whether they get along personally or not
I prefer to spend money on experiences rather than on possessions	I place great value on hard work, loyalty, and steadfastness
I prefer a creative life over financial well-being	I will meet my responsibilities, whether they give me a personal pleasure or not

---

Source: Adapted from Daniel Yankelovich, New Rules (New York: Random House, Inc., 1981).

Motivation to Work

Older people tend to work for money and security. Having lived through two world wars and the Great Depression, they know what it is like to be out of a job and to go without material possessions. They do not want to do this again. Therefore, they are inclined to define success in economic terms. On the other hand, young people tend to work for social and self-fulfillment goals, and they want work to be fun. Social researcher Daniel Yankelovich reports that nearly 80% of the American population is currently engaged in a search for higher level needs.[34]

Young people also work in order to have leisure. As recently as 1969, the majority of Americans believed that hard work always "paid off." Yet, as of 1976, most people no longer believed this to be true. This shift in thinking is due primarily to the attitudes of the young.[35] When young employees are given a three-day layoff for making mistakes on the job, they are likely to respond, "That's okay, I'll take five." This attitude is unthinkable to most older people. For older generations, a three-day layoff is severe and serious punishment.

Figure 2.6 shows the inverted order of priorities among younger and older Americans. In general, older Americans feel the need for survival first, relationships second, and personal growth third, while younger Americans invert this order — first comes personal growth, then relationships, and survival is taken for granted.

A recent study by researchers at AT&T supports the conclusion that the motivational makeup of younger managers differs from that of their

---

FIGURE 2.6

The Needs Felt by Older and Younger Americans

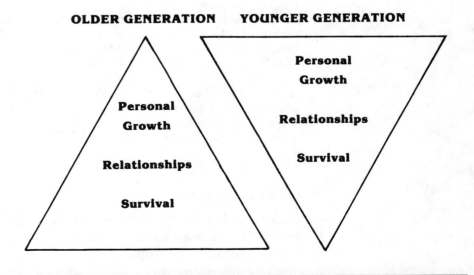

Source: Adapted from Daniel Yankelovich, New Rules *(New York: Random House, Inc., 1981), 33.*

older counterparts. In 1957, more than half of the managers in that company were motivated to achieve economic success and obtain the social prestige of holding top positions in the company. By 1977, fewer than one-third had the same goals. Although money and position remained important considerations, personal, family, and leisure-time activities were often more important. In other words, today the job must fit the life-style, whereas in the past, the job was likely to be the life-style.[36] Consider the following situation.

The New Generation Employee

Michael Donnelly is 36, married, the father of two, and an account executive for a Chicago insurance company. He always looks just a little strange in a conservative business suit and black wingtips; he seems made for jeans and sweaters. He is almost too serene for the business world, too easygoing. There is no hard edge to the man, no glint of raw ambition.

Michael is a native Chicagoan, and he's been a teacher and a salesman, among other things. In his current job he earns $35,000 a year, and he has been promoted three times in the last four years. On his last promotion, while discussing his future with his boss, he uttered words that would be heresy—unthinkable!—to the previous generation of managers. "I told my boss that I'm not particularly driven," he says. "I don't mind working 50 hours a week, but not 60 to 70, and not weekends."

His idea of a good time is doing absolutely nothing, and he tries to do it every chance he gets. "If I didn't have to work, I wouldn't," he says. What would he do? "I'd travel, and when I got that out of my system, I'd do some philanthropic work, which I enjoy." He pauses, relishing the thought. A smile begins around his eyes. "After that," he says, pausing portentously, "I'd probably write the Mediocre American Novel."

On the job, Michael is conscientious and efficient. He does good work but has no desire to get to the top. "The costs (of climbing to the top) are too great," he says. "And the reward is very small and mainly monetary. My wife and kids would have to be subordinate to my job because even people at the lower levels in the company, regional managers or whatever, spend a large amount of their time entertaining clients at night, flying to different parts of the country on weekends, using their time in other ways than with family. It is done to get ahead, but I really distrust that. I don't trust a person who puts business relationships ahead of personal ones."

Michael has plenty of company.[37]

Reaction to Change

Older people have created the world as it is today. Therefore, their typical reaction to change is to oppose it. On the other hand, young people have little sense of ownership of things as they are now; in addition, they are used to new experiences, having grown up in a world of constant innovation. So, young people are less reluctant to change, are more adaptive when it occurs, and will often create change.

Self-Gratification

Relatively few older people are accustomed to the immediate gratification of personal needs. As children, they were forced to make do with few toys and almost no luxuries — quilts were made from Dad's old suits, cut into squares. When they became adults, self-gratification generally took a back seat to the needs of younger family members. Contrast this with the fact that the majority of younger people in the United States today have not wanted for many things for very long.

Since the start of the Industrial Revolution, each generation has wanted to give its children all of the things Mom and Dad never had. But it wasn't until the 1950s that this goal could become a reality for large numbers of people. From this time onward, most American parents had more money and resources to spend on their children than had their parents, and it became common to hear, "My kids are going to have it better than I did."

Now, in the work setting and in the home, the children of the forties, fifties, sixties, and seventies have grown up expecting, and often demanding, immediate gratification of their desires. Self-sacrifice and the postponement of personal satisfaction are new experiences for these young people — a fact that is upsetting to many older adults. In place of the traditional ethic of self-denial and sacrifice, an ethic of self-absorption has been programmed into large numbers of young Americans.[38]

Respect for Authority

Older generations were taught, "Children should be seen and not heard," and "Children should obey their elders." Automatic respect for and obedience to authority figures were developed from an early age in these generations. In contrast, parents who were influenced by Dr. Benjamin Spock and other writers of the forties, fifties, and sixties have encouraged younger people to question what they see and hear and to reason for themselves. These young people have been taught by liberal teachers and by personal experience that respect must be earned. The task of leadership today is much harder than it used to be because loyalty and obedience, either at home or on the job, are not important values for large numbers of young people.

Dress and Hairstyle

When older people were growing up, it was common to hear, "Cleanliness is next to godliness," and two world wars fought by short-haired heroes reinforced the idea that if you were a good guy, you had to have short hair. Of course, there were important reasons for these heroes to have short hair: they couldn't fight a war with hair in their eyes, and it cost less to make standard sized helmets. In any case, for more than half a century, young men were conditioned to wear their hair short and to dress neatly.[39]

Then came the fifties and sixties, and young people who had the time and economic security to "search for their identity" found that long hair and jeans distinguished them from their elders. Indeed, hairstyle and dress became symbols of rebellion against the older generation. In the work setting today, dress and hairstyle continue to be a source of conflict between the generations, as older people wish younger people would be more tasteful in their appearance and young people wish older people would relax.

Respect for Property

It is not unusual for older people to put scraps of paper in their pockets until they find a trash can to throw them in. On the other hand, young people are often careless of and even destructive to property. This reflects the fact that many young people have not had to clean, fix, or replace the things they damaged or lost while growing up. If they made a mess, someone else would clean it up; if they broke something, someone else would fix it; if they lost something, someone would buy them a new one.

If a person does not have to work for something in the first place and is not held responsible for what is broken or lost, there is little incentive to take care of property. Property is simply not valued because it appears to be easily replaced. This point is important in the work setting because of the need to care for tools, equipment, buildings, and grounds. Often, there is no way to repair or replace something once it is gone.

Sex Roles

Older people tend to be stereotyped in their thinking concerning male and female social roles. Many older men are opposed to women working outside the home and would do almost anything to avoid having to report to a female supervisor. In contrast, younger people are more flexible about who does what; increasingly in recent years, young people have learned nondiscrimination and sexual equality so that who is the subordinate and who is the supervisor is not as emotional a question.

Consider that the average person's attitude about whether a wife should work outside the home reversed between the years 1938 and 1978 in favor of women working. An increasing tendency for young men to drop out of the work force at the same time that more women enter employment is evidence of further shifts in attitudes regarding sex roles. Between 1947 and 1977, the exodus from the work force of men in their prime working years doubled.[40]

Competition

History has taught older people the value of winning. Living through life-and-death situations in major wars, and working in a free market system in which the most aggressive businesses succeed, have taught older people to value competition. On the other hand, younger people tend to believe that "it is not whether you win or lose, but how you play the game, that counts." When these two views meet in the work setting, misunderstanding can occur as young people view older bosses as ruthless and older bosses question whether younger employees will produce when the going gets tough.

Patriotism

Older people grew up with national causes that they considered to be just — World War I and World War II. In contrast, younger people grew up with a cause they viewed as unjust — the Vietnam War. When an older person sees young people burning the American flag or protesting the draft, it is very disturbing; and when a young person hears patriotic slogans, suspicions are raised. Conflict over patriotism can occur between the generations both at home and on the job. Remember the many exchanges between Archie and Mike in "All in the Family"?

VALUES AND COMMUNICATION — FIVE
IMPORTANT POINTS

Misunderstanding over values can occur both on the job and in the home. What can be done to help? Keeping in mind the following points can help you to improve communication and create better relations:

- It is important to remember that the values people have are normal outgrowths of what they were exposed to during their formative years — ages one through twenty. Some values may be better than others, but in the sense that culture creates them, all values are normal.

- If you want to understand the values of another person, you should see things through that person's "cultural eyes." You should consider

ILLUS. 2.4

Clear communication can bridge the generation gap.

the forces and events that were in effect during the person's imprinting, identification, and socialization periods. Is materialism the result of being forced to do without things while growing up? Is intolerance in human relations the product of being taught that "black is black and white is white, and there are no shades of gray"? Is difficulty in working with a female supervisor the result of having only known women as sisters, girlfriends, and mother, never as the boss? Is a seeming inability to show emotion due to the belief that a person should be strong and that the display of emotion is a sign of weakness? Finally, is preference for rock 'n' roll music the result of having been socialized during the 1950s?

• The world is becoming smaller in the sense that more and more people live longer and longer, and these people have diverse value systems. This is particularly true of melting-pot societies such as America's. Multitudes of people have accepted the invitation engraved on the Statue of Liberty and have followed her lamp to these shores:

> Give me your tired, your poor,
> Your huddled masses yearning to breathe free,
> The wretched refuse of your teeming shore.
> Send these, the homeless, tempest-tost to me,
> I lift my lamp beside the golden door!

Today there are four generations of Americans representing at least 27 ethnic backgrounds, and they are all interdependent.[41] If people are to live and work in harmony, they must understand and adjust to many different value systems.

• Remember that once values are formed, they do not change easily, and what people are like during young adulthood tends to remain unchanged for the rest of their lives. In fact, it is very difficult for one person to alter another person's beliefs once they have developed. If you are over twenty-one, consider your own values—has anyone ever tried to change you? Were they successful?

As stated before, people change their world view only through a significant emotional experience. You should remember this if you seek to change others; otherwise, you must learn to live with people as they are.

• Values are communicated primarily by actions, less so by words. For example, young people who see elected officials convicted of crimes and then pardoned will form their own attitudes toward public officials and crime regardless of the speeches they hear. Respect for officials will be low, and they will learn, "It is not so wrong to do it as it is to get caught; and if you do get caught, that's okay—people will forgive and forget." At the family level, parents who say to their children, "We believe in respect for property, good health habits, and personal honesty," are teaching the opposite values when they throw paper out the car window, smoke cigarettes, and cheat on taxes.

Because people are influenced more by what they see than by what they hear, it is important for each person to consider, "What are my values?" and "Do I communicate these by my actions?" In your own case, where do you stand on the following?

A. Marriage: _____

_____

_____

_____

B. Work: _____

_____

_____

_____

C. Government: _____

_____

_____

_____

D. Education: _____

_____

_____

_____

E. Religion: _____

_____

_____

_____

What are your views on:

A. Language: _____

_____

_____

_____

B. Dress: _____

_____

C. Sex: _____

_____

_____

_____

D. Money: _____

_____

_____

_____

E. Any other issue regarding values: _____

_____

_____

_____

F. Do your actions reflect your values? Discuss. _____

_____

_____

_____

INTERACTION — THE WORLD WITHIN AND THE WORLD OUTSIDE

Neither the world within nor the world outside the person can, by itself, completely account for human behavior. The human being and the environment, working together and affecting each other, determine why people do what they do. Figure 2.7 shows this relationship.

A bit of doggerel describes the relationship between the individual, the environment, and human behavior:

> As you wander on through life,
> No matter what your goal —
> Keep your eye upon the doughnut,
> And not upon the hole.

The "doughnut" represents the critical area of interaction between the person and the world. Human behavior is determined in this interaction.

Two psychological experiments dramatically illustrate the interaction between the individual and the environment, proving that even what a person sees is influenced by this complex interplay.

FIGURE 2.7

The Relationship Between the Individual, the Environment, and Human Behavior

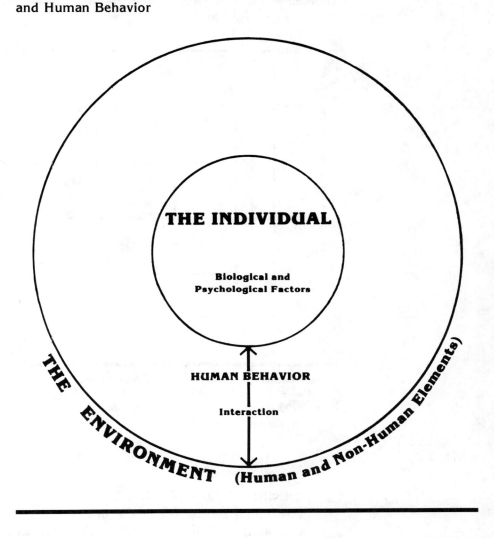

- *Pupillary dilation.* Pupillary dilation reveals the tendency to be more open to some experiences and to shut out others. When looking at interesting or pleasant stimuli, as opposed to neutral stimuli, the pupil dilates measurably. Which experiences are interesting and which ones are not is a function of the biology and motivation of the individual, interacting with values acquired through cultural experiences. Figure 2.8 shows how male and female subjects respond to different visual stimuli.

     The eyes are often referred to as "windows of the soul." Even if they are not windows of the soul, the eyes (more specifically, the pupils) do register certain activities of the nervous system, including, but not restricted to, the effects of visual stimulation. Evidence shows that deeply rooted personal attitudes may be laid bare by the

FIGURE 2.8

Changes in Pupil Size While Viewing Various Pictures
(Percentage of Decrease or Increase from Size While
Viewing Control Patterns)

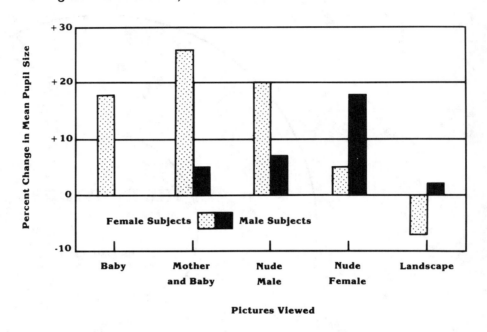

Source: Eckhard Hess and James Polt, "Pupil Size as Related to Interest Value of Visual Stimuli," Science, Vol. 132 (August 5, 1960), p. 350. Copyright © 1960 by The American Association for the Advancement of Science. Reprinted with the permission of AAAS.

activities of the pupils. In effect, they are physiological telltales of attitudinal states. When the nineteenth-century romantic writer Guillaume de Salluste described adoring looks between young lovers, this was the phenomenon being reported.[42]

• *The American flag.* In Figure 2.9, color the starred area with a bright yellow marker; color the white bars with a medium-blue marker, but leave the dot in the center white. Stare at the dot for 45 seconds; then look at the white rectangle below the flag. You should see a red, white, and blue American flag inside the white rectangle. Why? Because the environment does not act on an empty organism, nor can the organism create something without environmental input. A yellow, black, and blue figure (the environment), interacting with the rods and cones of the human eye (the individual), results in the perception of complementary colors as an afterimage on a white surface (the behavior).

FIGURE 2.9

What Do You See?

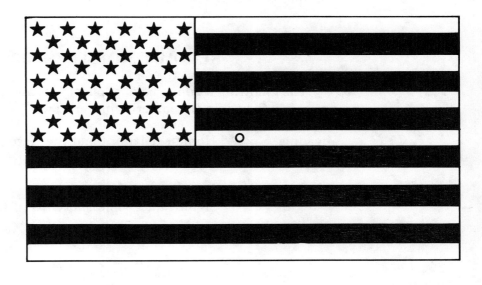

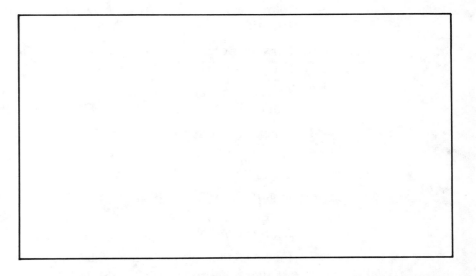

Source: American flag exercise adapted from John Rowan Wilson and the editors of Time-Life Books, The Mind *(New York: Time-Life, 1969), 54.*

As final evidence that who you are, what you do, and every other aspect of your behavior is a function of internal and external interacting forces, consider the legend of Pecos Bill:

As a baby, Pecos Bill was traveling west with his family when the wagon he was riding in hit a bump, and he fell out. The next day, a female coyote found him and took him home to raise with her newborn pups. Pecos lived with his coyote mother and brothers for 12 years before civilization saw him again. When people did see him, they could hardly believe the sight of a boy running on all fours, chasing rabbits, and acting like a coyote. But this unusual behavior was not strange to Pecos, who had been "raised that way." It should be noted too that Pecos had become the smartest of all the coyotes. Neither was this strange; for Pecos Bill was a human being.[43]

RECOMMENDED RESOURCES

The following reading, case, applications, and film are suggested for greater insight into the material in Part Two:

Reading	— Human Relations and the Nature of Man
Case	— The Satisfied Sales Representative
Applications	— Values Auction Significant People and Critical Events
Film	— What You Are Is Where You Were When

REFERENCE NOTES

1 John Watson, *Behaviorism* (New York: W. W. Norton & Co., Inc., 1925).

2 Bernard Berelson and Gary A. Steiner, *Human Behavior*, short ed. (New York: Harcourt, Brace & World, 1967), 142.

3 James C. Coleman, *Personality Dynamics and Effective Behavior* (Chicago: Scott, Foresman & Company, 1960), 53.

4 Coleman, *Personality Dynamics and Effective Behavior*, 53.

5 "Hunger Regulates Lives," *Science News Letter*, 58, no. 2 (1950): 21–22.

6 Melville J. Herskovits et al. *A Cross-Cultural Study of Perception* (Indianapolis: Bobbs-Merrill Co., Inc., 1969), in Peter Farb, *Humankind* (New York: Bantam/Houghton Mifflin, 1978), 285–86.

7 John Devine, "Evolution Revelation," *The Saturday Evening Post* (January–February 1982): 48, 112.

8 Coleman, *Personality Dynamics and Effective Behavior*, 44–73.

9 Coleman, *Personality Dynamics and Effective Behavior*, 44–73.

10 Margaret Mead, "The Concept of Culture and the Psychosomatic Approach," *Contributions Toward Medical Technology*, ed. Arthur Weider (New York: Ronald Press, 1953), 1:377–78.

11 Maury Smith, *A Practical Guide to Value Clarification* (La Jolla, Calif.: University Associates, Inc., 1977).

12 Morris Massey, *The People Puzzle: Understanding Yourself and Others* (Reston, Va.: Reston Publishing Co., 1979).

13   Coleman, *Personality Dynamics and Effective Behavior*, 65.

14   Arthur W. Combs and Donald Snygg, *Individual Behavior* (New York: Harper & Brothers, 1959), 136.

15   Harry Levinson, *Executive* (Cambridge, Mass.: Harvard University Press, 1981), 31.

16   Massey, *The People Puzzle*.

17   Levinson, *Executive*, 30.

18   Zick Rubin and Elton B. McNeil, *The Psychology of Being Human*, 3d ed, (New York: Harper & Row, Publishers, Inc., 1981), 360–64, and Didi Moore, "The Only Child Phenomenon," *The New York Times Magazine* 6 (January 18, 1981): 26.

19   Moore, "The Only Child Phenomenon," 26, and Rubin and McNeil, *The Psychology of Being Human,* 360–64.

20   Moore, "The Only Child Phenomenon," 26, and Rubin and McNeil, *The Psychology of Being Human*, 360–64.

21   U.S. Department of Labor, Office of the Secretary, Women's Bureau, *Facts on Women Workers* (Washington, D.C.: U.S. Government Printing Office, 1980).

22   Institute for Social Research, *ISR Newsletter* 7, no. 1 (Winter 1979), in Daniel Yankelovich, *New Rules* (New York: Random House, Inc., 1981), 97.

23   Yankelovich, *New Rules*, 103–4, and S. N. Wellborn, "When School Kids Come Home to an Empty House," *U.S. News and World Report* (September 14, 1981), 42, 47.

24   Farb, *Humankind*, 359.

25   Farb, *Humankind*, 338.

26   Farb, *Humankind*, 350.

27   Coleman, *Personality Dynamics and Effective Behavior*.

28   Farb, *Humankind*, 438.

29   Farb, *Humankind*, 374–80.

30   Massey, *The People Puzzle*, 95.

31   Massey, *The People Puzzle*, 120–21.

32   Massey, *The People Puzzle*, 97.

33   Bronislaw Malinowski, *Magic, Science and Religion and Other Essays* (Garden City, N.J.: Doubleday & Company, Inc., 1954), 14.

34   Yankelovich, *New Rules*, 78–84.

35   Massey, *The People Puzzle*.

36   Paul Weingarten, "The Not-Me Generation," *The Cincinnati Enquirer* — Magazine section (14 November, 1982): 9–10.

37 Weingarten, "The Not-Me Generation," 7–8. Reprinted with permission from Associated Press.

38 Massey, *The People Puzzle*, and Yankelovich, *New Rules*.

39 Massey, *The People Puzzle*.

40 Yankelovich, *New Rules*, xv.

41 U.S. Department of Labor, Bureau of the Census, *Census 1970*, Vol. 1, Table 193 (Washington, D.C.: U.S. Government Printing Office, 1973), 598–99.

42 Eckhard H. Hess, "Personal Communication," in Bernard Berelson and Gary A. Steiner, *Human Behavior: An Inventory of Scientific Findings* (New York: Harcourt, Brace & World, 1964), 104.

43 Edward O'Reilly, "The Saga of Pecos Bill," *The Century Magazine* 106, no. 6 (October 1923): 827–33, in B. A. Botkin, ed., *A Treasury of American Folklore* (New York: American Book–Stratford Press, 1944), 180–82.

STUDY QUIZ

As a test of your understanding and the extent to which you have achieved the objectives in Part Two, complete the following questions. See Appendix D for the answer key.

1. A significant emotional experience can change a person's value system, regardless of the person's age.

   a. True
   b. False

2. The socialization period has primary influence on:

   a. adults
   b. young children
   c. the elderly
   d. teenagers

3. Sexual inhibition in early years is seen primarily in the:

   a. middle class
   b. upper class
   c. lower class

4. The world outside includes:

   a. everyone except the individual
   b. how the individual relates to the environment
   c. all conditions, circumstances, and people that surround the individual
   d. psychological factors attributed to the individual's behavior

5. In the socialization period, what is the major cultural force influencing the teenager?

   a. Family
   b. Friends
   c. Heroes

6. Younger generations tend to work for social and self-fulfillment goals, and they want work to be fun.

   a. True
   b. False

7. One way to improve communication and create better relations is to recognize that the different values people have are normal outgrowths of what they were exposed to during their formative years (ages one through twenty).

   a. True
   b. False

8. The only way a person will change his or her basic values after the age of twenty-one is through a significant _____ experience.

   a. emotional
   b. occupational
   c. intellectual

9. All of the following are cultural periods during which the normal human being is influenced except:

   a. the imprinting period
   b. the socialization period
   c. the identification period
   d. the pseudo-sexual period

10. In order of importance, needs felt by most older people are:

   a. survival, relationships, personal growth
   b. personal growth, relationships, survival
   c. relationships, personal growth, survival

11. A phenomenon showing the effect of environment on psychological experience is known as the:

   a. Bolivian oxygen effect
   b. Sander parallelogram
   c. peripheral heart action

12. Cultural forces that influence human behavior include all of the following except:

   a. religion
   b. family
   c. social class
   d. intelligence

DISCUSSION QUESTIONS AND ACTIVITIES

The following questions and activities help personalize the subject. They are appropriate for classroom exercises and homework assignments.

1. What elements of the physical environment have influenced your life? Consider climate, weather, terrain, etc. _____

_____

_____

_____

2. What family factors were important during your imprinting period? Who were your heroes during your identification period? How did peer group members influence you during your socialization period? At what age did your values lock in? Where were you when your values became firm? _____

_____

_____

_____

3. Have you ever had a significant emotional experience that has changed your life? Explain. _____

_____

_____

_____

4. Are your values mostly traditional or mostly modern? What are your views on money, dress, work habits, drugs, etc.? Do your actions reflect your values? _____

_____

_____

_____

5. Give an example of how factors within you and forces in your world have interacted to determine your behavior. Do you think your behavior is determined mostly by external forces (environment) or mostly by internal forces (personal qualities)? Discuss. _____

_____

_____

_____

6. If you want to improve communication and have a better relation-ship with someone, what steps should you take? _____

    _____

    _____

    _____

7. Divide into small groups to discuss the remaining questions. Are society's values changing? In what direction — conservative, liberal? Do you approve? What individuals, events, and forces have influenced American values in recent years?

8. How have cultural forces affected you? Discuss the influences of family, social class, school, media, music, religion, and other institu-tions on your development.

9. Is human behavior determined primarily by forces inside the person (biology and motivation) or primarily by forces outside the person (other people, events, conditions)? Discuss the concept of locus of control.

PART THREE

Personality

Learning Objectives

After completing Part Three, you will better understand:

1. the nature of personality as the sum total of human behavior;

2. the importance of self-concept in the creation of personality;

3. your personality according to Freud's psychoanalytic theory;

4. the three domains of human behavior — feelings, cognitions, and motor movements;

5. the type of person you are, based on the personality traits of ascendency and sociability;

6. your personality according to cardinal, central, and secondary dispositions;

7. the eight defense mechanisms employed by the personality to preserve emotional health;

8. your use of ego-defense mechanisms;

9. your psychological health, and how to use a four-step procedure to improve personal and social adjustment;

10. the normal stages and tasks of personality development;

11. your status in personality development: tasks completed and tasks to do.

PERSONALITY IS PERSONAL AND SOCIAL

As a result of interaction between forces within and forces outside the individual, a personality develops. Personality is the sum total of human behavior, and it is both personal and social. The Dutch philosopher Baruch Spinoza describes the personal nature of personality: "To be what we are and to become what we are capable of becoming is the only end of life."[1] Psychologist Carl Rogers explains the importance of knowing who you are and becoming a person:

> As I follow the experience of many clients in the therapeutic relationship, it seems to me that each one has the same problem. Below the level of the problem situation about which the individual is complaining—behind the trouble with studies, or wife, or employer, or with his own uncontrollable or bizarre behavior, or with his frightening feelings, lies one central search. It seems to me that, at bottom, each person is asking: "Who am I, really? How can I get in touch with this real self, underlying all of my surface behavior? How can I become myself?" It appears that the goal the individual most wishes to achieve, the end that he knowingly or unknowingly pursues, is to become himself.[2]

As you consider your own personality, how would you describe your personal nature or being? Who are you, and where are you going? Explain briefly. _____

_____

_____

_____

_____

_____

Personality is also social, a series and integration of social roles. As Shakespeare writes:

> All the world's a stage,
> And all the men and women merely players:
> They have their exits and their entrances;
> And one man in his time plays many parts,
> His acts being seven ages.

Throughout our lives, we define ourselves as leaders, parents, citizens, students, and other social beings, adopting the goals, values, and other characteristics of these roles. Social roles can be so important that the individual may break down when roles are changed. Imagine the successful businessman who, on losing his fortune and prestige, commits suicide. Or imagine the homemaking mother who, having raised her children, becomes depressed and physically ill.[3]

In order to understand a person's behavior, it helps to understand the part social roles play. The following shows how social roles influence the behavior of young people.

Social Roles and Personality

Studies of boys' gangs show that the following roles typically develop:

Leaders. As a result of physical strength, intellectual ability, courage, or some other characteristic, one individual in the group tends to emerge as the leader. The leader gives instructions, settles disputes, coordinates activity, sets an example for the others, and often serves as a group conscience. When a member of the gang gets into trouble with outsiders, he may justify his behavior by blaming the leader: "He told me to do it."

Advocates. Often, there are youngsters who are more facile with words or ideas than the leader but who lack organizing ability or boldness in action. These group members may be cast in the role of negotiators with rival gangs or defenders of the group against adult disapproval. They are expected to be masters of the alibi and skilled at rationalization and clever negotiation. They play a role roughly analogous to that of lawyer or diplomat.

Clowns. Many juvenile groups have their court jester — a boy or girl who is expected to be funny. Sometimes this person differs from the others in physical appearance (for example, very tall, thin, or fat), and sometimes the person is below par in other skills demanded by the group. By combining humor and self-display, the clown can gain status in the group and the affectionate regard of other members.

Fall guys. Often there is a member whose alleged ineptness, mistakes, or simply bad luck get him blamed for almost everything that goes wrong for the group. The presence of such a scapegoat tends to relieve the others of the feelings of inferiority and insecurity that would otherwise result from group failures.

Mascots. In some cases, the group adopts a mascot — an individual who is younger, physically handicapped, or otherwise different from other members of the group in a way that they consider inferior. The mascot is usually well accepted by the group as long as he sticks to his role and does not attempt to participate in the group as a full-fledged member.[4]

When you were a child, what social roles did you play, and how has this influenced your life? What social roles do you play today, and how do these affect your personality? Explain briefly. _____

_____

_____

_____

_____

THE IMPORTANCE OF SELF-CONCEPT

Self-concept is the guiding light in the interaction between forces within you and forces outside you. Your self-concept is that constellation of central ideas and attitudes you have about yourself. People are thinking creatures who not only react to the world but are capable of originating behavior and making free choices. Indeed, as does no other known being, people influence the world and create themselves.[5] The following story shows the importance of self-concept.

The Mask

An ancient legend tells of a king who conquered and ruled over a vast domain. He was brave and respected, but no one loved him. This made him lonely, and his face reflected his inner bitterness. Deep, ugly lines developed around his mouth, and he never showed a smile.

One day the king saw a beautiful young lady and fell in love with her immediately. He decided to marry her. He clothed himself in his finest robes and placed a glittering crown on his head. But when he looked into the mirror, he saw only a cruel, hard face.

He was terribly distressed until he thought of a wonderful idea. He called for his magician and said: "Make me a mask, and paint it with your magic paints, so that it will make my face look kind and pleasant."

"This I can do," said the magician. "But on one condition: you must keep your real face in the same lines that I paint; one frown or display of anger, and the mask will be ruined."

"I will do anything you say in order to win the love of my lady. Tell me how to keep the mask from cracking."

"You must think kind thoughts," replied the magician, "and to do this, you must do kind deeds. You must strive to make your people happy rather than to acquire more territory. Be kind and courteous to all your subjects."

ILLUS. 3.1

To a large extent, what you think about yourself determines what you may try to accomplish.

The king agreed, and the magician made a mask of very thin wax and painted it skillfully. The king tried it on and he looked very handsome. He had little difficulty in winning the hand of the woman he loved.

The king was very careful not to spoil his mask, and his subjects were amazed at the change that had come over him. They gave all the credit to his wife who, they said, had made him over to be like herself.

Months went by, and as gentleness and thoughtfulness for others became a part of his personality, he was convinced that he should be more honest and not just pretend at it.

He began to regret that he had deceived his beautiful wife with his magic mask, and he called for his magician and cried out: "Remove this mask. Take it away. This false face is not my true one."

"If I do, I can never make another mask like it," warned the magician, "and you will have to remain with your own real face as long as you live."

The magician took off the mask, and the king ran to the mirror, full of fear and anguish over what he might see. To his amazement, he saw eyes that were bright and lips that were curved into a radiant smile. The old ugly lines around his mouth and the old frown had disappeared, and his face was the exact likeness of the mask he had worn for so long.

The king's wife never noticed the difference. She saw only the familiar features of the man she loved so dearly.[6]

As Figure 3.1 shows, self-concept mediates factors in the individual and elements in the environment as personality is formed. Self-concept influences the psychological needs you experience and determines whether you are deficiency motivated or growth motivated. Self-concept also influences the way you experience cultural forces and whether you perceive them as favorable, neutral, or adverse.

The philosopher Jean-Paul Sartre identifies the central goal of every person to be as follows: to be aware of who one is, and to take full

FIGURE 3.1

Personality Formation

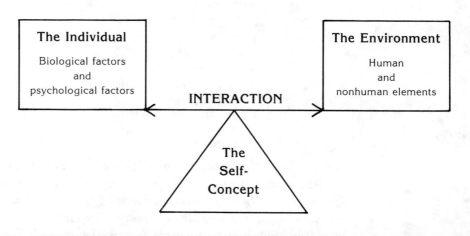

responsibility for one's own existence. The value of self-awareness and the importance of being responsible for your own life are the themes of the following poem:

Mirrors

When humans found the mirror
They began to lose their souls
The point of course is that
They began to concern themselves
With their images rather than
Their selves.

Other people's eyes are mirrors
But the most distorting kind
For if you look to them you
   can only see
Reflections of your reflections
Your warpings of their warpings

What then instead?

Do not look at yourself (except perhaps with amusement)
Feel yourself instead
As we did before mirrors
When we were young
And did not feel the need to please
But only to be
Experience how it is to be
Now

Where are your passions and desires?
Your knots and pains and anxious
   unattended muscles?
Where are your laughter and your tears
   that are deeper than your throat?

Where is what you want?
What you love and hate?
How do you reach and push away?
How do you waste your strength
   in self-holding constriction?
Keeping yourself against reaching
   and pushing away?

Be
And you will be involved in life
So involved in life
That you will afford no time
   or inclination
For staring with bulging
   or squinting eyes
At mirrors.[7]

To understand the importance of self-concept, think of your own life. How has your self-concept influenced you? Has your self-image changed over time or remained the same? Do you have a positive self-concept today? Can you identify elements in your personal nature and social roles that have helped to form your self-concept? Explain briefly.

PERSONALITY STRUCTURE
AND DYNAMICS

There are many theories of personality. Historically, the most influential has been the psychoanalytic theory of Sigmund Freud.

The Id, Ego, and Superego of
the Human Personality

Psychoanalytic theory identifies three systems or structures within the personality and attributes to each one certain functions and energies.

One of these structures is the id, within which are two powerful drives: a constructive drive (derived from sexual forces within the person) leading to love, growth, and integration of the personality with the surrounding world; and a destructive drive (derived from aggressive forces within the person) leading to feelings of hate, constriction of the personality, alienation from the surrounding world, and death. One of the major tasks of the personality is to fuse these drives so that the constructive drive is dominant. Also the site of repressed memories and experiences and of primitive wishes and impulses, the id comprises the uncivilized core of man that continually struggles for expression.

The job of the ego, considered to be the executive part of the personality, is to control and guide the powerful drives of the id. The ego is made up of the five senses, together with the abilities to concentrate, judge, form concepts, think reflectively, recall, learn, and act. The ego seeks to master the outside world so that the person can survive.

The third structure is the superego or, more colloquially, the conscience — an internal, self-governing agent with four functions:

Rules. As part of the process of growth, children identify with their parents and other important figures in their environment. In doing so, they assimilate many of their parents' rules for living — rules about expressing aggressive impulses and about giving and receiving love.

Values. By the same process of identification, children adopt and evolve certain values that become the basis for their attitudes about important aspects of living. These values range from such firmly and universally established ideals as the sanctity of human life to more specific ones that are part of a professional discipline, such as the values of privacy and confidentiality that govern the practice of medicine.

Ideals. The conscience spurs people on to attain an ego ideal, an internalized image of oneself at one's future best. This image is constructed from expectations held by parents and others, from aspirations children develop for themselves out of recognition of their capacities and abilities, and from identification with important figures in the environment. Mark Twain said, "It may be called the Master Passion, the hunger for self-approval." Concepts of "self-fulfillment" and "self-actualization" in part refer to a person's efforts to attain the ego ideal. However, the ego ideal, like a distant mountain peak, is beyond one's capacities so that it continues to serve as a goal toward which one is constantly striving. Various social models, ranging from presidents, artists, scholars, and saints on the one hand, to con men and drug dealers on the other — depending on the cultural milieu from which the child comes — serve as the raw material for the ego ideal, and their function as models is reinforced by history, literature, religion, myth, and folklore.

Judgments. The fourth function of the conscience, and the most evident, is the one that polices and makes judgments. Everyone has experienced pangs of conscience or twinges of guilt after having violated the rules or values by which he lives or when he has not met the demands of the ego ideal.[8]

Using Freud's model of personality structure and dynamics, can you identify the elements in your own behavior that seem to come from the id (sexual and aggressive drives)? Which of your values and actions can you trace to the superego or conscience (the influence of social programming and personal ideals)? How effective is your ego in balancing the physical drives of the id with the idealistic demands of the superego? Who is in control of your life — the id, ego, or superego?

ID, SUPEREGO, AND EGO — PERSONAL ANALYSIS

Directions

Use the spaces below to evaluate your personality according to Freud's psychoanalytic theory.

ID

Evaluate sexual (constructive) drives leading to love, growth, and creativity. To what degree do you feel these drives? What behaviors can be traced to these drives?

_____

_____

_____

_____

_____

Consider aggressive (destructive) drives leading to conflict, hate, and alienation. To what degree do you feel these drives? What behaviors can be traced to them?

_____

_____

_____

_____

_____

SUPEREGO

Evaluate the influence of society on the formation of your values (consider parents and teachers especially). Who has influenced you? What values were taught?

_____

_____

_____

_____

_____

Consider your conscience. What principles and standards guide you? Describe your personal ideals.

_____

_____

_____

_____

_____

EGO

How effective is your ego? Are the physical drives of the id in balance with the idealistic demands of the conscience? Evaluate yourself at this point in time.

_____

_____

_____

_____

_____

CONSCIOUS AND SUBCONSCIOUS BEHAVIOR

Imagine the human personality as an iceberg. Below the waterline is the mass of the iceberg, and below the level of consciousness is the mass of personality. See Figure 3.2.

FIGURE 3.2

Conscious and Subconscious Personality

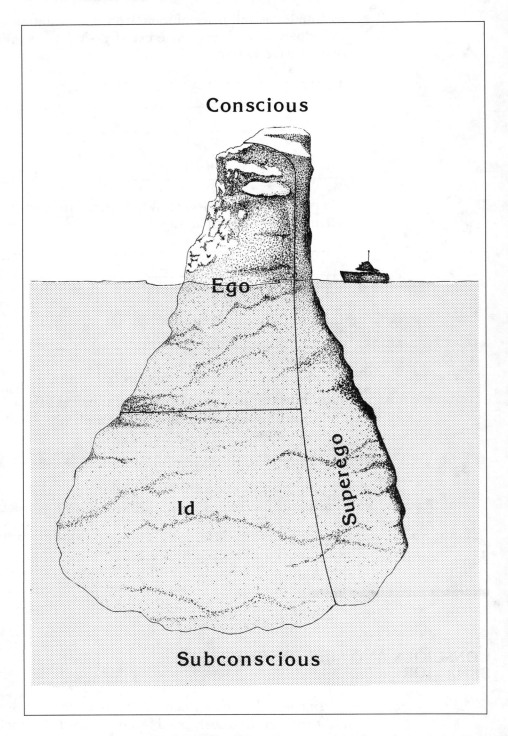

Just as you can only see the tip of the iceberg, so is conscious behavior only the "tip" of the human personality. Below the water level lies the subconscious, the dwelling place of things forgotten because of poor memory and things repressed because they are unpleasant or threatening. Both positive and negative experiences and feelings live in the subconscious.

If you are to fully understand and deal with human behavior — your own and that of others — you should recognize that people often do what they do for subconscious reasons. A person may dress or speak in a certain manner, and the subconscious motive may be to be accepted by others; a person may shout or make an emotional display, and the subconscious reason may be to gain attention; a person may distrust others, and the subconscious reason may be to avoid being hurt.

Demonstrations like the following show the role of subconscious behavior:

> During hypnosis, the subject was instructed that after he awakened, Dr. D. would begin talking to him about some abstruse subject in which he was not at all interested, and that, although he would actually be profoundly bored, he would try to appear interested. He was told that he would want very much to close the conversation, that he would wish for some way of shutting off this interminable flow of words, that he would look around in the hope of finding some distraction, and that he would feel that Dr. D. was terribly tiresome.
>
> The subject was then awakened, whereupon Dr. D. began the conversation. Although the subject appeared to be politely attentive, Dr. D. would occasionally say, "Perhaps you're not interested?" The subject would reply with excessive emphasis, "Oh, yes, certainly, I'm very much interested." Now and then, he would interrupt Dr. D., trying to pin him down to some definite point for discussion, but each time this effort was evaded.
>
> At length the subject began glancing about the room and was noted casually to observe an open door. Finally, he interrupted Dr. D., saying, "Excuse me, I feel an awful draft," and got up to close the door. As he did so, he was asked what he was doing. He replied, "The air seems to be awfully hot ('hot air'); I thought I would shut off the draft." When the hypnotist pretended not to understand and asked him what he was doing, the subject replied, "Why, I just shut the bore."[9]

How much of your own behavior is motivated below the level of consciousness? Do you understand why you do what you do? Is your subconscious composed of positive experiences and feelings, thus providing a source of strength, or is your subconscious filled with negative attitudes and unresolved problems? Discuss. _____

_____

_____

_____

_____

The human personality falls into three domains—feelings, cognitions, and motor movements. Statistically, all behavior within these domains falls within a curve of normality, often referred to as the "bell-shaped curve." On any human trait, most people cluster around the middle of this curve, with few extremes. For example, most people enjoy music, but few devote their lives to a career as a musician; most people have average intellectual ability, while few are at the genius level; and most people are able to run a mile at an average speed, while few are able to run a mile in less than four minutes. Figure 3.3 shows the bell-shaped curve for human traits.

An explanation of each of the three domains of human behavior and their interrelationship is as follows:[10]

Feelings

The autonomic nervous system (sympathetic and parasympathetic) and the endocrine system (glands and hormones) form the physiological basis for feelings. All feelings fall along a continuum of pleasant, neutral, and unpleasant sensations. Feelings reflect emotions, such as love and hate, trust and suspicion, happiness and depression, contentment and anxiety. Feelings also reflect biological states, such as pleasure, pain, wellness, and illness. See Figure 3.4.

Emotions and biological states are interrelated, as seen in a person who feels less pain when in a state of happiness and in a person who is unable to feel loving because of illness. Elements of personality that are

---

FIGURE 3.3

Curve of Normality for Any Human Trait

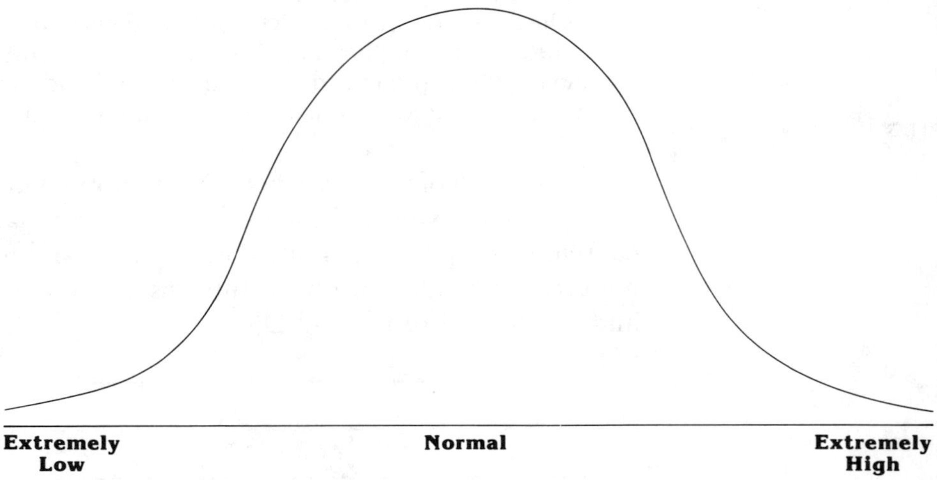

| **Extremely Low** | **Normal** | **Extremely High** |

FIGURE 3.4

Continuum of Feelings

PLEASANT SENSATIONS	←········ NEUTRAL SENSATIONS ········→	UNPLEASANT SENSATIONS
	Emotions	
Love	←---------------------------→	Hate
Trust	←---------------------------→	Suspicion
Happiness	←---------------------------→	Depression
Contentment	←---------------------------→	Anxiety
	Biological Stress	
Pleasure	←---------------------------→	Pain
Wellness	←---------------------------→	Illness

influenced by the feelings domain include personal temperament, value orientations, interest patterns, and social opinions. Any behavior that is an expression of attitude has its roots in the feelings domain and can be an important factor of personality, helping to explain basic optimism or negativism as a world view, as well as less basic, yet important, political preference.

Feelings develop according to an emotional timetable. The normal sequence in which emotions first appear, from birth to age fifteen, is shown in Figure 3.5.

Cognitions

The central nervous system (nerve cells, pathways, spinal column, and brain) forms the physiological basis of the cognitive domain. All thinking processes, including simple awareness (such as whether it is raining outside) and complex mental reasoning (verbal comprehension, mathematics, and interpersonal judgments), are functions of this domain of human behavior. Cognitive activity falls along a continuum of simple to complex, as seen in Figure 3.6.

Any behavior that is an expression of mental capacity, such as knowledge of history, mechanical aptitude, creative thinking, or general problem-solving ability, has its roots in the cognitive domain.

FIGURE 3.5

An Emotional Timetable

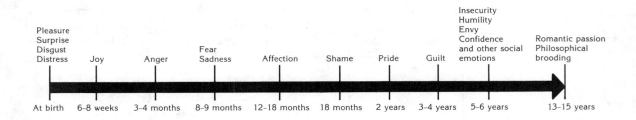

									Insecurity Humility Envy	
Pleasure Surprise Disgust Distress	Joy	Anger	Fear Sadness	Affection	Shame	Pride	Guilt	Confidence and other social emotions	Romantic passion Philosophical brooding	
At birth	6–8 weeks	3–4 months	8–9 months	12–18 months	18 months	2 years	3–4 years	5–6 years	13–15 years	

Source: p. 425 from Psychology: The Frontiers of Behavior, *3rd edition, by Ronald E. Smith, Irwin G. Sarason, and Barbara Sarason. Copyright © 1986. Reprinted by permission of Harper and Row, Publishers, Inc.*

Motor Movements

Motor movements fall along two continua: simple to complex and general to specific. See Figures 3.7 and 3.8.

Motor movements represent skills that can play major roles in defining personality. Indeed, skills may be the dominant dimension of personality during the working years. Consider sports figures, musicians, actors, and artists.

FIGURE 3.6

Continuum of Cognitions

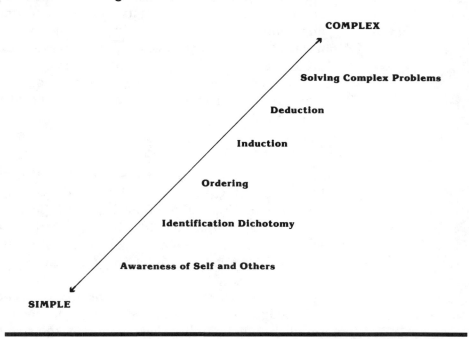

COMPLEX

Solving Complex Problems

Deduction

Induction

Ordering

Identification Dichotomy

Awareness of Self and Others

SIMPLE

FIGURE 3.7

Continuum of Motor Movements—Simple to Complex

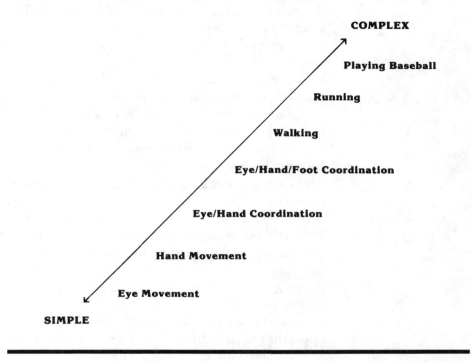

COMPLEX

Playing Baseball

Running

Walking

Eye/Hand/Foot Coordination

Eye/Hand Coordination

Hand Movement

Eye Movement

SIMPLE

FIGURE 3.8

Continuum of Motor Movements—General to Specific

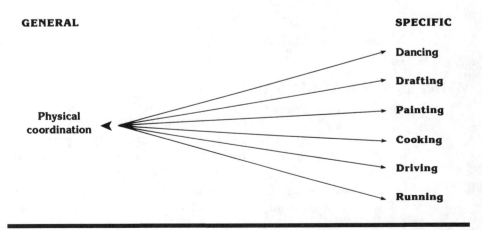

GENERAL

SPECIFIC

Physical coordination

Dancing

Drafting

Painting

Cooking

Driving

Running

Interrelationships

Each domain of human behavior influences and is influenced by the others, and all are affected by environment, so personality is multidimensional and multidetermined. Imagine an individual whose temperament is aggressive, whose value orientation is aesthetic, who is interested in working with tools and materials, who has knowledge of design, art, and construction, and who has an aptitude for drawing. With supportive environmental conditions, the individual might become a productive and creative architect. If any factor in any behavioral domain, or in the environment, were changed, the same individual would develop a different personality and different behavior.

What if this person were less vigorous or aggressive by temperament (productivity would probably be reduced); or what if the value orientation were economic instead of aesthetic (creations would probably not be as beautiful); or what if the person were interested in working with people instead of with things (the person might manage other architects instead of personally doing the work); or what if the person never learned design, art, and construction (lack of knowledge would probably affect the quality of work); or what if an aptitude for music, rather than for drawing, had been developed (the person would probably be a musician); and what if the environment were hostile, such as a difficult boss, a depressed economy, or personal problems at home (the loss of energy, opportunity, and time would reduce achievements). Each domain of human behavior is interdependent, and all of these are influenced by environment.

Consider your own personality; how would you describe your personal temperament, value orientation, and interest pattern? What special knowledge, aptitude, or other mental capacity do you possess? What unique skills and motor movements have you acquired? How has your environment acted to support or hinder your development in each of the behavioral domains? Discuss. _____

_____

_____

_____

_____

WHAT IS YOUR PERSONALITY TYPE?

Two traits of personality that have their roots primarily in the feelings domain and that are especially important in human relations are ascendancy (the tendency to be peaceful or dominant) and sociability (the tendency to be introverted or extroverted). For an evaluation of your own personality on these important traits, complete the following questionnaire.

TYPES OF PEOPLE—
DIFFERENT STROKES FOR
DIFFERENT FOLKS

Directions

The following survey includes questions about your personality on two important traits: ascendancy and sociability. It measures how dominant or peaceful you are and how introverted or extroverted you are. There are no right or wrong answers on this questionnaire. Answer each question as accurately as possible. If you are uncertain about a question, give your first natural response. Read each question, decide how you feel about it, and circle your answer as follows:

Circle 1 for *never*.
Circle 2 for *rarely*.
Circle 3 for *sometimes*.
Circle 4 for *often*.
Circle 5 for *always*.

Questions	*Responses*				
	Never	Rarely	Sometimes	Often	Always
1. Are you a strong-willed person?	1	2	3	4	(5)
2. Are you quiet and reserved in new social situations?	1	(2)	3	4	5
3. Do you find it easy to forgive and forget?	1	2	3	(4)	5
4. Are you spontaneous and outgoing?	1	2	3	(4)	5
5. Do you continue arguments when you know the other person has had enough?	(1)	2	3	4	5
6. Do you embarrass easily?	1	(2)	3	4	5

Source: Developed by Jerri Thomas, Northern Kentucky University, 1982, based on the works of Gordon Allport and Carl Jung. Reprinted with permission.

Questions	Never	Rarely	Sometimes	Often	Always
			Responses		
7. Do you find it hard to say "no" to a salesperson, even when you really do not want the product?	(1)	2	3	4	5
8. Are you at ease meeting new people?	1	2	3	4	(5)
9. Will you ask to see someone higher up when your requests are not met?	1	2	(3)	4	5
10. Would you prefer to read a character study over an adventure story?	1	2	(3)	4	5
11. Is it difficult for you to ask for something for yourself?	1	(2)	3	4	5
12. Do you find it easier to express yourself in conversation than in writing?	1	2	(3)	4	(5)
13. Are you critical of the ideas, opinions, and behavior of others?	1	2	(3)	4	5
14. Do you think about the meaning of life?	1	2	(3)	4	5
15. Do you want things settled and secure in your life?	1	(2)	3	4	5
16. Do you enjoy giving speeches?	1	(2)	3	4	5
17. Are you action oriented?	1	2	3	(4)	5
18. Are you attentive to details?	1	2	3	4	(5)
19. Will you sit at a restaurant table you do not like rather than request a better one?	(1)	2	3	4	5
20. Do you like to be the center of attention?	1	2	(3)	4	5
21. Among your colleagues, are you the one who decides what the group will do?	1	2	3	(4)	5

Questions	Never	Rarely	Sometimes	Often	Always
			Responses		
22. Do you prefer to listen in social situations?	1	(2)	3	4	5
23. Are competitive situations unpleasant to you?	(1)	2	3	4	5
24. Do you like social activities, such as parties and meetings?	1	2	3	4	(5)
25. Do you control the various groups in which you participate?	1	2	(3)	4	5
26. Are you a quiet person?	(1)	2	3	4	5
27. If you have a disagreement with someone, do you try to smooth things over?	1	2	3	(4)	5
28. Do people usually remember you?	1	2	(3)	4	5
29. With your family and friends, are you the one "in charge"?	1	2	(3)	4	5
30. Do you prefer a more planned than spontaneous life?	1	(2)	3	4	5
31. Is it hard for you to express anger toward others?	1	2	3	(4)	(5)
32. Do you like to work with people?	1	2	3	4	(5)
33. Do you step in and make decisions for others?	1	(2)	3	4	5
34. Do you prefer to do a perfect job when you know less would be acceptable?	1	2	3	(4)—(5)	
35. Are you cautious in approaching new or difficult problems?	1	2	(3)	4	5
36. Do you like to talk about yourself?	1	2	(3)	4	5

Questions	Never	Rarely	Sometimes	Often	Always
37. Do personal restrictions upset you?	1	2	3	4	(5)
38. Is privacy important to you?	1	2	3	(4)	5
39. Do arguments upset you?	1	2	(3)	4	5
40. Do you make friends easily?	1	2	3	4	(5)
41. Do you try to persuade other people to your way of thinking?	1	2	(3)	4	5
42. Do you prefer to work alone?	1	(2)	3	4	5
43. Are you easygoing?	1	2	3	4	(5)
44. Do you enjoy it when people talk about you?	1	2	(3)	4	5
45. Do you like to create events and "make things happen"?	1	2	(3)	4	5
46. Do you find it easier to express yourself in writing than in speaking?	1	2	(3)	4	5
47. Is it easy for you to relax?	1	2	3	(4)	5
48. Do you overlook details because of other interests?	1	(2)	3	4	5
49. Once you have made a decision, is it difficult for you to change your mind?	1	2	3	4	(5)
50. Do you show your emotions less than most people?	1	2	3	4	(5)
51. Do you have trouble saying "no" to people?	(1)	2	3	4	5
52. Do you enjoy people?	1	2	3	4	(5)
53. Are you an opinionated person?	1	2	3	4	(5)
54. Do you enjoy the pleasures of solitude such as reading, writing, and					

Responses

Questions	Responses				
	Never	Rarely	Sometimes	Often	Always
thinking, over social activities?	1	2	3	(4)	5
55. Do you believe people are basically good?	1	2	3	(4)	5
56. Do you like to show affection?	1	2	3	(4)	5
57. Are you achievement oriented?	1	2	3	4	(5)
58. Do you make decisions only after gathering all available facts?	1	2	3	(4)	5
59. Are you a good team player?	1	2	3	4	(5)
60. Do you feel comfortable in social situations?	1	2	3	4	(5)
61. Do you consider yourself to be a leader rather than a follower?	1	2	3	(4)	5
62. Are you patient and methodical in problem-solving situations?	1	2	3	(4)	5
63. Are power and prestige unimportant to you?	1	(2)	3	4	5
64. Do you like variety in your social life?	1	2	3	(4)	5
65. Are you a forceful person?	1	2	(3)	4	5
66. Do others find you hard to understand?	1	(2)	3	4	5
67. Do you try to avoid inter-personal conflict?	1	2	(3)	4	5
68. Do you enjoy selling your ideas?	1	2	3	(4)	5
69. Do you like competitive situations?	1	2	3	(4)	5
70. Do you rewrite your let-ters, reports, and other assignments?	1	2	(3)	4	5
71. Are you a soft-spoken person?	1	(2)	3	4	5

	Responses				
Questions	Never	Rarely	Sometimes	Often	Always
72. Would you prefer going to a party over reading a book?	1	2	3	4	(5)
73. If you were waiting in a line, would you confront someone who crowded ahead of you?	1	2	(3)	4	5
74. Are you neat and orderly?	1	2	3	(4)	5
75. Does it upset you to say unpleasant things to others?	1	(2)	3	4	5
76. Do you make decisions impulsively?	1	2	(3)	4	5
77. Are you persistent in pursuing your goals?	1	2	3	4	(5)
78. Do you keep your feelings private?	1	2	3	(4)	5
79. Are you tactful in your relations with others?	1	2	3	(4)	5
80. Do you talk more than you listen?	1	2	(3)	4	5

SCORING

To find your score on the Types of People test, first place the number you circled for each question in the appropriate space in the answer key that follows. Then, obtain the totals for dominance, peacefulness, introversion, and extroversion, and divide each of these by 2.

Questionnaire Answer Key

Ascendency				*Sociability*			
Dominance		**Peacefulness**		**Introversion**		**Extroversion**	
1. _5_ 41. _3_		3. _4_ 43. _5_		2. _2_ 42. _2_		4. _4_ 44. _3_	
5. _1_ 45. _3_		7. _1_ 47. _4_		6. _2_ 46. _3_		8. _5_ 48. _2_	
9. _3_ 49. _5_		11. _2_ 51. _1_		10. _3_ 50. _5_		12. _3_ 52. _5_	
13. _3_ 53. _5_		15. _2_ 55. _4_		14. _3_ 54. _4_		16. _2_ 56. _4_	
17. _4_ 57. _5_		19. _1_ 59. _5_		18. _5_ 58. _4_		20. _3_ 60. _5_	

21. 4 61. 4 23. 1 63. 2 22. 2 62. 4 24. 5 64. 4
25. 3 65. 3 27. 4 67. 3 26. 1 66. 2 28. 3 68. 4
29. 3 69. 4 31. 4 71. 2 30. 2 70. 3 32. 5 72. 5
33. 2 73. 3 35. 3 75. 2 34. 4 74. 4 36. 3 76. 3
37. 5 77. 5 39. 3 79. 4 38. 4 78. 4 40. 5 80. 3

___ + ___   ___ + ___   ___ + ___   ___ + ___

= 73 / 2   = 57 / 2   = 63 / 2   = 76 / 2

= 36.5   = 28.5   = 31.5   = 38

Next, chart your scores for dominance, peacefulness, introversion, and extroversion on the "personality profile" in Figure 3.9. When you have placed your scores in the appropriate locations, draw a line from each score to create a picture of your personality type, as shown in Figure 3.10.

INTERPRETATION

"Types of People — Different Strokes for Different Folks" measures two important traits of personality: ascendancy and sociability. The following describes the dimensions of each trait.

Ascendancy

Dominance. The dominant person expresses emotions in a forceful way and is concerned with obtaining results. Dominant people enjoy competitive situations and can become demanding when trying to complete a task. They usually take a direct approach to obtaining results. The following are characteristics of the dominant personality:

- likes to be in command;
- prefers to be the leader;
- often is critical of the ideas and opinions of others;
- usually is forceful in dealings with others; often is stubborn;
- is persistent in obtaining goals, strong willed, and opinionated;
- enjoys having power and prestige;
- enjoys competitive situations;
- becomes impatient when requests are not met;
- makes things happen; takes a direct approach;
- enjoys difficult assignments; is achievement oriented;
- looks for opportunities to advance; accepts challenges;
- questions the status quo; seeks positions of authority.

FIGURE 3.9

Personality Profile

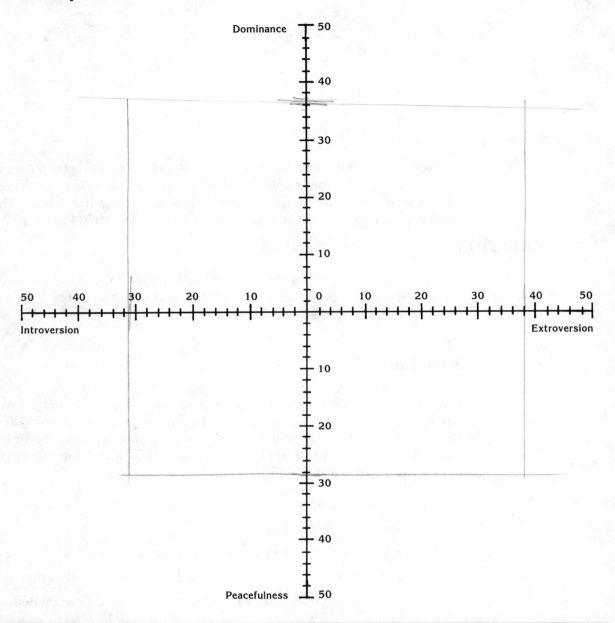

FIGURE 3.10

Sample Personality Profile

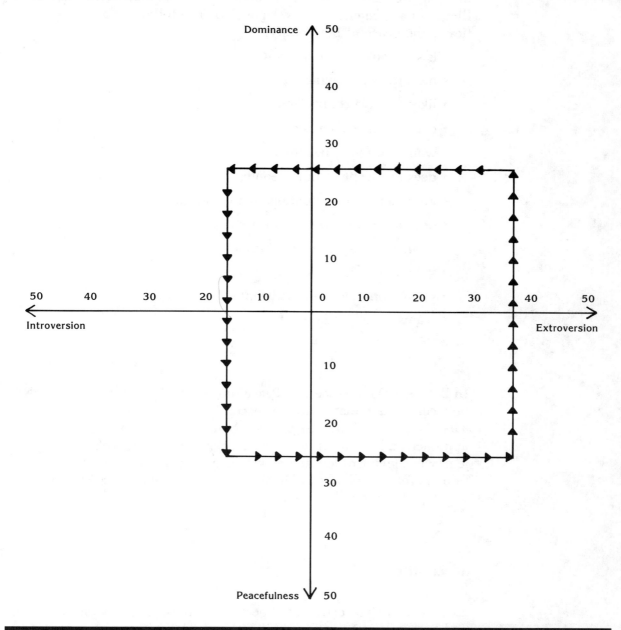

Peacefulness. The peaceful person expresses emotions in a quiet and calm manner. Peaceful people conduct human relations and business dealings in a low-pressure way and avoid direct confrontation, interpersonal conflict, and arguments whenever possible. The following are characteristics of the peaceful personality:

- is soft spoken and easygoing;
- has difficulty saying "no";
- likes to have things secure;
- does not like arguments;
- wants harmony in human relations;
- does not want to hurt people;
- approaches new situations with caution;
- does not value power and prestige;
- is sincere in human relations;
- values love;
- shows consideration for people;
- wants to help others.

In Between Dominance and Peacefulness. The personality that falls in between the dominant and the peaceful is a balance of the two extremes. The "in-between" person pursues goals with a relaxed but persistent approach and demonstrates consideration for people's feelings and problems when giving orders and making decisions. He or she prefers cooperation in problem solving and involves others whenever possible when taking steps to accomplish goals.

Sociability

Extroversion. The extroverted person is comfortable in social situations and genuinely enjoys people. Extroverts find it easy to express their feelings. They like variety and enjoy talking about themselves and their activities. In a sense, extroverts "wear their hearts on their sleeves" and are likely to behave in an impulsive and spontaneous way. The following are characteristics of the extroverted personality:

- makes new friends easily;
- likes to talk; laughs readily;
- dislikes details; does not take particular care of personal possessions;

- generates enthusiasm; has a high energy level;
- feels comfortable in groups;
- enjoys human interaction;
- likes to work with people;
- stimulates others;
- responds to public praise;
- likes attention;
- usually is self-confident;
- avoids direct controls and routine work.

Introversion. The introverted person does not readily express emotion and feels comfortable working alone. Introverts like to see the results of their own efforts. They are conscientious, precise, and systematic in their work and value self-control and self-reliance. Introverts are individualistic and reserved in their relations with others. The following are characteristics of the introverted personality:

- values independence;
- likes to work alone;
- dislikes social functions;
- moves deliberately; does not like to be hurried;
- is a perfectionist about work;
- is uncomfortable in groups; values privacy;
- is slow in making new friends;
- struggles with a problem rather than ask for help;
- appears aloof;
- is self-conscious in social situations;
- values self-discipline;
- prefers books and solitary activities.

In Between Extroversion and Introversion. The "in-between" person is a balance of the two extremes, extrovert and introvert. Such people feel equally comfortable in social situations and solitary activities. They are flexible and can usually adapt to situations that require perfectionist behavior as well as situations that require tolerance of imperfections.

The two traits of personality (ascendancy and sociability) and their four dimensions (dominance, peacefulness, introversion, and extroversion) interact to create four personality types: social/leader; social/charm; decisive/analytical; and detail/supportive. We all have qualities of each personality type; however, usually one type is most characteristic of each of us.

Each personality type has unique qualities and requires different treatment to bring out its best. Typical characteristics and the most effective way to lead each are as follows.

The Social/Leader Personality Type

Figure 3.11 shows the personality profile for the social/leader type. This personality type has high levels of dominance and sociability and directs these traits toward the competency motive. This person wants to make things happen and create events involving people and things rather than wait passively for circumstances to take shape.

The social/leader personality responds to personal challenge, is comfortable with people, enjoys variety, and is stimulated by change. Optimistic and socially outgoing, this person is self-confident and enjoys daily

ILLUS. 3.2–3.5

Your personality type requires unique treatment to bring out your best.

FIGURE 3.11

Personality Profile for the Social/Leader Type

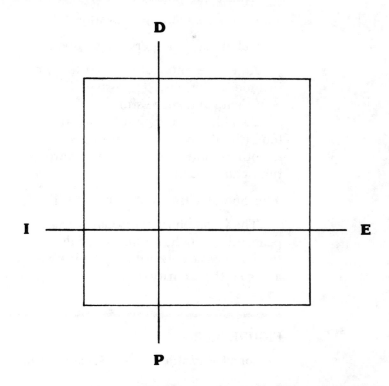

contact with people. Possessing initiative and drive, the social/leader personality leads by persuasion and contagious enthusiasm. Although independent and firm in thought, this person can appreciate and accept the views and contributions of others and has the ability to motivate people to work together. The social/leader type has many natural leadership traits.

The social/leader personality wants:

- responsibility;
- challenge;
- prestige;
- social influence;
- variety;
- achievement;
- opportunity for advancement.

The correct way to lead this personality type is to:

- provide opportunity for leadership; give the person full authority with corresponding responsibility;

- require excellence; provide rewards for good performance;
- provide demanding assignments; judge according to results;
- place the person in charge of developing others;
- offer freedom of operation;
- challenge the person's competitive spirit.

Adjectives most often used to describe the social/leader personality include ambitious, aggressive, flexible, variety loving, forceful, self-confident, and successful.

Possible work problems include: (1) talking too much and listening too little; (2) overlooking important details; (3) overpowering or inhibiting others; and (4) a tendency toward overscheduling and taking on more than can be done.

The Social/Charm Personality Type

The social/charm personality (see Figure 3.12) is both extroverted and peaceful. As such, important goals are affiliation and security. This person has a basic concern for people's welfare. Helping others is important, and so is the security of having personal beliefs shared and confirmed by

FIGURE 3.12

Personality Profile for the Social/Charm Type

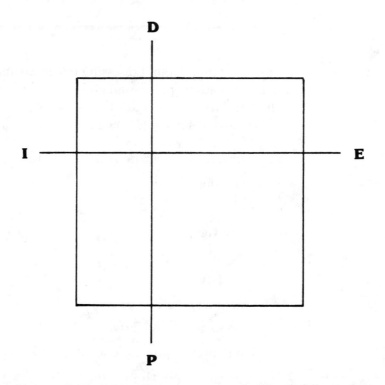

others. Outgoing and friendly, such people enjoy working with and through others, and their polite and helpful manner helps them to be quickly accepted. This type is somewhat cautious when dealing with new or difficult problems and usually demonstrates a good sense of timing. The social/charm personality requires a harmonious work atmosphere, avoids interpersonal conflict, and tries to keep things running smoothly. Relaxed and interested, this person likes to be sought out in time of need and enjoys playing a counseling role. The social/charm personality is a good listener and a good team player.

The social/charm personality wants:

- to work with people;

- opportunity for discussion;

- warmth and support;

- human interaction;

- a chance to motivate others;

- social recognition.

The correct way to lead this personality type is to:

- provide a warm and supportive emotional environment;

- provide opportunities for talking about ideas, people, and activities;

- provide a means for transferring talk into action;

- allow time for stimulating activities and social interaction;

- provide participative job relationships; include the person in the decision-making process;

- provide social incentives for taking on tasks;

- demonstrate consideration for human feelings and welfare.

Adjectives most often used to describe the social/charm personality include friendly, sociable, altruistic, considerate, helpful, understanding, and supportive.

Possible work problems include (1) trying too hard to please; (2) being easily hurt; (3) not attending to details; and (4) lacking job focus and task completion.

The Decisive/Analytical Personality Type

The decisive/analytical personality (see Figure 3.13) is both dominant and introverted. This person has a strong desire to do things "the right way" and is not always people oriented. This person tends to have a questioning, philosophical attitude and is most productive when there is ample time for private reflection, unencumbered by social considerations. Independent and self-assured, the decisive/analytical person enjoys challenging situations and takes pride in handling problems alone. Placing

FIGURE 3.13

Personality Profile for the Decisive/Analytical Type

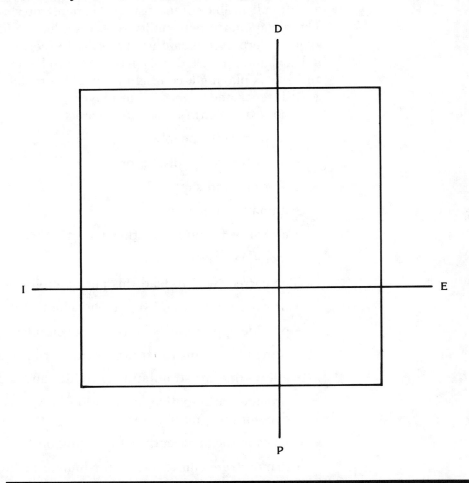

a high value on privacy, this person prefers others to take the social initiative and does not mind working alone. This person is exacting in work behavior and is reluctant to delegate to others. In any field — business, science, art — the decisive/analytical personality is seen as an independent and strong-willed person with little patience in human relations and a tendency to be brusque and even abrasive. When sufficiently motivated, the decisive/analytical personality is capable of significant personal accomplishments.

The decisive/analytical personality wants:

- privacy;

- personal accomplishment;

- independence;

- self-reliance;

- difficult assignments;
- few restrictions.

The correct way to lead this personality type is to:

- challenge the person's intellect;
- provide individual rewards for individual accomplishments;
- recognize the individual's personal independence;
- praise past performances, set deadlines — then let go;
- stick to business; be brief and to the point;
- provide difficult tasks that require independent accomplishment.

Adjectives most often used to describe the decisive/analytical personality include creative, persistent, thinking, opinionated, independent, rigid, immodest, stubborn, and perfectionist.

Possible work problems include (1) insensitivity in human relations; (2) impatience in decision making; (3) unwillingness to listen to other people; and (4) failure to delegate.

The Detail/Supportive Personality Type

The detail/supportive personality (see Figure 3.14) is quiet and peaceful and works best in an environment that permits order and stability. Willing to help others, this person will usually turn a hand to anything that is requested, often at the expense of personal desires. Basically cautious by nature, this person is slow to accept the new and experimental until it is proven completely. Preferring established ways, there is a tendency toward conservatism and traditional values and an appreciation of the importance of policy and precedent in dealing with problems. The detail/supportive personality likes a dependable work environment and avoids situations in which many things are "up in the air," with little predictability of results. Work goals include being correct and precise, specializing in areas of special competencies, and performing duties well. Rewards include being an accepted, appreciated member of the work group or organization and being respected for special talents.

The detail/supportive personality wants:

- order;
- stability;
- no sudden changes;
- precise job descriptions;
- recognition for loyalty and dependability;
- detailed instructions;
- personal respect.

FIGURE 3.14

Personality Profile for the Detail/Supportive Type

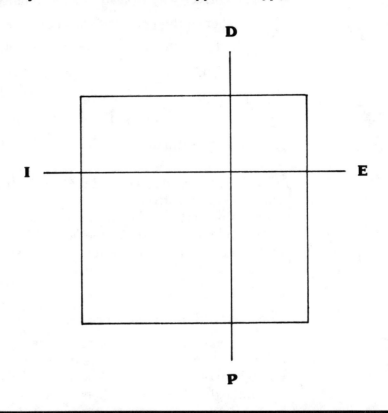

The correct way to lead this personality type is to:

- provide a secure work environment;
- ask questions to obtain the person's involvement; use participative management;
- be patient in drawing out his or her ideas;
- clearly define goals and roles;
- present new ideas or departures from status quo in a nonthreatening manner; give the person a chance to adjust; support changes with detailed and accurate data;
- if criticism is in order, provide constructive recommendations; disagree with the facts, not with the person — and do so in private;
- provide leadership that is clear and logical;
- give thorough training, explaining why things are done as they are;
- show appreciation for length of service and personal loyalty.

Adjectives most often used to describe the detail/supportive personality include cautious, quiet, modest, structured, reserved, cooperative, and dependable.

Possible work problems include (1) unwillingness to make unpopular decisions; (2) difficulty in delegating; (3) a tendency to be too cautious or conservative; and (4) a tendency to become buried in detail.

What is your personality type? Are you a social/leader, social/charm, decisive/analytical, or detail/supportive person? Does your world match your personality type? Are you right for your job? Do your family and friends understand your personality and support your needs? Discuss.

_____

_____

_____

_____

_____

_____

_____

_____

_____

_____

_____

_____

_____

PERSONALITY TRAITS

Years ago, Gordon Allport of Harvard University analyzed the English language and found 18,000 traitlike terms used to designate distinctive forms of behavior. Allport believed that this rich collection of terms provided a way to capture the uniqueness of each individual and that this uniqueness could be described in terms of personal dispositions. He identified three levels of strength or dominance of personal dispositions: cardinal dispositions, central dispositions, and secondary dispositions.

When an individual has a cardinal disposition, almost every aspect of his or her life is influenced by it. The person's entire identity is shaped by this powerful disposition. People who have a cardinal trait are often labeled with names or adjectives derived from historical or fictional characters, such as Christlike, Machiavellian, Quixotic, Scrooge, or Don Juan.

Few people have one cardinal disposition. Ordinarily, the personality develops around several outstanding central dispositions. These central traits form the dominant characteristics and tendencies of the personality.

Allport believed that these central characteristics of personality were likely to be those you would mention in writing a letter of recommendation — dependable, intelligent, kindhearted, and resourceful are examples.

A third level of personality traits is that of secondary dispositions. Secondary dispositions function more on the periphery of the personality. They are less significant, less conspicuous, and less consistent than central dispositions or cardinal traits, but they are important in personal adjustment and interpersonal relations. "Likes chocolate," "likes to travel," and "prefers blondes" are examples of secondary traits.[11]

To personalize the subject of personality traits, complete the following exercise.

CARDINAL, CENTRAL, AND SECONDARY TRAITS — PERSONAL EVALUATION

Directions

In this exercise, you will evaluate the dispositions that exist in your own personality. Answer the following questions in the spaces provided.

Identify and briefly describe your cardinal disposition. (If your life is not dominated by a "ruling passion" or cardinal trait, describe the cardinal disposition of a family member, friend, or acquaintance.)

_____

_____

_____

_____

Think about your central dispositions. Identify the most significant central traits in your personality, and give an example of how these traits affect your life. In a study by Allport, the average number of central traits was seven. How many central traits do you have in your personality?

_____

_____

_____

_____

_____

_____

_____

Identify your secondary dispositions—do you enjoy music, are you fond of animals, do you like to read, etc.?

_____

_____

_____

_____

_____

_____

_____

_____

_____

DEFENSE MECHANISMS

People use defense mechanisms to preserve both biological and emotional health. Biological protection ranges from the large muscle movements that allow you to fight off physical attack to the microscopic efforts of white blood corpuscles that enable you to combat infection and disease. In a healthy person, such biological defenses are natural and automatic reactions to physical threat. In a similar way, you preserve emotional well-being through psychological defense mechanisms. This is often subconscious behavior brought into operation to protect feelings of self-worth and a positive self-concept.

Everyone uses defense mechanisms, and they can be helpful as you adjust to life's demands. However, psychological defenses can be overused and can actually harm your personality by distorting reality and preventing you from dealing with problems effectively. The following is a discussion of eight common psychological defense mechanisms.[12]

Denial

If the truth is too threatening, you can deny it. Although this can give you needed comfort in the short term, it is the equivalent to lying to yourself, and when carried to an extreme, denial of reality can be harmful. People can deny physical illness, and this can help them get through the day. But at some point, they must face and correct the reality of physical illness, or greater harm may result.

Fantasy is a common form of denial and can be a pleasant escape. Through fantasy, you can deny unpleasant experiences and conditions and can imagine the world as you would like it to be. Although a certain

Denial can prevent
you from coping with
reality.

amount of fantasizing is normal and healthy, it can be harmful if practiced so much that you confuse a fantasy world with the real world. Constant denial of important facts, faults, or failures prevents you from coping successfully with reality. Denial is usually seen in adults only under severe stress.

Sublimation

If you have goals or desires that are unacceptable, a psychological defense is to redirect your behavior into more acceptable areas. In this way, you preserve your self-image, social reputation, and emotional health. This process is called sublimation.

People of all ages and in all areas of life use sublimation. A tackle executed on the football field may represent sublimated aggression; a painting of a nude may represent sublimated sexuality; and working in an orphanage may represent sublimated parental urges for the person who does not have children. Freud viewed sublimation as the most constructive of the defense mechanisms.

Displacement

If you transfer emotions toward one person or thing to another person or thing, you are using displacement as a defense mechanism. Sometimes this can be constructive, and sometimes not. It would not be constructive to shout at your spouse, strike your children, or kick the cat because you are upset about your work. However, it may be helpful to relieve your frustration by punching a bag or lifting weights.

It is usually best to deal with the source of emotional concern, even when this is difficult or unpleasant. If your spouse upsets you, channel your energy into solving your problems together rather than displacing the negative emotions onto your children or other innocent bystanders.

Regression

Regression is a retreat from an unpleasant current situation to a more pleasant past. If you go backward and return to childhood, you do not have to feel as responsible for your actions or for other people. You can be playful, spontaneous, irresponsible, and even selfish without feeling guilty.

Regression is a common defense mechanism when the personality is under stress. Psychologist Bruno Bettelheim describes the general regression to infantile behavior seen in many of the prisoners at Dachau and Buchenwald during World War II:

> The prisoners lived, like children, only in the immediate present. They became unable to plan for the future or to give up immediate pleasure satisfactions to gain greater ones in the near future. They were boastful, telling tales about what they had accomplished in their former lives, or how they succeeded in cheating foremen or guards, and how they sabotaged the work. Like children, they felt not at all set back or ashamed when it became known that they had lied about their prowess.[13]

More common examples of regression are the wife who goes home to her mother every time she and her husband quarrel and the student who indulges in candy and ice cream when the going gets tough, grades are low, and the world seems generally overwhelming.

As a defense mechanism, regression is good to the extent that it results in spontaneity and other healthy traits associated with childhood, and harmful to the extent that it results in selfishness or other unhealthy behavior.

Identification

You can feel good about yourself through identification. If the individual, family, country, company, or team you identify as your own is successful, you can take satisfaction and pride in that success. When practiced in moderation, identification is normal and healthy. However, when exercised to an extreme, or when used in place of experiencing personal self-worth, identification can be harmful. The father who lives life through his son's achievements places an undue burden on the son for his own happiness and fails to experience life on a firsthand basis. People who rely solely on the success of others for their own sense of worth usually experience frustration and dissatisfaction in the long run.

Repression

Repressing thoughts and feelings into the subconscious is a common defense mechanism that can be helpful. If it is not helpful to dwell on some embarrassing incident or failure, why do it? Better to keep it repressed and free your mind for constructive activities. In this way, the personality remains undamaged.

Some experiences are so traumatic that one represses them into the subconscious to prevent personality breakdown. This is the case of the battle-fatigued soldier who can remember everything up to the point of physical combat, but who has repressed the experiences of fear, killing, and death that he has undergone.

On the other hand, repression can be harmful if you fail to deal with the thoughts and feelings satisfactorily before repressing them, or if you repress so much of your personality that you do not know who you are, where you have been, or where you are going. In such a case, repression harms personality development.

Undoing

Sometimes you are sorry for harmful things you do. By going through the process of undoing, you can feel better about yourself and thus preserve your psychological health. For example, you may cause another person pain, extra work, or unhappiness. In order to undo this, you may take extraordinary steps to help them or to otherwise make up for your actions. The unfaithful husband may suddenly shower his wife with gifts to atone for his behavior; the businessman may seek to undo unethical business practices by giving large sums of money to the church or community; or the selfish mother may try to compensate by buying expensive presents and toys for her children.[14]

The process of undoing can be harmful if it becomes habitual behavior. People lose patience and respect for the person who constantly makes mistakes and seeks forgiveness by undoing.

Rationalization

"It wasn't important anyway," "What is meant to be will be," and "If only . . . ," are three common rationalizations. Rationalization is one of the psychological defense mechanisms most often used to justify actions, explain failures, and alleviate frustrations. Examples include the rejected lover who says, "I wasn't ready to settle down anyway"; the job applicant who says, "It would have been a terrible job," after learning that someone else has been selected; and the man, losing his hair, who reminds you that Don Juan was completely bald.

In some instances, rationalization can be helpful, as it helps preserve self-worth and self-confidence. However, rationalization is often used to justify unsatisfactory behavior and mistakes in judgment, and this can be harmful. The person who justifies cheating by pointing out that everyone does it and the individual who rationalizes speeding in a car to make a business appointment on time are examples.[15] When used to extreme, rationalization results in a person who constantly justifies mistakes, does not take responsibility for personal actions, and, ultimately, has a low self-image.

Which defense mechanisms are you most likely to use? Can you cite a time when defense mechanisms helped to preserve your mental health? Can you recall a time when defenses were improperly used, resulting in reduced personal and social adjustment? Complete the following exercise to evaluate your use of defense mechanisms.

EGO-DEFENSE MECHANISMS

We all use psychic defensive strategies to protect ourselves from anxiety. For Freud, the concept of psychic defense was a major factor explaining why people do what they do. He referred to defense mechanisms as the protective processes used by the ego to defend the personality from painful and unacceptable thoughts and impulses.

Directions

Before beginning this exercise, be sure the definition of each defense mechanism is clear in your mind. Then consider each one and the role it plays in your life. Under each defense mechanism, indicate on a scale of 1 to 10 how important you feel it is as a current ego defense (1 is low; 10 is high). Place an asterisk (*) next to the defense mechanisms you use the most.

Denial

| 1 | 2 | 3 | 4 | 5 | 6 | 7 | 8 | 9 | 10 |

Example: _____

_____

_____

_____

Sublimation

| 1 | 2 | 3 | 4 | 5 | 6 | 7 | 8 | 9 | 10 |

Example: _____

_____

_____

_____

Displacement

1   2   3   4   5   6   7   8   9   10

Example: _____

_____

_____

_____

Regression

1   2   3   4   5   6   7   8   9   10

Example: _____

_____

_____

_____

Identification

1   2   3   4   5   6   7   8   9   10

Example: _____

_____

_____

_____

Repression

1   2   3   4   5   6   7   8   9   10

Example: _____

_____

_____

_____

Undoing

1   2   3   4   5   6   7   8   9   10

Example: _____

_____

_____

_____

Rationalization

1	2	3	4	5	6	7	8	9	10

Example: _____

_____

_____

_____

People are vulnerable creatures, and ego defense mechanisms can serve a valuable purpose. However, they can become disruptive and self-defeating. In general, defense mechanisms distort reality and can seduce you into inaccurate perceptions and inappropriate behavior. If certain defenses become habitual, they can impair personal growth and adjustment. Do you feel that your use of a given defense mechanism is destructive to you or has interfered with your life in any important way? Discuss.

_____

_____

_____

_____

_____

EMOTIONAL HEALTH

A physical checkup is used to evaluate biological health, and a psychological checkup can help evaluate emotional health. For a review of your emotional health, complete the following questionnaire.

EMOTIONAL HEALTH—
HOW DO YOU MEASURE UP?

Directions

For each question, answer yes or no. Sometimes you will have trouble deciding, but choose the answer that best describes conditions at this time.

1. I am generally happy with myself.   yes _____   no _____

2. I am reasonably able to handle daily problems; either I overcome them, or I make successful compromises.   yes _____   no _____

3. I am emotionally stable, having few mood swings.   yes _____   no _____

4. My memory is fairly good. Although I forget things now and then, it is rare for me to draw a complete blank.   yes _____   no _____

5. My energy level is too low.   yes _____   no _____

6. I have a need for order that is excessive and counter-productive.   yes _____   no _____

7. I have trouble applying myself to productive activity.   yes _____   no _____

8. I am not usually afraid of things such as open places, dogs, or heights.   yes _____   no _____

9. I have a need to dominate that is harmful in my relations with others.   yes _____   no _____

10. I rarely waste time in arguing, complaining, envying, or resenting others.   yes _____   no _____

11. I readily take responsibility for my life.   yes _____   no _____

12. Pressures are getting me down.   yes _____   no _____

13. Making choices upsets me.   yes _____   no _____

14. I am realistic in my evaluation of other people. I see them as they are, as opposed to seeing them in overly negative or overly positive terms.   yes _____   no _____

15. I profit from experiences, as opposed to making the same mistakes over and over again.   yes _____   no _____

16. I hear voices, see visions, or smell odors that others do not.   yes _____   no _____

17. I am reliable. If I say I will do something, people can depend on me.   yes _____   no _____

18. I often talk to myself, even when others are present.   yes _____   no _____

19. I find myself thinking people are plotting against me, talking about me, or watching me.   yes _____   no _____

Source: Based on William C. Menninger and Harry Levinson, Human Understanding in Industry *(Chicago: Science Research Associates, 1956), 86–88.*

20. I have trouble understanding myself.　　　　　　　yes _____　　　no _____

21. I rarely have headaches, stomach pains, or other physical symptoms of too much stress.　　　　　　　yes _____　　　no _____

22. I am able to accept frustrations. When things go wrong, or someone doesn't do what I want, I take things calmly and try to find a better way.　　　　　　　yes _____　　　no _____

23. I often do dangerous or foolish things.　　　　　　　yes _____　　　no _____

24. I am usually able to adjust to the people with whom I live and work.　　　　　　　yes _____　　　no _____

25. I have bodily ailments that seem impossible to have.　　　　　　　yes _____　　　no _____

26. I don't seem to care about anything or anybody.　　　　　　　yes _____　　　no _____

27. My job is generally satisfying.　　　　　　　yes _____　　　no _____

28. In addition to my work, I have other interests that provide satisfaction — family, home, hobby, sports, pets, community activities.　　　　　　　yes _____　　　no _____

29. I feel in control of my life.　　　　　　　yes _____　　　no _____

30. I am not overly obsessed about anything, such as money, sex, or work.　　　　　　　yes _____　　　no _____

31. I am not overly compulsive in my behavior, such as having to wash my hands constantly.　　　　　　　yes _____　　　no _____

32. I do not displace emotions onto innocent parties (such as releasing my hostility on co-workers because of home problems, or vice versa).　　　　　　　yes _____　　　no _____

33. I have a positive attitude toward myself and toward life.　　　　　　　yes _____　　　no _____

34. I am not overly critical of the shortcomings of others.　　　　　　　yes _____　　　no _____

35. I am too submissive, and rarely exert my own ideas or wishes.　　　　　　　yes _____　　　no _____

36. I can easily give recognition and credit to somebody else, as opposed to requiring all of the attention and praise myself.　　　　　　　yes _____　　　no _____

37. I am relatively free of tension and anxiety.　　　　　　　yes _____　　　no _____

38. I have trouble sharing with others.　　　　　　　yes _____　　　no _____

39. I am too security conscious; I am afraid to take risks.　　　　　　　yes _____　　　no _____

40. I have an excessive need for approval from others.　　　　　　　yes _____　　　no _____

SCORING

Give yourself one point for each of the following items answered yes:

1. ____	24. ____
2. ____	27. ____
3. ____	28. ____
4. ____	29. ____
8. ____	30. ____
10. ____	31. ____
11. ____	32. ____
14. ____	33. ____
15. ____	34. ____
17. ____	36. ____
21. ____	37. ____
22. ____	

Give yourself one point for each of the following items answered no:

5. ____	20. ____
6. ____	23. ____
7. ____	25. ____
9. ____	26. ____
12. ____	35. ____
13. ____	38. ____
16. ____	39. ____
18. ____	40. ____
19. ____	

Enter your total score: _____. Note that 40 is a perfect score.

INTERPRETATION

It is good to evaluate emotional health, but what do you do when you see the need to improve? How do you make changes? The following are actions you should take:

- *Understanding.* Try to understand why you behave the way you do. What are the forces in you and in your world that have formed your personality and influenced your behavior?

- *Decision making.* Consider the behaviors that you want to change and why you want to change them. What will be the rewards of making the change? Decide whether the change and the rewards are worth the effort. If so, resolve to improve.

- *Planning.* Plan a program to improve, and set a timetable. This may involve changes in your environment, as well as changes within you. If low job satisfaction is harming your personality (for example, causing frustration, irritability, aggressiveness, drinking, and overeating), changing your occupation may help. However, this may require the development of personal skills you do not presently have. If so, you may need to continue your education or practice more in your trade or profession.

  Often, however, you can improve your psychological health without making major environmental changes, such as change of job, residence, or school. In many cases, what is needed is to improve your personal or social habits. Examples of problem areas include poor physical condition, fingernail biting, poor work or study habits, interrupting others, poor family relations, and inability to relax.

- *Improving.* A four-step procedure should be used to make improvements in personal and social behaviors.

  First, identify your problem area and set a behavioral goal that will represent improvement. Figure 3.15 presents examples of problem areas and behavioral goals.

  Next, prepare a "time and achievement chart" for your problem area and behavioral goal. See Figure 3.16.

  The third step in the procedure is to keep a record of your experiences. For each day you complete the behavioral goal, place a check mark in the space provided. Continue this until the new behavior becomes a habit or an essential part of your personality, or until you have reached your goal.

  The fourth step is to reward your success. The reward may be intrinsic to the behavior itself. If so, enjoy the fact that you have improved and are a better person. On the other hand, reward for improving may be extrinsic. For example, if you identify health habits as a problem area and the behavioral goal is to quit smoking, and you succeed, an extrinsic reward may be to do or get something you have wanted. If so, take that vacation, buy that new dress, or have a hot fudge sundae. You deserve it.

Mental health professionals use a system to classify abnormal behavior. The *Diagnostic and Statistical Manual of Mental Disorders* Washington, D.C.: American Psychiatric Association, 1980 (also known as the DSM III) is used by researchers, clinicians, government agencies, and insurance companies. See Figure 3.17 on page 138.

FIGURE 3.15

Identifying Problems and Setting Goals

Problem Area	Behavioral Goals
1. Poor physical condition	1. Three times a week—warm up by stretching, jog two miles, do 20 push-ups, and do 20 sit-ups*
2. Nail biting	2. Daily—eliminate all fingernail biting
3. Poor work and study habits	3. Daily—finish all current work or study assignments
4. Interrupting others	4. Daily—hold any comments until the other person has finished talking, thus improving listening habits
5. Poor family relations	5. Daily—improve relations with children by increasing the time spent with them
6. Inability to relax	6. Nightly—reduce tension through meditation and muscle relaxation

*Consult your physician before embarking on an exercise program.

STAGES AND TASKS OF PERSONALITY DEVELOPMENT

Psychologist Erik Erikson identifies eight stages of personality development from birth to old age. During each stage, the individual must accomplish certain tasks—physical, psychological, and social tasks of life. The successful completion of these developmental tasks results in self-satisfaction, social approval, and positive personality growth. The failure to meet the tasks of any of life's stages leads to unhappiness, disapproval by others, and difficulty with later personality development.[16] Figure 3.18 on page 140 shows the eight stages and tasks of personality development.

At every stage of life, you are faced with three objectives: (1) to resolve issues unsolved in previous stages; (2) to accomplish the critical tasks of the present stage; and (3) to prepare for the next stage. Just as constructing a solid base when building with blocks provides a firm foundation to support the structure, meeting the developmental tasks of each stage of life provides a foundation for further development. Your behavior in fulfilling these tasks may be personal or social, conscious or subconscious, normal or abnormal, emotionally constructive or destructive; in any case, self-concept influences personality development.

FIGURE 3.16

Time and Achievement Chart

Problem Area: Improve Family Relations

Period: One Week*

Behavioral Goals**	Mon	Tues	Wed	Thurs	Fri	Sat	Sun
1. Daily — Improve relations with children by spending at least 20 minutes with each child individually in an activity of interest to the child, excluding spectator activities such as TV***							

*Most behavior requires more than one week to change. Therefore, a time and achievement chart should be prepared for each weekly period.

**Behavioral goals should be as specific as possible. Vague goals, such as "I want to be a better parent," usually lead to frustration and lack of improvement. When trying to improve behavior, it is important to be able to see and measure success.

***Research supports the claim that the quality of time spent with a child is at least as important as the quantity of time. Thus, if improving relations is your goal, the child might gain more by tossing a football with you for 20 minutes than by sitting with you in the living room watching a professional game on TV for several hours.

The eight stages and developmental tasks of personality formation are as follows:[17]

Trust Versus Mistrust

The first stage of personality development occurs during infancy (the first one or two years of life). A newborn needs stimulation and affection. If these needs are satisfied, the infant will develop trust—a sense that the world is a safe and secure place and that other people (particularly parents) will provide protection. On the other hand, if a baby's needs for stimulation and affection are not satisfied and the child is ignored or abused, mistrust will result. The baby will learn to view the world as a hostile place, requiring self-protective behavior rather than openness toward others.

The major developmental tasks of infancy are (1) giving and receiving affection and (2) achieving a loving, reliable relationship with the mother or primary caretaker.

FIGURE 3.17

Major Categories of Psychological Disorder

Category	General Description	Examples of Specific Disorders
Anxiety disorders	Disorders in which anxiety is the main symptom, or in which the symptom seems to be an attempt to defend against anxiety	Panic attacks Phobias Obsessive-compulsive disorders
Affective disorders	Disturbances of mood that color one's entire life	Depression Bipolar disorder (alternating mania and depression)
Schizophrenic disorders	Disorders involving serious alterations of thought and behavior that represent a split from reality	Disorganized, catatonic, paranoid, and undifferentiated types of schizophrenia
Disorders arising in childhood or adolescence	Disorders that are usually first evident in infancy, childhood, or adolescence	Hyperactivity (attention deficit disorder) Infantile autism Mental retardation
Dissociative disorders	Sudden alteration in the normally integrated functions of consciousness or identity	Amnesia (when not caused by an organic mental disorder) Multiple personality
Personality disorders	Deeply ingrained, inflexible, and maladaptive patterns of thought and behavior	Antisocial personality disorder
Organic mental disorders	Psychological or behavioral abnormalities associated with a temporary or permanent dysfunction of the brain	Senile dementia Korsakoff's syndrome
Substance use disorders	Undesirable behavioral changes associated with drugs that affect the central nervous system	Alcohol abuse or dependence Amphetamine abuse or dependence Cannabis (marijuana) abuse or dependence
Somatoform disorders	Disorders marked by physical symptoms for which no physical causes can be found, and which may be linked to psychological stresses or conflicts	Conversion disorder (physical symptoms that cannot be explained by known physical causes) Psychogenic pain disorder (severe pain that cannot be explained by known physical causes)

FIGURE 3.17 — *continued*

Category	General Description	Examples of Specific Disorders
Psychosexual disorders	Disorders of sexual functioning or sexual identity	Sexual dysfunctions, e.g., impotence; inhibited orgasm
		Transsexualism
Adjustment disorders	Impairment of functioning due to identifiable life stresses, such as family or economic crises	Adjustment disorder with depressed mood
		Adjustment disorder with anxious mood
Factitious disorders	Physical or psychological symptoms that are voluntarily produced by the patient, often involving deliberate deceit	Factitious disorder with psychological symptoms
		Factitious disorder with physical symptoms

Source: Zick Rubin and Elton B. McNeil, Psychology: Being Human, *4th ed. (New York: Harper & Row, Publishers, Inc., 1985), 392. Table based on the* Diagnostic and Statistical Manual of Mental Disorders, *3d ed. (Washington, D.C.: American Psychiatric Association, 1980).*

Autonomy Versus Doubt

The second stage of personality development usually occurs during young childhood (from about two to four years of age). If a young child learns to explore and to do things independently during this period, a sense of personal power and self-confidence will develop — the sense that "I can do it myself." On the other hand, if the child does not succeed at such tasks as eating or controlling body functions and is continually criticized for making a mess, shame and self-doubt will result.

The major developmental tasks of this period are (1) to achieve physical self-control and (2) to view oneself as an independent and worthy person. The young child who has learned trust and autonomy is better prepared for all subsequent stages of life.

Initiative Versus Guilt

The third stage of personality development is associated with the preschool years (from about four to six years of age). Language develops and motor skills and physical coordination improve during this stage. It is an extension of the previous stage, when autonomy can develop into initiative, or doubt can deteriorate into guilt and fearfulness. If a five-year-old proclaims, "I am going to climb that tree," and succeeds in this initiative, self-confidence and mastery of the environment are reinforced. On the other hand, if the child is discouraged from trying, or is ridiculed

FIGURE 3.18

Stages and Tasks of Personality Development

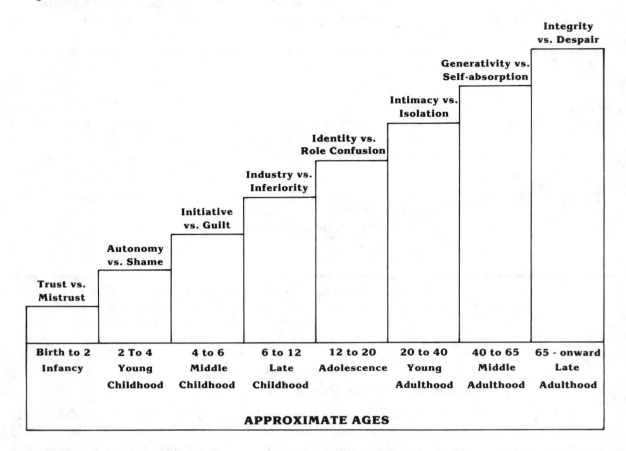

							Integrity vs. Despair
						Generativity vs. Self-absorption	
					Intimacy vs. Isolation		
				Identity vs. Role Confusion			
			Industry vs. Inferiority				
		Initiative vs. Guilt					
	Autonomy vs. Shame						
Trust vs. Mistrust							
Birth to 2 Infancy	2 To 4 Young Childhood	4 to 6 Middle Childhood	6 to 12 Late Childhood	12 to 20 Adolescence	20 to 40 Young Adulthood	40 to 65 Middle Adulthood	65 - onward Late Adulthood

APPROXIMATE AGES

for failing, the child will feel guilt and will be reluctant to attempt anything new or difficult again. The small child has dreams of being a giant and a tiger, but may, in these same dreams, run in terror for dear life.[18]

Important developmental tasks of this period include (1) learning personal care; (2) learning to be a member of a family or social group; and (3) beginning to distinguish right from wrong. The favorable outcomes of satisfying these tasks are self-confidence, direction, and purpose.

Industry Versus Inferiority

The fourth stage of personality development usually occurs during later childhood (from about six to twelve years of age). If scholarship, craftsmanship, and social skills are learned successfully during this period, a child develops a sense of industry and feelings of accomplishment. Tremendous self-worth is created by succeeding in schoolwork, animal care, athletics, music, hobbies, and other activities. On the other hand, feelings of inferiority (the feeling that "I can't do anything right") result from failure. This is why it is important for a child to be encouraged and to receive recognition in areas of greatest aptitude during this period of life.

Feelings of industry or inferiority formed during this period represent an advantage or a handicap for all subsequent personality development. The sphere of activity during this stage of personality development usually extends beyond the family and includes the neighborhood, school, and other social institutions. Scouting, sports, and hobby clubs are examples.

Important developmental tasks of this period include (1) developing a conscience and a system of values; (2) learning mental, physical, and interpersonal skills; (3) learning to compete and cooperate with age-mates; and (4) learning how to win and lose gracefully. Satisfying these tasks successfully results in competence and effective work and social habits.

Identity Versus Role Confusion

The fifth stage of personality development occurs during adolescence (from about 12 to 20 years of age). The greatest task of this period is to develop a sense of personal identity. The feeling that "I know and like who I am" is the goal. Included in the definition of "self" is a healthy sexual identity (there are boys and girls, and I am glad I am a girl), moral identity (there is right and wrong, and I believe I know what is right), and a life plan (I want to work with my hands, have a family, and live in the country). The concern with discovering and being oneself occurs concurrently with the concern for establishing satisfying human relationships and sharing with others. Belonging to a peer group and giving and receiving affection are important to the adolescent.

The young person who suffers from either role confusion or a lack of love wanders through the teen years without self-understanding, without clear goals, and in an unhappy state. Adolescence is a critical period of life and is often filled with stress, not only for the individual, but for family and friends. This is due primarily to the teenager's natural efforts to escape from parental dominance and to establish an independent identity.

Important developmental tasks of this stage include (1)adjusting to body changes; (2) achieving emotional independence from parents; (3) making new friends of both sexes; (4) developing intellectual skills; and (5) selecting and preparing for an occupation. The satisfactory completion of these tasks results in feelings of self-acceptance, fidelity in human relations, and optimism toward life.

Intimacy Versus Isolation

The sixth stage of personality development is usually associated with young adulthood and includes the ages from about 20 to 40. During this period, the individual typically "leaves the family nest" psychologically and economically. During this stage, balance must be found between two opposing challenges. The many possibilities of adult life must be explored, keeping options open; at the same time, the young adult must achieve basic occupational success.

Meaningful relationships are sought with people outside the family during this period. A major goal of these relationships is to establish a sense of intimacy, a feeling of closeness and commitment with another person. A relationship in which one can be oneself and can experience unconditional love is what is meant by intimacy. For most young people, intimacy consists of a loving relationship with a person of the opposite sex.

Economically, the young adult begins earning a livelihood. As this is done, assets developed during earlier periods (autonomy, initiative, industry, and identity) will be of immense help, while doubt, guilt, inferiority, and role confusion will be liabilities as a career is pursued.

Without a loving relationship and meaningful work, the young adult typically experiences a sense of isolation and feeling of being unimportant. Freud identified the central issues of this stage of development to be love and work.[19] Also, during the period of young adulthood, important personal and social values solidify as the individual considers the purpose of existence and the meaning of life. Finally, young adulthood is usually a period of starting a family and nurturing children. Concern for an independent self expands to include concern for dependent others.

Important developmental tasks of this stage include (1) finding a satisfying social group; (2) selecting and learning to live with a mate; (3) starting a family and meeting the physical and psychological needs of young children; (4) getting started in an occupation; and (5) defining personal and social values. Successfully meeting these challenges results in loving relationships, social responsibility, and economic independence.

Generativity Versus Self-Absorption

The seventh stage of personality development is associated with middle adulthood, approximately forty to sixty-five years of age. With personal affairs in order, the adult who achieves generativity directs attention toward other people—the family as well as the larger community. The person becomes concerned about the state of the world and the well-being of future generations. There is the need to be needed and the desire to contribute to the welfare of others. Productivity, creativity, and responsibility are important values of the person who exhibits generativity during middle adulthood.

In contrast, a person who has not developed generativity experiences self-absorption, the feeling that "I come first before anyone or anything else." Oscar Wilde portrayed such self-absorption in *The Picture of Dorian Gray*, a story about a vain young man who received his wish to remain young forever. He used other people and was cruel to those who loved him. A portrait of him reflected all of his misdeeds, and this evil image haunted him. In the end, he stabbed the picture, then died. Wilde's story is a parable that illustrates the disaster of self-absorption.[20]

Developmental tasks of middle adulthood include (1) relating to one's spouse as a person; (2) helping young people to become happy and self-sufficient adults; (3) adjusting to aging parents; (4) establishing economic security for one's remaining years; (5) developing leisure-time activities; (6) providing leadership in social, economic, religious, and other institutions; and (7) adjusting to the physical changes of aging. The satisfactory resolution of these tasks leads to a sense of contribution, social stability, and peace of mind.

Integrity Versus Despair

The last stage of personality development occurs during later adulthood, from about sixty-five years of age onward. This is the period of reflection, summing up, and ending life. The central task of this stage is to achieve integrity and inner peace. The older person with integrity feels that life has been good and the years have been used well. There is a sense of fulfillment.

On the other hand, the elderly person who has not achieved integrity feels that life has been wasted, is filled with regret, and feels personal despair. The older person with integrity cares about future generations and seeks to help other people, while the older person with despair dwells on personal problems of the past, thinking, "If I could only live my life over, I would do things differently."

The developmental tasks of later adulthood include (1) adjusting to decreasing physical strength; (2) adjusting to retirement and a reduced income; (3) maintaining interests beyond oneself; (4) adjusting to the deaths of family and friends; and (5) accepting one's own impending death.

As you consider the eight stages of personality development, where do you stand? What developmental tasks have you met, and which ones lie ahead? Complete the following exercise to evaluate your position.

DEVELOPMENTAL TASKS — WHERE DO YOU STAND?

Directions

As you consider your life, where are you in the stages and tasks of personality development? Put a check mark next to those tasks you have achieved, and indicate the level of achievement (1 is low; 10 is high).

Trust Versus Mistrust
(Infancy: Birth to Age Two)

Task	Achieved	Level
Give and receive affection	_____	_____
Experience a loving, reliable relationship with a primary caretaker	_____	_____

Autonomy Versus Doubt
(Young Childhood: Age Two to Four)

Task	Achieved	Level
Develop physical self-control	_____	_____
View oneself as an independent and worthy person	_____	_____

Initiative Versus Guilt
(Middle Childhood: Age Four to Six)

Task	Achieved	Level
Learn personal care	_____	_____
Learn family and group membership roles	_____	_____
Distinguish right from wrong	_____	_____

Industry Versus Inferiority
(Late Childhood: Age Six to Twelve)

Task	Achieved	Level
Develop a conscience and a system of values	_____	_____
Learn mental, physical, and interpersonal skills	_____	_____
Learn to compete and cooperate with age-mates	_____	_____
Learn to win and lose gracefully	_____	_____

Identity Versus Role Confusion
(Adolescence: Age Twelve to Twenty)

Task	Achieved	Level
Adjust to body changes	_____	_____
Achieve emotional independence from parents	_____	_____
Make new friends of both sexes	_____	_____
Develop intellectual skills	_____	_____
Select and prepare for an occupation	_____	_____

Intimacy Versus Isolation
(Young Adulthood: Age Twenty to Forty)

Task	Achieved	Level
Find a satisfying social group	_____	_____
Select and learn to live with a mate	_____	_____
Start a family and meet the needs of young children	_____	_____
Get started in an occupation	_____	_____
Define personal and social values	_____	_____

Generativity Versus Self-Absorption
(Middle Adulthood: Age Forty to Sixty-Five)

Task	Achieved	Level
Relate to one's spouse as a person	_____	_____
Help young people to become happy and self-sufficient	_____	_____
Adjust to aging parents	_____	_____
Establish income security	_____	_____
Develop leisure-time activities	_____	_____
Provide leadership in society's institutions	_____	_____
Adjust to physical changes of aging	_____	_____

Integrity Versus Despair
(Late Adulthood:
Age Sixty-Five Onward)

Task	Achieved	Level
Adjust to decreasing physical strength	_____	_____
Adjust to retirement and a reduced income	_____	_____
Maintain interests beyond oneself	_____	_____
Adjust to deaths of family and friends	_____	_____
Accept one's own impending death	_____	_____

INTERPRETATION

Erikson's model of personality development is very useful in understanding your current status, whether you are happy or not, how you got this way, and what challenges lie ahead. In short, it provides a review of past development, a diagnosis of present conditions, and a preview of future tasks.

SUMMARY

As a summary of the subject of personality, consider the following questions:

- Do you know who you are as a person? Are you satisfied with the social roles you play?

- How has your self-concept influenced your life?

- Is there a healthy balance between the id, ego, and superego of your personality; does your ego-ideal include both personal pleasure and social responsibility?

- How much do you know about your personality, and how much have you forgotten or repressed? Does your subconscious behavior support your conscious goals?

- What are the feelings, cognitions, and motor skills that make you, you? Which of these are average, and which are high or low?

- What is your personality type—social/leader, social/charm, decisive/analytical, or detail/supportive? Does your environment allow the full flowering of your personality?

- Which defense mechanisms do you employ—denial of reality, sublimation, displacement, regression, identification, repression, undoing, rationalization? Do your defenses support or harm your emotional well-being?

- Do you have emotional health; do you have coping skills to deal with personal and interpersonal problems?

- At which stage in life are you — early, middle, or late? What developmental tasks have you met, which ones are you dealing with now, and which ones lie ahead?

CONCLUSION

In this book, we have considered the nature and dynamics of why people do what they do. In particular, the roles and interrelationships of motivation, values, and personality have been discussed. We hope that you have learned much that you can use both on the job and in the home. We hope, too, that we have raised questions that will make the subject of human behavior a matter of lifelong interest to you. In this spirit, we conclude with D.H. Lawrence's thought-provoking and enigmatic poem, "What Is He?"

What Is He?

What is he?
—A man, of course.

Yes, but what does he do?
—He lives and is a man.

Oh quite. But he must work. He must have a job of some sort.
—Why?

Because obviously he's not one of the leisured classes.
—I don't know. He has lots of leisure. And he makes quite
 beautiful chairs.

There you are then. He's a cabinet maker.
—No, no.

Anyhow, a carpenter and joiner.
—Not at all.

But you said so.
—What did I say?

That he made chairs, and was a joiner and carpenter.
—I said he made chairs, but I did not say he was a carpenter.

All right then, he's just an amateur?
—Perhaps. Would you say a thrush was a professional flautist, or just
an amateur?

I'd say it was just a bird.
—And I say, he is just a man.

All right. You always did quibble.[21]

RECOMMENDED RESOURCES

The following reading, cases, application, and films are suggested for greater insight into the material in Part Three:

Reading	— The Abrasive Personality at the Office
Cases	— Bruce, the Behavior Mod Landlord
	You Need Connections to Be Obnoxious
Application	— Personal and Interpersonal Growth
Films	— Freud: The Hidden Nature of Man
	Rock-a-Bye Baby
	Men's Lives
	I'm a Fool
	Sticky My Fingers, Fleet My Feet
	Hard Choices: Death, Dying, and Grieving

REFERENCE NOTES

1 Baruch Spinoza, as quoted in Will Forpe and John McCollister, *The Sunshine Book: Expressions of Love, Hope and Inspiration* (Middle Village, N.Y.: Jonathan David Publishers, Inc., 1979), 41.

2 Carl Rogers, *On Becoming a Person* (Austin, Tex.: University of Texas, Hogg Foundation for Mental Hygiene, 1958), 9–10.

3 James C. Coleman, *Personality Dynamics and Effective Behavior* (Glenview, Ill.: Scott, Foresman & Company, 1960), 63–64.

4 Fritz Redl and W. W. Wattenberg, *Mental Hygiene in Teaching* (New York: Harcourt Brace Jovanovich, Inc., 1951), in Coleman, *Personality Dynamics and Effective Behavior*, 256–57.

5 Clark E. Moustakas, ed., *The Self: Explorations in Personal Growth* (New York: Harper & Row, Publishers, Inc., 1956), 91.

6 Forpe and McCollister, *The Sunshine Book*, 35.

7 S. Herman and N. Korenick, *Authentic Management*, Copyright © 1977, Addison-Wesley Publishing Company, Inc., Reading, Mass. Pg. 72. Reprinted with permission.

8 Harry Levinson, with the assistance of Cynthia Lang, *Executive* (Cambridge, Mass.: Harvard University Press, 1981), 18–19.

9 Milton H. Erickson, "Experimental Demonstrations of the Psychopathology of Everyday Life, "*The Psychoanalytic Quarterly*, 8 (1939): 340–41.

10 David Krathwohl, Benjamin S. Bloom, and Bertram B. Masia, *Taxonomy of Educational Objectives* (New York: McKay, 1964).

11 Gordon Allport, *Personality: A Psychological Interpretation* (New York: Henry Holt & Co., 1937), and Gordon Allport, *Pattern and Growth In Personality* (New York: Holt, Rinehart & Winston, 1961).

12 Coleman, *Personality Dynamics and Effective Behavior*, 198–207; Anna Freud, *The Ego and the Mechanisms of Defense* (London: Hogarth Press and The Institute for Psychoanalysis, 1937); Sigmund Freud, *Civilization and Its Discontent* (London: Hogarth Press, 1930); Sigmund Freud, *The Problem of Anxiety* (New York: W. W. Norton & Co., Inc., 1936); and James F. Calhoun and Joan Ross Acocella, *Psychology of Adjustment and Human Relationships* (New York: Random House, Inc., 1978), 66–68.

13 Coleman, *Personality Dynamics and Effective Behavior*, 200.

14 Coleman, *Personality Dynamics and Effective Behavior*, 203.

15 Coleman, *Personality Dynamics and Effective Behavior*, 198–99.

16 Coleman, *Personality Dynamics and Effective Behavior*, 90; E. H. Erikson, *Childhood and Society*, 2d ed. (New York: W. W. Norton & Co., Inc., 1963); and Robert J. Havighurst, *Developmental Tasks and Education* (New York: Longmans, Green and Co., 1952).

17 Coleman, *Personality Dynamics and Effective Behavior*; Erikson, *Childhood and Society*; Havighurst, *Developmental Tasks and Education*; Ernest R. Hilgard and Richard C. Atkinson, *Introduction to Psychology*, 4th ed. (New York: Harcourt, Brace & World, 1967), 74; and Louis H. Janda and Karen E. Klenke-Hamel, *Psychology: Its Study and Uses* (New York: St. Martin's Press, Inc., 1982), 205–7.

18 Erikson, *Childhood and Society*.

19 Coleman, *Personality Dynamics and Effective Behavior*, 81–91.

20 Oscar Wilde, *The Picture of Dorian Gray* (New York: Charterhouse Press, 1904; Brentano's, 1906).

21 Vivian de Sola Pinto and F. Warren Roberts, eds., *The Complete Poems of D. H. Lawrence*, vol. 1 (London: Heinemann, 1964).

STUDY QUIZ

As a test of your understanding and the extent to which you have achieved the objectives in Part Three, complete the following questions. See Appendix D for the answer key.

1. A relationship in which one can be oneself and can experience unconditional love is what is meant by intimacy.

   a. True
   b. False

2. The feeling that "I come first before anyone or anything else" is typical of a person who has achieved generativity.

   a. True
   b. False

3. The older person with despair dwells on personal problems of the past, thinking, "If I could only live my life over, I would do things differently."

   a. True
   b. False

4. Sublimation serves to direct behavior toward areas that are more unacceptable than acceptable.

   a. True
   b. False

5. Behavioral goals should not be specific because then they become impossible to accomplish.

   a. True
   b. False

6. Regression is a defense response to stress.

   a. True
   b. False

7. The first stage of personality development occurs between:

   a. birth and two years of age
   b. birth and four years of age
   c. two and four years of age
   d. three and six years of age

8. In the second stage of personality development, it is important that the child learns to:

a. develop trust
b. explore and do things independently
c. develop a sense of personal identity
d. explore the many possibilities of adult life

9. The person who helps others even at personal expense is considered:

   a. extroverted
   b. detail/supportive
   c. decisive/analytical
   d. introverted

10. Unwillingness to accept reality is called:

    a. regression
    b. rationalization
    c. denial
    d. repression

11. If a person has a hard day at work, comes home, and starts shouting at the family, feelings are said to be:

    a. repressed
    b. sublimated
    c. rationalized
    d. displaced

12. Undoing can be a positive way of preserving psychological health, but it can also be harmful by:

    a. undoing the positive things and repeatedly doing negative things
    b. making a habit of it, consequently alienating people
    c. saying you are sorry when you really don't mean it
    d. habitually making a practice of avoiding commitments

13. More than any other defense mechanism, we tend to use:

    a. undoing
    b. repression
    c. rationalization
    d. denial

14. The founder of psychoanalytic theory was:

    a. Maslow
    b. Freud
    c. Adler
    d. Massey

15. Human personality falls into three domains of behavior, including:

    a. actions, thinking, and reactions
    b. feelings, actions, and results

    c. feelings, cognitions, and motor movements

    d. cognitions, motor activity, and actions

16. The central question of clients seen in therapy is:

    a. Who am I?

    b. Where have I been?

    c. What should I do?

17. Self-concept is:

    a. ideas and attitudes developed in early childhood

    b. ideas and attitudes we think others have about us

    c. ideas and attitudes others have about us

    d. ideas and attitudes we have about ourselves

18. What does not belong in the "continuum of cognitions"?

    a. Deduction

    b. Induction

    c. Awareness of self and others

    d. Coordination

19. "All the world's a stage, / And all the men and women merely players: / They have their exits and their entrances; / And one man in his time plays many parts, / His acts being seven ages" was written by:

    a. William Shakespeare

    b. B. F. Skinner

    c. Erik Erikson

    d. Sigmund Freud

20. Id, ego, and superego are terms coined by:

    a. Carl Jung

    b. Gordon Allport

    c. Sigmund Freud

    d. B. F. Skinner

21. The autonomic nervous system (sympathetic and parasympathetic) and the endocrine system (glands and hormones) form the physiological basis of feelings.

    a. True

    b. False

22. What defense mechanism is a retreat from the unpleasant current situation to the pleasant past?

    a. displacement

    b. rationalization

    c. repression

d. regression

e. all of the above

23. The process of pushing thoughts and feelings into the subconscious is called:

    a. rationalization
    b. undoing
    c. identification
    d. displacement
    e. repression

24. A newborn has needs for stimulation and affection. If these needs are satisfied, the infant will develop _____.

    a. identity rather than role confusion
    b. autonomy rather than doubt
    c. trust rather than mistrust
    d. integrity rather than despair
    e. initiative rather than guilt

25. The most effective way to motivate the social/leader personality type is to:

    a. provide demanding assignments and judge according to results
    b. provide the opportunity for leadership with restrictions on authority
    c. provide time for stimulating activities and social interaction
    d. stick to business; be brief and to the point

26. A decisive/analytical person has a:

    a. tendency to be hurt easily
    b. strong desire to do things "the right way"
    c. basic interest in people
    d. need to be in charge

27. The detail/supportive person likes to work in an environment that is:

    a. unstructured
    b. competitive
    c. stable
    d. fast paced

28. The social/charm person likes:

    a. stimulating activities and social interaction
    b. challenge and the opportunity to compete
    c. privacy and time for personal reflection
    d. clearly defined goals and roles

29. According to Gordon Allport, the most dominant personality dispositions are:

   a. cardinal
   b. secondary
   c. central

30. Jean-Paul Sartre says the goal for every person should be:

   a. to achieve material success
   b. to be politically active
   c. to accept personal responsibility
   d. to live a socially rewarding life

31. According to Erikson, there are three objectives to every stage of life. Which of the following is not included?

   a. to accomplish critical tasks of the present stage
   b. to consider variable alternatives
   c. to prepare for the next stage
   d. to resolve issues remaining from past stages

32. Romantic passion and philosophical brooding are emotional states normally experienced at:

   a. five to seven years of age
   b. eight to ten years of age
   c. eleven to twelve years of age
   d. thirteen to fifteen years of age

33. The DSM III is a system of:

   a. classifying abnormal behavior
   b. counseling people with emotional problems
   c. evaluating normal personality traits

DISCUSSION QUESTIONS AND ACTIVITIES

The following questions and activities help personalize the subject. They are appropriate for classroom exercises and homework assignments.

1. What are the major personal qualities and social roles that describe you?

   _____

   _____

   _____

2. Do you have a positive, neutral, or negative self-concept? Explain.

   _____

   _____

   _____

3. Describe yourself using Freud's terms id, ego, and superego. Which is the biggest component of your personality?

   _____

   _____

   _____

4. What are the cardinal, central, and secondary traits of your personality? Do you see the primary influence of biology or environment here?

   _____

   _____

   _____

5. Do you have a "favorite" defense mechanism? Is this helping or hurting you?

   _____

   _____

   _____

6. Where are you in the stages and tasks of personality development? Are you on track or behind? Is your development on the upswing, holding steady, or losing momentum?

   _____

   _____

   _____

7. Describe yourself using the concepts of sociability and ascendency. What does this indicate regarding your life-style and occupational plans?

_____

_____

_____

8. Use the three domains of human behavior — feelings, cognitions, and motor movements — to write a one-paragraph description of yourself. What is the role of each of these in determining your occupational and social identity?

_____

_____

_____

9. Gather into groups to discuss the following questions. What social roles do different individuals play — family, occupational, community? How has self-concept affected the lives of various group members?

10. Discuss birth order as a factor in personality formation: (a) Do oldest children tend to be serious, responsible, and achievement oriented? (b) Do middle children tend to have difficulty with role identification during their teenage years? (c) Do youngest children tend to be spoiled and irresponsible? (d) Do only children tend to be independent and difficult to lead? What family sizes do group members prefer?

11. Which has been more important for members of the group, early life experiences or later life experiences? Discuss the different effects of childhood experiences and life long learning.

12. Discuss the concept of personality traits. What are the cardinal, central, and secondary tendencies of various group members? What environmental and genetic factors can members identify to explain their cardinal and central tendencies?

13. Discuss emotional health. Give examples of poor emotional health and good emotional health. How would group members deal with personal adjustment problems?

14. Critique the concept of developmental stages and tasks. Could it be argued that low self-esteem can be traced to unfinished developmental tasks and that high self-esteem comes from completing tasks on time? Who in the group is ready for love; ready for work; ready for parenthood; ready for social contribution; ready for death?

READINGS

Abraham Maslow and the New Self

He wrote with none of the dark grandeur of a Freud or the learned grace of an Erik Erikson or the elegant precision of a B. F. Skinner. He was not a brilliant speaker; in his early years he was so shy he could hardly bring himself to mount the podium. He traveled little; Brooklyn was his home for nearly half his life. The branch of psychology he founded has not achieved a dominant position in the colleges and universities. He died in 1970, but a full-scale biography remains to be written.

And yet, Abraham Maslow has done more to change our view of human nature and human possibilities than has any other American psychologist of the past fifty years. His influence, both direct and indirect, continues to grow, especially in the fields of health, education, and management theory, and in the personal and social lives of millions of Americans.

Maslow confronts us with paradoxes. He started out as a behaviorist, a skilled experimenter, and then went on to demonstrate the crippling limitations of just that kind of psychology in the study of human affairs. He coauthored a textbook on abnormal psychology, a classic in its field, and then went on to investigate, not the pathological, but the exceptionally healthy person. Considering himself a Freudian, he went on to take Freudian psychology out of the basement of warring drives and inevitable frustration, up into the spacious, previously unexplored upper stories of the human personality, where entirely different, non-Freudian rules seemed to prevail.

Working ten to twelve hours a day in the shadow of a heart condition that was to kill him at sixty-two, Maslow produced a rich and varied body of work, one that has altered our way of thinking about human needs and motivations, neurosis and health, experience and values. Some of his theories are still controversial, especially in their particulars, but no one can deny that this dogged and daring explorer has radically revised our picture of the human species and has created a vastly expanded map of human possibilities.

Abraham H. Maslow was born on April 1, 1908, in a Jewish slum in Brooklyn, the first of seven children. His father, a cooper by trade, had come to America from Kiev, then had sent for a hometown cousin to join him as his wife. Young Maslow's childhood was generally miserable. He

Source: By George Leonard. Reprinted by permission of The Sterling Lord Agency, Inc. Copyright © 1983 by George Leonard.

was alienated from his mother ("a pretty woman, but not a nice one," he later told English writer Colin Wilson) and afraid of his father ("a very vigorous man, who loved whiskey and women and fighting"). His father's business succeeded, and when Abe was nine the family moved out of the slums and into the first of a series of lower-middle-class houses, each slightly more comfortable than the one preceding it. But these moves took the family into Italian and Irish neighborhoods and made Abe the victim of terrifying anti-Semitism. He was not only Jewish but also, by his own account, a peculiar-looking child, so underweight that the family doctor feared he might get tuberculosis. "Have you ever seen anyone uglier than Abe?" his father mused aloud at a family gathering.

Reading was his escape, the library his magic kingdom. And when he chose to go to Brooklyn Borough High School, an hour-and-a-half's journey from his home, Abe got his first taste of success. He became a member of the chess team and of the honor society Arista. He edited the Latin magazine and the physics magazine, for which, in 1923, at the age of fifteen, he wrote an article predicting atom-powered ships and submarines. In terms of sheer, raw intelligence, Maslow was a true prodigy. Tested years later by the psychologist Edward L. Thorndike, he registered an IQ of 195, the second highest Thorndike ever encountered.

At eighteen, Maslow enrolled in New York's City College. It was free and his father wanted Abe to study law. But Maslow found the school impersonal and the required courses dull. He skipped classes, made poor grades, and was put on probation for the second semester.

No matter. Maslow was intoxicated with the rich artistic and intellectual life of New York City in the vintage year of 1927. He discovered the music of Beethoven and the plays of Eugene O'Neill. He went to two concerts a week at Carnegie Hall and sold peanuts to get into the theater. He attended lectures by Will Durant and Bertrand Russell and Reinhold Niebuhr. Like most young American intellectuals of that period, he became a socialist and an atheist.

But if Maslow was in love with the life of the mind, he was even more in love—blissfully, hopefully—with his cousin Bertha. And it was during the year he was nineteen that he experienced two of the great moments of his life, the kinds of moments he was later to call "peak experiences." The first came when he read William Graham Sumner's *Folkways*, a book that introduced him to the idea of cultural evolution, forever disabused him of the assumption that his own society was the "fixed truth from which everything else was a foolish falling away," and triggered a lifelong interest in anthropology. By his own account, he was never again the same.

The second peak experience of that year came when he kissed Bertha. Previously, he had never dared to touch her. His frustration was indeed so painful that it drove him to leave New York City for a semester at Cornell. When he returned, Bertha's sister Anna took matters into her own hands by literally pushing him into Bertha's arms. "I kissed her," Maslow later told Colin Wilson, "and nothing terrible happened—the heavens didn't fall, and Bertha accepted it, and that was the beginning of a new life. . . . I was accepted by a female. I was just deliriously happy with her. It was a tremendous and profound and total love affair."

By now it was clear that Maslow would not become a lawyer, and he went away to the University of Wisconsin to study psychology in earnest. A few lonely, frustrated months later, Abe wired Bertha that they were going to get married. The wedding took place in New York during the December holidays of 1928. Bertha returned to Wisconsin with him and enrolled as a student.

Thus began Abraham Maslow's life as a psychologist. It was a life that would be graced with an extraordinary succession of mentors, distinguished scholars who were somehow drawn to this shy, brilliant young man and wanted him to work with them; they invited him to meals, drove him to meetings, helped get him jobs. One might say that these mentors served an emotional function as surrogate mothers and fathers, but if the Fates had conspired to choose ideal professional influences, they could not have done a better job.

As an undergraduate, Maslow became a lab assistant to William H. Sheldon, who later was to achieve fame with his theory of constitutional types (endomorph, mesomorph, ectomorph). Sheldon and other professors provided a solid grounding in classical laboratory research. Professor Harry Harlow, the noted primate researcher, eventually became Maslow's chief mentor at Wisconsin. In 1932 Harlow shared authorship of a paper on the intelligence of primates with Maslow, and the twenty-four-year-old undergraduate was so inspired by seeing his name in print in the *Journal of Comparative Psychology* that he spent all of his next summer vacation, helped by Bertha, repeating the experiment with every primate in the Bronx Park Zoo.

As a graduate student at Wisconsin, Maslow came up with a truly original line of research. He discovered that the incessant mounting behavior of primates, which involved males mounting males, females mounting females, and females mounting males, as well as the "conventional" mounting of females by males, had more to do with dominance than with sexuality. This activity was, in fact, a means of sorting out the hierarchy of the primate horde. What's more, he learned that the ferocity involved in dominance behavior tends to fade away as one goes up the primate intelligence scale: the monkey uses its dominance position to tyrannize; the chimpanzee, to protect.

Maslow moved from Wisconsin to Columbia University as the eminent behaviorist Edward Thorndike's research associate. And he continued his work on dominance and sexuality, going from simple dominance in animals to dominance-feeling in humans to the relationship between self-esteem and sexuality. In 1936, while still at Columbia, he began doing Kinsey-type interviews with female college students, possibly inspiring Kinsey's own work, which began some two years later. Maslow's interviews showed that highly dominant women, regardless of their sex drives, are more likely to be sexually active and experimental than are less dominant women. But he also found—and this is important in terms of his later work—that "any discussion of dominance must be a discussion of insecure people, that is, of slightly sick people. . . . Study of carefully selected psychologically secure individuals indicates clearly that their sexual lives are little determined by dominance-feeling." Here was a hint, a seed: there seems to exist a state of psychological health that transcends at least one lower drive.

During this period of inspired excitement and feverish work, Maslow continued to collect mentors. One of them was Alfred Adler, an early disciple of Freud who eventually broke with his master.

Maslow also sat at the feet of such eminent psychologists and anthropologists as Erich Fromm, Kurt Goldstein, Karen Horney, and Margaret Mead—some of them refugees from the Nazi terror. It was the late Thirties and New York was both an exciting and a sobering place for a Jewish intellectual.

Of all his mentors, Ruth Benedict, the anthropologist, and Max Wertheimer, the founder of the European Gestalt school of psychology, had the greatest influence on Maslow's life. Both became good friends and often came to dinner with him and Bertha at their modest Brooklyn home. Maslow admired Benedict and Wertheimer inordinately. Not only were they giants in their fields, but they were also, to put it simply, wonderful human beings. He began making notes on these exceptional people. Nothing he had learned in psychology equipped him to understand them. How could they be what they so clearly were in a world of savage, repressed Freudian drives and Nazi horrors? Who was the real human species-type, Hitler or Benedict and Wertheimer?

These questions helped set the stage for the major turning point in Maslow's life, one that was to change psychology and our view of the human personality for all time. The year, as best as it can be reconstructed, was 1942; the place, New York City. By now, though not a great lecturer, Maslow was a beloved teacher, so popular that the college newspaper characterized him as the Frank Sinatra of Brooklyn College. He was working very hard, sometimes teaching nights as well as days for the extra income. He adored his daughters, who were now two and four; their innocence and potential in a darkening world sometimes moved him to tears. And the war was always in the back of his mind. He was too old to be drafted for military service but he wanted to make his contribution in the fight against Hitler. He wanted somehow to enlist himself in the larger enterprise of helping create a world in which there would be no Hitlers, in which "good people" would prevail.

It was in that emotional climate that he happened upon a parade of young American servicemen on their way to combat duty. And he was overcome by the evils of war, the needless suffering and death, the tragic waste of human potential. He began weeping openly. Against the backdrop of those times, the conventional, step-by-step psychology he had been doing was entirely inadequate. He knew he would have to change his life and career. It would have been easy enough to stay on his present course. His research credentials were firmly established. His recently published

Principles of Abnormal Psychology, co-authored with Bela Mittelmann, was being well received. Maslow was undoubtedly on his way to a successful career in mainstream psychology. But now, tears streaming down his cheeks, he determined to take a more difficult, more uncertain course.

The direction of his exploration was set by a flash of insight that came to him while he was musing over his notes on Ruth Benedict and Max Wertheimer, trying to puzzle out the pattern that made these two people so very different from the neurotic, driven people who are usually the subject of psychological study. As he wrote years later, "I realized in one wonderful moment that their two patterns could be generalized. I was talking about a kind of person, not about two noncomparable individuals. There was a wonderful excitement in that. I tried to see whether this pattern could be found elsewhere, and I did find it elsewhere, in one person after another."

Like many historic breakthroughs, this one, in retrospect, seems obvious, so simple a child might have hit upon it: Up until that time, the field of psychology had by and large concentrated on mental illness, neglecting or entirely ignoring psychological *health*. Symptoms had been relentlessly pursued, abnormalities endlessly analyzed. But the normal personality continued to be viewed primarily as a vague, gray area of little interest or concern. And *positive* psychological health was terra incognita.

From the moment of the turning point at the parade in New York City, Maslow would devote his life and his thought to the exploration of this unknown land, of what he called in his last book "the farther reaches of human nature." In this exploration, he would find it necessary to leave his mentors behind. Though he would go on to form his own network of colleagues and supporters, he would find himself increasingly alone out on the frontiers of human knowledge. He was to become, in his words, "a reconnaissance man, a Daniel Boone," one who enjoys being "first in the wilderness."

Maslow stayed at Brooklyn College until 1951, then went to Brandeis University, in Waltham, Massachusetts, where he became chairman of the psychology department. In 1969 he moved to Menlo Park, California. A special fellowship set up by an industrialist would give him unlimited time for writing. But time was short; he died a year later. Still, in the twenty-seven years after the turning point in his career, he published close to a hundred articles and books that add up to a great synthesis, a bold and original psychological theory.

Maslow's theory is built upon his finding that human needs can be arranged in a hierarchy, beginning with the physiological needs for oxygen, water, food, and the like, then moving up through the needs for safety, belongingness, love, and esteem. Each lower need is, in Maslow's term, "prepotent" to the one above it. A very hungry person, for example, will quickly forget hunger if deprived of oxygen. Generally, each of the lower needs must be met before the one above it emerges. Taken this far, his "hierarchy of needs" is a useful but not particularly shattering formulation.

For one thing, it avoids the twists and turns in the Freudian notion that all so-called higher feelings and actions are merely disguised versions of the primary drives of sex and ego-need; tenderness, for example, is seen by Freud as nothing more than "aim-inhibited sexuality." But Maslow goes even further: After all of the "deficiency-needs" listed above are fairly well satisfied, then a need for "self-actualization" emerges. This "being-need" is just as real, just as much a part of human nature as are the deficiency-needs.

The concept of self-actualization crystallized during Maslow's moment of insight about Ruth Benedict and Max Wertheimer, but it evolved and developed through years of studying exceptionally healthy and success-ful individuals. Self-actualization is, in short, the tendency of every human being—once the basic deficiency-needs are adequately fulfilled—to *make real* his or her full potential, to become everything he or she can be. The self-actualizing person is the true human species-type; a Max Wertheimer is a more accurate representation of the human species than is a Hitler. For Maslow, the self-actualizing person is not a normal person with some-thing added, but a normal person with nothing taken away. In a "syner-gic" society—the term is Benedict's—what is good for the development and well-being of the individual is also good for the development and well-being of the society. Our type of society is obviously not synergic, which accounts for the rarity of self-actualizing people. Though the physiological needs of most of our citizens are fulfilled, the safety needs are hardly to be taken for granted, what with the prevalence of dog-eat-dog competition and crime. And many lives are lacking in an adequate supply of belongingness, love, and esteem. Maslow sees these lacks, these "holes" in the development of a person, as a prime cause of mental ill-ness. Indeed, for Maslow, neurosis can be viewed largely as a deficiency disease. Thus, the Maslovian thesis cries out against the injustice that deprives so many people of their most basic needs and suggests major reforms in our ways of relating, especially in the family.

For those people who somehow transcend the deficiency-needs, self-actualization becomes a growth process, an unfolding of human nature as it potentially could be. Maslow defines this "true" human nature in terms of the characteristics of self-actualizing people, using not just per-sonal interviews but also the study of such historical figures as Thomas Jefferson, Albert Einstein, Eleanor Roosevelt, Albert Schweitzer, and Jane Addams.

One of the most striking characteristics of these people is that they are strongly focused on problems *outside* of themselves. They generally have a mission in life; they delight in bringing about justice, stopping cruelty and exploitation, fighting lies and untruth. They have a clear per-ception of reality, along with a keen sense of the false, the phony. They are spontaneous and creative, sometimes displaying what might be called a mature childlikeness, a "second naiveté." They are autonomous, not bound tightly to the customs and assumptions of their particular culture. Their character structure is highly democratic, so that their friendships tend to cut across the dividing lines of class, education, politics, and ethnic background. At the same time, they are marked by a certain detachment and a need for privacy; they generally limit themselves to a relatively small circle of close friends. Significantly, they do not lump people or ideas in the usual categories but rather tend to see straight through "the man-made mass of concepts, abstractions, expectations, beliefs and stereotypes that most people confuse with the world."

Self-actualizing people, Maslow discovered, are far more likely than others to have peak experiences — that is, episodes of delight and heightened clarity and even revelation, during which all things seem to flow in perfect harmony. Through numerous interviews and questionnaires, he found that even ordinary people take on self-actualizing qualities during peak experiences. He also comes very close to saying that such experiences provide a glimpse into the realm of Being, into ultimate reality itself.

Here is another paradox: Maslow the self-proclaimed atheist insisting upon the importance of a class of human experience that includes the experiences of the greatest religious figures back through the ages. But he himself was always filled to the brim with a religious wonder, with a profound sense of what Rudolf Otto calls *das Heilige*, "the holy"; and he never shrank from presenting the transcendent realm of Being forcefully, even if he did so in a secular, psychological context. At the turn of the century William James had written eloquently about the mystic experience, but most psychologists ignored this entire aspect of human life or dismissed it as some kind of compensation mechanism. For Freud, who confessed he had never had such an experience, the "oceanic feeling" is mere infantile regression. Maslow's courage in bringing the peak experience out of the closet has since been validated by several studies and polls showing its universality and value.

When people reach the stage of self-actualization, according to Maslow, many of the assumptions of conventional psychology are overturned. For example, human motivation prior to Maslow was generally treated in terms of tension reduction, and impulses were considered to be dangerous. But Maslow points out that this is true only in the realm of the lower needs. The "growth-needs" of the self-actualizing person are not mere itches to be relieved by scratching. The higher tensions (problems to be solved, human relations to be deepened) can be pleasurable. Creative impulses, then, are to be welcomed and trusted.

By opening up the previously hidden area of psychological health, Maslow provides a new kind of guidance for the human journey. Self-actualizing people, he argues, are good choosers. When given an opportunity, they gravitate toward what is good for them and, in his view, good for the human race. "So far as human value theory is concerned," Maslow writes in his 1962 book, *Toward a Psychology of Being*, "no theory will be adequate that rests simply on the statistical description of the choices of unselected human beings. To average the choices of good and bad choosers, of healthy and sick people, is useless. Only the choices and tastes and judgment of healthy human beings will tell us much about what is good for the human species in the long run."

In the 1950s Maslow began to see his work as part of a Third Force in psychology, representing a decisive, positive move beyond standard Freudian psychology, with its sickness-oriented view of humankind, and beyond behaviorism, which tends to treat the individual as a mere point between stimulus and response. With his generous, inclusive spirit, Maslow viewed Third Force psychology as large enough to hold Adlerians, Rankians, Jungians, Rogerians, neo-Freudians, Talmudic psychologists, Gestaltists, and many others. In 1961 his mailing list, which had long been used to circulate papers and ideas, became the basis for the *Journal of Humanistic Psychology*. A year later Maslow was a guiding force in starting the Association for Humanistic Psychology, whose founding members included Charlotte Bühler, Kurt Goldstein, David Riesman, Henry Murray, and Lewis Mumford. Two of the most influential founders were Rollo May, who was instrumental in introducing European existential psychology to the U.S., and Carl Rogers, whose humanistic, client-centered approach to psychotherapy and counseling has since spread throughout the world.

The summer of 1962 was to see two events that would play a major role in Maslow's influence on the culture. The first involved his appointment as a visiting fellow to Non-Linear Systems, a high-tech plant in Del Mar, California. Here, Maslow first realized that his theories could be applied to management. He discovered that there were just as many self-actualizing people in industry—perhaps more—than in the universities, and he got the idea that a humane, enlightened management policy devoted to the development of human potential could also be the most effective. He called this concept "eupsychian management," which became the title of his 1965 book on the subject. As it turned out, Maslow's ideas foreshadowed those that are now associated with the best of Japanese management, and it is hard to find a book on management theory today that does not give a prominent place to Abraham Maslow.

The second event of that summer was synchronistic—to use a word coined by Jung to describe coincidences that are more than just that. Abe and Bertha were driving down California's Highway 1 for a holiday, and their progress was slower than anticipated on that spectacular and tortuous coast road. Looking for a place to spend the night, they saw a light and drove off the road down a steep driveway toward what they took to be a motel. They were astonished to find that almost everybody there was reading the recently published *Toward a Psychology of Being* and enthusiastically discussing Maslovian ideas.

The Maslows had stumbled upon what was to become Esalen Institute on the eve of its opening to the public. The institute's cofounder, Michael Murphy, had just bought a dozen copies of the book and given them to the members of his staff. Later, Maslow and Murphy became close friends and Maslow became a major influence on Esalen and on the entire counterculture of the 1960s.

This association was to raise some eyebrows among Maslow's conservative colleagues. The first press reports on the newly minted human-potential movement were, to be as charitable as possible, sensationalized and uninformed, and a less courageous man might have pulled back. But Maslow was not one to flinch under fire. "Esalen's an experiment," he told Bertha. "I'm glad they're trying it." And later, in public symposia, Maslow called Esalen "potentially the most important educational institution in the world."

Maslow's influence on America, transmitted through this lineage, can hardly be overstated. What has happened is that the counterculture of the 1960s has become a major and influential segment of the mainstream culture of the 1980s. This development has been largely ignored by the established journals of opinion but is clearly seen in the surveys of Louis Harris and Daniel Yankelovich, in the sophisticated Trend Reports of John Naisbitt, and in Naisbitt's recent best seller, *Megatrends*.

It is also becoming clear that while the quest for self-actualization might lead some people to a narrow preoccupation with the self, the number who go to this extreme is small, and the "me first" stage is generally temporary, a way station on the journey to social consciousness. This is seen in the Values and Lifestyles (VALS) Program of SRI International, a California-based research and consulting organization, which has adapted Maslow's hierarchy of needs to an analysis of the U.S. population and which numbers some of the nation's most successful corporations among its subscribers. The VALS study shows that the "Inner-Directeds," those who might be said to be on the path toward self-actualization, now make up 21 percent of all Americans and represent the fastest-growing segment of the population. Of this 21 percent, only 3 percent are in the self-centered, narcissistic "I-am-me" category. The Inner-Directeds, for the most part, tend to move inexorably toward social consciousness, service to others, and personal integration—which should come as no surprise to anyone who has given Maslow more than a cursory reading.

Critics argue that Maslow did not adequately deal with the problem of evil, with humanity's darker side, and there is something to this criticism. But Maslow himself was aware that he had much more work to do, "at least two hundred years' worth," he told Bertha shortly before his death. True, Maslow's theory might not be complete, but it never fails to challenge us with a spine-tingling vision of individual potential and health and of a synergic society.

Despair is often comfortable, in some circles even fashionable, and it is easy enough to dismiss or even ridicule Maslow's challenge. After all, nothing is more difficult or painful than to look clearly at your own wasted potential, then start doing something about it. But ever-increasing numbers of Americans are taking the challenge. For example, the fastest-growing movement in health management today involves the field of holistic, health-oriented approaches to the physical that Maslow applied to the psychological. If anything can solve the crisis of medical depersonalization and rising costs, it is this classically Maslovian shift: more and more people working against a pathogenic environment and society while taking personal responsibility for their own positive good health.

In spite of his unorthodox views, Maslow was elected to the presidency of the American Psychological Association in 1967, and now, more than twelve years after his death, his voice is still being heard, even if indirectly, even if by people who barely know his name. Warren Bennis, professor of management at USC, recalls it as "that incredibly soft, shy, tentative, and gentle voice making the most outrageous remarks." Bennis also remembers Maslow for "a childlike spirit of innocence and wonder — always wearing his eyebrows (as Thomas Mann said about Freud) continually raised in a constant expression of awe."

Still, it takes another characteristic to join the shyness, the outrageousness, and the awe into a complete human being, and that is courage, which is the essence of Abraham Maslow's story. Psychologist James F. T. Bugental, who served as the first president of the Association for Humanistic Psychology, lived near Maslow during the last year of his life. "Abe used to go for his walks," Bugental recalls, "and he'd come by our house. We had this myth that one of the cans of beer in the refrigerator was his, and he'd always say, 'Is my beer cold?'

"And he'd drink his beer and get a little sentimental and sometimes show us pictures of his granddaughter and weep because she was so beautiful and innocent and would have to lose her innocence. And sometimes he would talk about the time in his childhood when he'd have to go through a tough Irish neighborhood to get to the library, and about how he would plan his route and sometimes get chased and sometimes get beat up. But he never let that stop him. He went to the library even though he might have to get beat up.

"That's the way I see his life. He never stopped doing what he thought he had to do, even though he might get beat up. He had courage, just plain courage."

QUESTIONS

1. Do you identify with humanistic psychology? Have Maslow's ideas had an impact on you?

   _____

   _____

   _____

2. Do you know a person who is like Maslow's self-actualized personality?

   _____

   _____

   _____

3. Have you had a "peak experience" in your life? Describe.

_____

_____

_____

The Human Side of Enterprise

The conventional conception of management's task in harnessing human energy to organizational requirements can be stated broadly in terms of three propositions. In order to avoid the complications introduced by a label, let us call this set of propositions "Theory X":

1. Management is responsible for organizing the elements of productive enterprise — money, materials, equipment, people — in the interest of economic ends.

2. With respect to people, this is a process of directing their efforts, motivating them, controlling their actions, modifying their behavior to fit the needs of the organization.

3. Without this active intervention by management, people would be passive — even resistant — to organizational needs. They must therefore be persuaded, rewarded, punished, controlled — their activities must be directed. This is management's task. We often sum it up by saying that management consists of getting things done through other people.

Behind this conventional theory there are several additional beliefs — less explicit, but widespread:

4. The average man is by nature indolent — he works as little as possible.

5. He lacks ambition, dislikes responsibility, prefers to be led.

6. He is inherently self-centered, indifferent to organizational needs.

7. He is by nature resistant to change.

8. He is gullible, not very bright, the ready dupe of the charlatan and the demagogue.

The human side of economic enterprise today is fashioned from propositions and beliefs such as these. Conventional organization structures and managerial policies, practices, and programs reflect these assumptions.

Source: By Douglas McGregor. Reprinted, by permission of the publisher, from Management Review, *November 1957. Copyright © 1957 American Management Association, New York. All rights reserved.*

In accomplishing its task—with these assumptions as guides—management has conceived of a range of possibilities.

At one extreme, management can be "hard" or "strong." The methods for directing behavior involve coercion and threat (usually disguised), close supervision, tight controls over behavior. At the other extreme, management can be "soft" or "weak." The methods for directing behavior involve being permissive, satisfying people's demands, achieving harmony. Then they will be tractable, accept direction.

This range has been fairly completely explored during the past half century, and management has learned some things from the exploration. There are difficulties in the "hard" approach. Force breeds counterforces: restriction of output, antagonism, militant unionism, subtle but effective sabotage of management objectives. This "hard" approach is especially difficult during times of full employment.

There are also difficulties in the "soft" approach. It leads frequently to the abdication of management—to harmony, perhaps, but to indifferent performance. People take advantage of the soft approach. They continually expect more, but they give less and less.

Currently, the popular theme is "firm but fair." This is an attempt to gain the advantages of both the hard and the soft approaches. It is reminiscent of Teddy Roosevelt's "speak softly and carry a big stick."

IS THE CONVENTIONAL VIEW CORRECT?

The findings which are beginning to emerge from the social sciences challenge this whole set of beliefs about man and human nature and about the task of management. The evidence is far from conclusive, certainly, but it is suggestive. It comes from the laboratory, the clinic, the schoolroom, the home, and even to a limited extent from industry itself.

The social scientist does not deny that human behavior in industrial organization today is approximately what management perceives it to be. He has, in fact, observed it and studied it fairly extensively. But he is pretty sure that this behavior is not a consequence of man's inherent nature. It is a consequence rather of the nature of industrial organizations, of management philosophy, policy, and practice. The conventional approach of Theory X is based on mistaken notions of what is cause and what is effect.

Perhaps the best way to indicate why the conventional approach of management is inadequate is to consider the subject of motivation.

PHYSIOLOGICAL NEEDS

Man is a wanting animal—as soon as one of his needs is satisfied, another appears in its place. This process is unending. It continues from birth to death.

Man's needs are organized in a series of levels — a hierarchy of importance. At the lowest level, but pre-eminent in importance when they are thwarted, are his physiological needs. Man lives for bread alone, when there is no bread. Unless the circumstances are unusual, his needs for love, for status, for recognition are inoperative when his stomach has been empty for a while. But when he eats regularly and adequately, hunger ceases to be an important motivation. The same is true of the other physiological needs of man — for rest, exercise, shelter, protection from the elements.

A satisfied need is not a motivator of behavior! This is a fact of profound significance that is regularly ignored in the conventional approach to the management of people. Consider your own need for air: Except as you are deprived of it, it has no appreciable motivating effect upon your behavior.

SAFETY NEEDS

When the physiological needs are reasonably satisfied, needs at the next higher level begin to dominate man's behavior — to motivate him. These are called safety needs. They are needs for protection against danger, threat, deprivation. Some people mistakenly refer to these as needs for security. However, unless man is in a dependent relationship where he fears arbitrary deprivation, he does not demand security. The need is for the "fairest possible break." When he is confident of this, he is more than willing to take risks. But when he feels threatened or dependent, his greatest need is for guarantees, for protection, for security.

The fact needs little emphasis that, since every industrial employee is in a dependent relationship, safety needs may assume considerable importance. Arbitrary management actions, behavior which arouses uncertainty with respect to continued employment or which reflects favoritism or discrimination, unpredictable administration of policy — these can be powerful motivators of the safety needs in the employment relationship at every level, from worker to vice president.

SOCIAL NEEDS

When man's physiological needs are satisfied and he is no longer fearful about his physical welfare, his social needs become important motivators of his behavior — needs for belonging, for association, for acceptance by his fellows, for giving and receiving friendship and love.

Management knows today of the existence of these needs, but it often assumes quite wrongly that they represent a threat to the organization. Many studies have demonstrated that the tightly knit, cohesive work group may, under proper conditions, be far more effective than an equal number of separate individuals in achieving organizational goals.

Yet management, fearing group hostility to its own objectives, often goes to considerable lengths to control and direct human efforts in ways that are inimical to the natural "groupiness" of human beings. When man's social needs — and perhaps his safety needs, too — are thus thwarted, he behaves in ways which tend to defeat organizational objectives. He becomes resistant, antagonistic, uncooperative. But this behavior is a consequence, not a cause.

EGO NEEDS

Above the social needs — in the sense that they do not become motivators until lower needs are reasonably satisfied — are the needs of greatest significance to management and to man himself. They are the egoistic needs, and they are of two kinds:

1. Those needs that relate to one's self-esteem — needs for self-confidence, for independence, for achievement, for competence, for knowledge.

2. Those needs that relate to one's reputation — needs for status, for recognition, for appreciation, for the deserved respect of one's fellows.

Unlike the lower needs, these are rarely satisfied; man seeks indefinitely for more satisfaction of these needs once they have become important to him. But they do not appear in any significant way until physiological, safety, and social needs are all reasonably satisfied.

The typical industrial organization offers few opportunities for the satisfaction of these egoistic needs to people at lower levels in the hierarchy. The conventional methods of organizing work, particularly in mass-production industries, give little heed to these aspects of human motivation. If the practices of scientific management were deliberately calculated to thwart these needs, they could hardly accomplish this purpose better than they do.

SELF-FULFILLMENT NEEDS

Finally — a capstone, as it were, on the hierarchy of man's needs — there are what we may call the needs for self-fulfillment. These are the needs for realizing one's own potentialities, for continued self-development, for being creative in the broadest sense of that term.

It is clear that the conditions of modern life give only limited opportunity for these relatively weak needs to obtain expression. The deprivation most people experience with respect to other lower-level needs diverts their energies into the struggle to satisfy those needs, and the needs for self-fulfillment remain dormant.

MANAGEMENT AND MOTIVATION

We recognize readily enough that a man suffering from a severe dietary deficiency is sick. The deprivation of physiological needs has behavioral consequences. The same is true—although less well recognized—of deprivation of higher-level needs. The man whose needs for safety, association, independence, or status are thwarted is sick just as surely as the man who has rickets. And his sickness will have behavioral consequences. We will be mistaken if we attribute his resultant passivity, his hostility, his refusal to accept responsibility to his inherent "human nature." These forms of behavior are symptoms of illness—of deprivation of his social and egoistic needs.

The man whose lower-level needs are satisfied is not motivated to satisfy those needs any longer. For practical purposes they exist no longer. Management often asks, "Why aren't people more productive? We pay good wages, provide good working conditions, have excellent fringe benefits and steady employment. Yet people do not seem to be willing to put forth more than minimum effort."

The fact that management has provided for these physiological and safety needs has shifted the motivational emphasis to the social and perhaps to the egoistic needs. Unless there are opportunities at work to satisfy these higher-level needs, people will be deprived; and their behavior will reflect this deprivation. Under such conditions, if management continues to focus its attention on physiological needs, its efforts are bound to be ineffective.

People will make insistent demands for more money under these conditions. It becomes more important than ever to buy the material goods and services which can provide limited satisfaction of the thwarted needs. Although money has only limited value in satisfying many higher-level needs, it can become the focus of interest if it is the only means available.

THE CARROT-AND-STICK APPROACH

The carrot-and-stick theory of motivation (like Newtonian physical theory) works reasonably well under certain circumstances. The means for satisfying man's physiological and (within limits) his safety needs can be provided or withheld by management. Employment itself is such a means, and so are wages, working conditions, and benefits. By these means the individual can be controlled so long as he is struggling for subsistence.

But the carrot-and-stick theory does not work at all once man has reached an adequate subsistence level and is motivated primarily by higher needs. Management cannot provide a man with self-respect, or with the respect of his fellows, or with the satisfaction of needs for self-fulfillment. It can create such conditions that he is encouraged and enabled to seek such satisfaction for himself, or it can thwart him by failing to create those conditions.

But this creation of conditions is not "control." It is not a good device for directing behavior. And so management finds itself in an odd position. The high standard of living created by our modern technological know-how provides quite adequately for the satisfaction of physiological and safety needs. The only significant exception is where management practices have not created confidence in a "fair break"—and thus where safety needs are thwarted. But by making possible the satisfaction of low-level needs, management has deprived itself of the ability to use as motivators the devices on which conventional theory has taught it to rely — rewards, promises, incentives, or threats and other coercive devices.

The philosophy of management by direction and control — regardless of whether it is hard or soft — is inadequate to motivate because the human needs on which this approach relies are today unimportant motivators of behavior. Direction and control are essentially useless in motivating people whose important needs are social and egoistic. Both the hard and the soft approach fail today because they are simply irrelevant to the situation.

People, deprived of opportunities to satisfy at work the needs which are now important to them, behave exactly as we might predict — with indolence, passivity, resistance to change, lack of responsibility, willingness to follow the demagogue, unreasonable demands for economic benefits. It would seem that we are caught in a web of our own weaving.

A NEW THEORY OF MANAGEMENT

For these and many other reasons, we require a different theory of the task of managing people based on more adequate assumptions about human nature and human motivation. I am going to be so bold as to suggest the broad dimensions of such a theory. Call it "Theory Y," if you will.

1. Management is responsible for organizing the elements of productive enterprise — money, materials, equipment, people — in the interest of economic ends.

2. People are not by nature passive or resistant to organizational needs. They have become so as a result of experience in organizations.

3. The motivation, the potential for development, the capacity for assuming responsibility, the readiness to direct behavior toward organizational goals are all present in people. Management does not put them there. It is a responsibility of management to make it possible for people to recognize and develop these human characteristics for themselves.

4. The essential task of management is to arrange organizational conditions and methods of operation so that people can achieve their own goals best by directing their own efforts toward organizational objectives.

This is a process primarily of creating opportunities, releasing potential, removing obstacles, encouraging growth, providing guidance. It is what Peter Drucker has called "management by objectives" in contrast to "management by control." It does not involve the abdication of management, the absence of leadership, the lowering of standards, or the other characteristics usually associated with the "soft" approach under Theory X.

SOME DIFFICULTIES

It is no more possible to create an organization today which will be a full, effective application of this theory than it was to build an atomic power plant in 1945. There are many formidable obstacles to overcome.

The conditions imposed by conventional organization theory and by the approach of scientific management for the past half century have tied men to limited jobs which do not utilize their capabilities, have discouraged the acceptance of responsibility, have encouraged passivity, and have eliminated meaning from work. Man's habits, attitudes, expectations — his whole conception of membership in an industrial organization — have been conditioned by his experience under these circumstances.

People today are accustomed to being directed, manipulated, controlled in industrial organizations and to finding satisfaction for their social, egoistic, and self-fulfillment needs away from the job. This is true of much of management as well as of workers. Genuine "industrial citizenship" — to borrow again a term from Drucker — is a remote and unrealistic idea, the meaning of which has not even been considered by most members of industrial organizations.

Another way of saying this is that Theory X places exclusive reliance upon external control of human behavior, while Theory Y relies heavily on self-control and self-direction. It is worth noting that this difference is the difference between treating people as children and treating them as mature adults. After generations of the former, we cannot expect to shift to the latter overnight.

STEPS IN THE RIGHT DIRECTION

Before we are overwhelmed by the obstacles, let us remember that the application of theory is always slow. Progress is usually achieved in small steps. Some innovative ideas which are entirely consistent with Theory Y are today being applied with some success.

Decentralization and Delegation

These are ways of freeing people from the too-close control of conventional organization, giving them a degree of freedom to direct their own activities, to assume responsibility, and, importantly, to satisfy their egoistic needs. In this connection, the flat organization of Sears, Roebuck and Company provides an interesting example. It forces "management by objectives," since it enlarges the number of people reporting to a manager until he cannot direct and control them in the conventional manner.

Job Enlargement

This concept, pioneered by I.B.M. and Detroit Edison, is quite consistent with Theory Y. It encourages the acceptance of responsibility at the bottom of the organization; it provides opportunities for satisfying social and egoistic needs. In fact, the reorganization of work at the factory level offers one of the more challenging opportunities for innovation consistent with Theory Y.

Participation and Consultative Management

Under proper conditions, participation and consultative management provide encouragement to people to direct their creative energies toward organizational objectives, give them some voice in decisions that affect them, provide significant opportunities for the satisfaction of social and egoistic needs. The Scanlon Plan is the outstanding embodiment of these ideas in practice.

Performance Appraisal

Even a cursory examination of conventional programs of performance appraisal within the ranks of management will reveal how completely consistent they are with Theory X. In fact, most such programs tend to treat the individual as though he were a product under inspection on the assembly line.

A few companies — among them General Mills, Ansul Chemical and General Electric — have been experimenting with approaches which involve the individual in setting "targets" or objectives for himself and in a self-evaluation of performance semiannually or annually. Of course, the superior plays an important leadership role in this process — one, in fact, which demands substantially more competence than the conventional approach. The role is, however, considerably more congenial to many managers than the role of "judge" or "inspector" which is usually forced upon them. Above all, the individual is encouraged to take a greater responsibility for planning and appraising his own contribution to organizational objectives; and the accompanying effects on egoistic and self-fulfillment needs are substantial.

Applying the Ideas

The not infrequent failure of such ideas as these to work as well as expected is often attributable to the fact that management has "bought the idea" but applied it within the framework of Theory X and its assumptions.

Delegation is not an effective way of exercising management by control. Participation becomes a farce when it is applied as a sales gimmick or a device for kidding people into thinking they are important. Only the management that has confidence in human capacities and is itself directed toward organizational objectives rather than toward the preservation of personal power can grasp the implications of this emerging theory. Such management will find and apply successfully other innovative ideas as we move slowly toward the full implementation of a theory like Y.

The Human Side of Enterprise

It is quite possible for us to realize substantial improvements in the effectiveness of industrial organizations during the next decade or two. The social sciences can contribute much to such developments; we are only beginning to grasp the implications of the growing body of knowledge in these fields. But if this conviction is to become a reality instead of a pious hope, we will need to view the process much as we view the process of releasing the energy of the atom for constructive human ends — as a slow, costly, sometimes discouraging approach toward a goal which would seem to many to be quite unrealistic.

The ingenuity and the perseverance of industrial management in the pursuit of economic ends have changed many scientific and technological dreams into commonplace realities. It is now becoming clear that the application of these same talents to the human side of enterprise will not only enhance substantially these materialistic achievements, but will bring us one step closer to "the good society."

QUESTIONS

1. Have you worked in a Theory X management system? Describe.

_____

_____

_____

2. Have you worked in a Theory Y management system? Discuss.

_____

_____

_____

3. If you were a manager, which system would you use, Theory X or Theory Y? Explain.

_____

_____

_____

Demotivation—Its Cause and Cure

There is little disagreement that employee-related costs are soaring, that productivity, both qualitative and quantitative, is far from capacity potential, and that employee commitment continues to decline. But what is the cause behind these symptoms? Their very existence makes it difficult to comprehend why previous research and broad-based solutions have not yet been put to work. We find, instead, that costly Band-Aids are being applied to the situation, further escalating operating expenses, imposing a broader hiatus of disparity between domestic and foreign manufacturing costs, and increasing general employee apathy.

In order to address this dilemma, it is necessary to examine three factors affecting productivity and resulting profitability: psychological contracts, employee orientation, and motivation. In other words, we must go back to the beginning of the employer/employee relationship and consider certain basic steps, which when mishandled, result in demotivation, a condition which negatively affects the entire business community. Fortunately, solutions to this problem do exist, if we can only take the time to refocus our energies.

DEMOTIVATION IN BRIEF

It is the author's opinion that we are not capitalizing on all available resources and that as a result, a counterproductive process called demotivation takes place, undermining the best intentions of the employer and the employee. This win-or-lose situation can begin the day an organization interviews a prospective hire and can continue straight through to retirement.

When the author first published the demotivation theory, its breadth of application was not yet recognized; it was merely a process theory. Since then, its implications have been more thoroughly explored, and the demotivation process is now considered a good indicator of internal unrest. Predicting EEO suits and union activity, it also serves as a predictor of deadwood and employee apathy. All of us—from executives to blue-collar workers—experience the results of demotivation, yet as a business community, we have not responded accordingly.

Source: By Mary Coeli Meyer. Reprinted with the permission of Personnel Journal; *all rights reserved.*

Why should such a state of affairs exist? First of all, it should be quickly acknowledged that supervisors are not always to blame for the diminishment of motivation, as is popularly supposed. It is the power of construct itself which brings about the situation. Thus, it could be a supervisor, an indirect manager, the board of directors, or a combination of people that is affecting the perceived success of the employee. The theory of demotivation is founded on the principle that employees come motivated for many reasons, many of which are not expressed to employers. So, it is entirely feasible that the demotivation process is an outgrowth of underestimating profit and product potential. In brief, we have looked at only the obvious potential, rather than considering all the alternatives for organizational success.

The first error in judgment occurs when "we" presume to understand those things which motivate people and then respond to those superficial identifications. This is not only costly but time-consuming and futile. Furthermore, to the degree that organizations make long-range plans, they would probably look not only at product and profit information, but at human resource information as well, including skills base, production needs correlated to the number of people available on-site and off-site, training and development needs, etc. Such has not been the case, and thus the Theory Y proposition that employees come motivated is replaced historically by the notion that the Great Jackass Fallacy is the effective way to manage. In other words, push, pull, prod, promise, and bait will yield productivity. Consequently, a cure is always being sought to a problem which is made to exist but which did not actually exist before the assumption.

Several factors lead to loss of motivation. These factors are either individual or organizational in nature and include:

- Lack of constructive feedback

- Inconsistent behavior by those who directly affect success

- Lack of sensitivity to individual needs

- Denial of sufficient information

- Lack of behavioral and psychological support

- Intrusion into predefined psychological and actual job space.

To understand the transaction of motivational diminishment, we need to examine one of the most significant points of departure — the psychological contract between employer and employee which is made during the initial interview.

PSYCHOLOGICAL CONTRACTS

The subject of psychological contracts is not a new one, although little attention is given to it outside the academic circle. Perhaps this neglect is due to the jargonlike terminology; but regardless, it is not given sufficient consideration by business. A psychological contract is a commitment, a mutual agreement, silently defined by the expectations of the employer and the employee. Very few organizations or employees consciously acknowledge its presence, even though it is a cornerstone in the realization of profit and personal success. There is virtually no situation where a psychological commitment does not take place. Thus, its application is not nearly so academic as it is business-related.

To understand the psychological contract, it is necessary to examine Herzberg's two-factor theory. According to Herzberg, there are hygiene factors and motivating factors. Hygiene factors include items such as pay, benefits, and environment. Not satisfying them brings about dissatisfaction. To oversatisfy them does nothing more than leave an employee neutral, certainly not more motivated. To oversatisfy them also obliges the company to spend more than is required on employee-related items. This perhaps explains why 60 to 80% of an operating budget is related to employee costs, while human productivity approaches only 30% of capacity.

Now consider the motivating factors: responsibility, recognition, achievement opportunity, and accomplishment opportunity. They are profit-producing and cost-effective; and to implement them requires an attitude change, rather than a financial investment. Doing nothing about these factors leaves an employee neutral, which is a reasonably safe activity but not profitable. To provide even marginal support of motivators reinforces the original motivation and results in substantial end results which benefit the organization as well as the individual. We, however, have universally focused our attention on hygiene items only, rather than the motivators. That alone may partially explain the increase in foreign competition with U.S. manufacturing costs.

THE INTERVIEW AND ITS IMPLICATIONS

Applying this information to the formulation of a psychological contract brings us to the process of interviewing. A candidate comes in for an interview having identified those specific needs and expectations she wants satisfied. These needs can be virtually anything: many are expressed to the interviewer, but most go unstated. Those acknowledged items include salary, the nature of the position, benefits and related skill-base characteristics. Notice that all are hygiene factors. We have been socialized to discuss these matters rather than motivation items.

The interviewer has similar screening items to consider and interviews according to the anticipated organizational needs. More important, however, is the fact that neither the interviewer nor the interviewee discusses the real motivators of the interviewee, nor the true concerns of the organization, simply because the present system does not espouse this open dialogue. In fact, during the interview, both the interviewer and the interviewee are listening with their psychological ears for predefined answers to predefined questions, inadvertently distorting the received information. As a result, the psychological contract is based on those perceptions and established on this minimal amount of information. At the same time, the organization and the employee make an overt agreement based on what is "said" during the interview.

This psychological contract is a strong commitment. It is founded on both organizational and individual need fulfillment. However, what remains unsaid provides the initial impetus for the dissolution of the psychological contract and thus initiates the demotivation process. This process is further encouraged by weak orientation programs.

THE EMPLOYEE ORIENTATION PROGRAM

The organization subconsciously responds to these gaps in information when it installs either an informal or formal employee orientation program. During the employee orientation program, the employee is told in more direct terms what is expected from her; what the rules are, the rewards of living up to the expectations of the organization; and particular specifics, such as how to find the washroom, the cafeteria, the time clock—and, of course, the products. She doesn't learn about the real politics of the organization: the fact that a merger is being discussed behind the closed doors, that there is an impending layoff, that her position might be temporary if the new computer is purchased, or that soon her department will merge with another, making her new position redundant. Similarly, the organization doesn't know that this new employee accepted the job because she wanted to reduce stress, complete a B.S. degree at company expense, and use this company as a stepping stone to the next higher position outside.

Another contributing factor is follow-up information. If any of the information provided in the orientation program doesn't agree with the original content of the interview, it has a divisive effect, and the demotivation process will advance as the psychological contract is diminished or altered. This is especially true when the persons interviewing differ from those orienting.

Demotivation is further encouraged when the orientation program doesn't take place within the first day a new person reports to work. Those organizations that put the program off until there are at least 15 people to be "handled," or until the individual has become more familiar with the company, run the risk of the employee's gaining information without the appropriate organizational interpretation, sorting it out solely on the basis of her expectations and her brief acquaintance with the firm. Some of this information may even come from a new "buddy" who is already immersed in the demotivation process. It can be safely assumed that the new employee will be influenced by this demotivated employee, thereby speeding up the demotivation process. Since the new employee seeks to belong, this friendly individual with the inside scoop will have more credibility than the faceless entity, namely the organization, that has not provided her with the necessary success information.

It is not unusual, then, that most employee orientation programs negate the original psychological contract and thereby diminish any commitment to the organizational objectives that were outlined during the interview. This negation is a significant contributing factor to the numerous discrimination suits that arise soon after an employee is hired.

The second great blunder is the employee orientation package. Consider its content. The personnel department briefs the employee on the various benefit programs and options, advises the employee of rules and regulations, and provides her with a folder of other hygiene items. She has probably also been informed of EEO, safety regulations, time frames, etc., none of which support her original motivation nor reinforce the psychological contract. Between 68 and 70 % of all employee orientations are carried out in this manner, whether they are formal or informal in nature.

The motivating factors which would strengthen the employee's commitment — recognition, responsibility, the opportunity to accomplish and achieve — are overlooked. The supervisor of the department, who actually governs the employee's success, is at best only slightly involved in the orientation. Yet identification is one of the strongest existing motivators. However, because it has behavioral overtones, the identification factor is often dismissed as unessential to the product and profit of the organization. Rather, the new employee is given a folder full of impersonal information and then escorted to an alien environment and expected to produce.

The new employee's colleagues are seldom briefed regarding her arrival, adding to the strangeness of the new environment. Thus, overall departmental recognition of the new employee tends to be sketchy and does little to reinforce her original psychological commitment. In short, she has a general knowledge of expectations, a general knowledge of the company, and many unknowns to deal with in her first few hours, let alone days.

THE DEMOTIVATION PROCESS

Demotivation can be more specifically examined as a step-by-step, six-phase process when we trace the evolution of the employee's attitude toward the organization and her work.

Phase 1 — Confusion

The employee is saying to herself, "What the . . . did I get myself into? It wasn't so bad at XYA Company. I knew my job, the people there were nice, and at least I felt comfortable." Every new employee likes to think that he or she can make a contribution and be important to the success of the company. The attention given to the person during the interview supports this desire, only to be further reinforced by the fact of being selected and hired. In fact, the company has convinced the suitable applicant with the following incentive: "Here is a place where your talents will be recognized and challenged, where growth opportunity is significant, and where management is truly concerned with each employee." As a result, when the applicant accepts the position, an attitudinal stage is established based on her personal perceptions of the psychological contract; that is, based on the idea of her individual worth and importance.

Thus, her introduction to the realities of the company provides the first mixed message and often conflicts with her original expectations. For example, she is oriented with a group of people, not as an individual, which only negates her sense of identity and consequence. Somewhat bewildered, the new employee now begins to ask questions in order to sort out the confusion and adjust for mixed messages and perceptions. This, of course, accounts for lower-than-expected productivity. This behavior is typical of phase one.

To respond to this initial phase of demotivation, we need to examine the actual orientation process. The attitudinal stage is established when the employee accepts a position based on her personal perceptions of the psychological contract. A return to individual (as opposed to group) orientation is necessary if full productivity is to be realized by the organization. Both the individual and the organization need to reinforce the contract and dissipate any potential or actual confusion which has developed. This is done with a follow-up program.

This is a one-to-one interface between the individual who instituted the psychological contract and the new employee. The setting should be comfortable and relaxed, so that the worker feels free to express himself or herself. The purpose of this meeting is to clarify any questions, mixed messages, or difficulties encountered in the first few weeks of employment. It is highly advisable to arrange this follow-up session no later than six weeks after the hire date. Information collected at this meeting needs to be fully utilized in order to re-evaluate the hiring and orientation process. Difficulties that are expressed regarding acceptance into the department need to be analyzed with regard to their frequency within that department. Any misunderstanding needs to be sorted out, its origin identified, and again, the information fed back into the system. Thus, preventive measures can become active planning items.

For new employees, this timely clarification and reinforcement of motivators interrupts the demotivation process and sets them up to succeed for the organization and themselves. Should action not be taken during this confusion stage, the employee will rapidly move on to phase two.

Phase 2 — Anger

Since the employee has not been with the company for a significant amount of time, this phase is rather important. The anger is first of all directed at herself. She will wonder why she's not controlling the situation. She will appear to be under stress and withdraw from the stream of office affairs briefly while trying to get control of the situation. Because of her short acquaintance with the organization, the answers she seeks to this discomfort will be more difficult to access, since the information system, grapevine, relationships, et al., will not be developed. Therefore, this anger will quickly change focal points and later be directed at the supervisor in phase three. Normally an employee reaching phase two would appear to be a workaholic. However, because this person lacks information to work with, stress symptoms will soon supersede workaholic symptoms. The supervisor, perceiving the stress, can easily remedy this problem and at the same time develop a truly productive working relationship with the employee.

By calling the employee to his office and assuming a friend-counselor posture, the supervisor can encourage the employee to explain her situation. Her need to belong, to be productive and successful, further enhances the effectiveness of this method. The supervisor, now knowledgeable of the psychological commitment, though not necessarily knowledgeable of the particulars, should spend some time defining the commitments and answering questions that have arisen. This facilitates the "identification element" of which we spoke earlier. Too, the supervisor wants to re-establish the psychological commitment and help this employee fit comfortably into the department so that he, too, can be successful in the eyes of the organization and with his reporting employees.

The new employee sees herself as an early failure in her new position and is naturally disappointed. The supervisor can dispel this notion of failure because of his position of authority and can further remedy fears by careful and analytical thinking: responding to the individual, re-establishing priorities, clarifying information voids, and establishing a working relationship with the employee that enables a continuing dialogue to take place. Thus, the action that the supervisor initiates can disrupt the demotivational process and enhance the productivity of the department with relatively little time and effort, and little, if any, cost.

Phase 3 — Subconscious Hope

The new employee is now rapidly losing motivation. She feels that the supervisor, by not taking action to improve the situation, has forsaken her. Consequently, anger at herself (phase two) is redirected at the supervisor. She becomes defensive and her stress is internalized. Productivity stays normal, i.e., mediocre, since it has never had the opportunity to reach full capacity. An experienced employee would withhold information at this point, which would undermine the supervisor, but the new employee devises other strategies to gain control of her situation.

The supervisor is usually disappointed with the new worker and may complain to the personnel department, perhaps requesting that they straighten out the problem. Because organizations frequently have employees on probation for the first three to six months, there is a safety valve for errors which occur, but it benefits the organization, not the employee, who is often considered completely responsible for the confusion. Such is not the case in foreign enterprises where heavy employee representation provides alternative safety valves. It is little wonder that the employee becomes uncommunicative and defensive about her plight. She realizes the implications of the situation but can do nothing about it. She is extremely disappointed, yet above all, she hopes that the situation will change.

If this phase is reached by an employee, the proper corrective action would be to sit down with an open mind and to identify the problems that confront the individual. After all, what the employee perceives is real, regardless of the facts which surround the issue. If it is worth the recruitment and orientation costs to recoup this employee, then she needs to be heard. This may reduce some excessive costs to the organization as well.

Again, the supervisor is the most suitable person to carry out this meeting, since it is he who is now having the problem. He is not getting what he expected from this employee — productivity — and so production rates are adversely affecting decision making and administration, not to mention reflecting on his managerial skills and responsibilities. Furthermore, the employee has transferred her anger to the supervisor, and the problem along with it. Working out these conclusions takes a certain amount of analytical skill on the part of the supervisor, but it will facilitate his next meeting with the employee. Taking stock of the situation in this manner also takes into consideration the current expectations of the employee and can turn a losing situation into a more positive one. The most effective viewpoint to take is that which has been tacitly indicated by the employee. This having been done, the supervisor should assume a listening posture to determine exactly how the employee perceives the situation. A subsequent dialogue between the two should then establish priorities, redefine a new psychological contract, and establish a working relationship which will enhance their opportunities for success. Assuming that this isn't done, the employee will move to phase four.

Phase 4 — Disillusionment

It is logical that the new employee will become disillusioned at this point if no action or attention has been given to her situation. Impacting the speed with which this stage is reached are the employee's self-concept, energy level, and substantive value system. When these factors are strong, the employee reaches disillusionment much more rapidly than the individual with a weaker self-concept. . . . She now realizes that remaining with this particular organization will demand sacrifice of her values and sense of self-worth. Productivity, of course, goes down, and her whole physical appearance — dress, facial expression, and body movements — reflects internal conflict and diminishing commitment to the company. If there is another dissatisfied worker in the department, the employee will spend more time with this person, being in need of reassurance and friendship. Last of all, she has most likely refurbished her resume and openly indicated her desire to leave the organization.

If the supervisor notices the situation at this phase of demotivation, a firm plan of action needs to be developed with identifiable end results. Assuming the posture of "I have a problem," he confronts the employee with his own distress over the situation. He solicits the new employee's help in resolving the discomfort and then listens for all information, sorting out that which is emotional and nonsubstantive and saying that which will illuminate the overall situation and help resolve the issues. Too, this information should be given to the personnel department, avoiding the name of the employee but advising them of the information which would make recruitment, selection, placement, and orientation more effective in the future. With the employee, the supervisor needs to listen and then decide what he must do to strengthen the relationship. In other words, the supervisor is assuming his share of the responsibility for the situation. Once this has been accomplished, the conversation is returned to the employee, who may then want to re-evaluate her responsibilities in light of what the supervisor just told her. She should also feel free to state her position clearly without fear of losing the job for her candidness. It should be noted here that when a new employee leaves a job soon after being hired, it is because the environment for free dialogue has not been established. Thus, the supervisor must strive for such open communication if he expects to retrieve this employee.

Phase 5 — Uncooperativeness

This phase is identified with the long-term employee by the following characteristics: He defines his job in language such as "It's not my job. . . . if you'd wanted me to do this, you should have told me when you hired me!" He takes negative risks without considering the consequences. He increases the amount of fraternization with employees in order to snowball the situation and have allies. He reconfirms his social need to belong and his rightness as opposed to the organization's wrongness (not the supervisor's wrongness). But because the new employee doesn't know the system, she doesn't have the same alternatives as the more tenured employee, although the phase is the same for both.

Productivity now reaches its lowest minimum level of acceptance. The employee will fraternize with those colleagues who share her grievance, most likely those who have "assisted" her in understanding the workings of the department. Her mind is not on the work but on other, external matters, such as talking with other companies, placement services, or search firms. She is not doing the job for which she was hired, but at this point it no longer really seems important. Due to her newness, it is not unusual for the organization to terminate this employee under the "probationary" policy, rather than to determine the cause of the situation which has evolved. This is conducive to EEO and union activity.

Resolution of phase five can be accomplished with either third-party intervention or direct employee-supervisor confrontation. The third-party intervention may be used when the rapport between the supervisor and the employee has reached an impasse. One other alternative for resolution is following the same procedure as for phase four, or letting the personnel department handle the situation. This last action is the least successful, for personnel is not viewed as a neutral party.

The third-party intervention is effective only if the supervisor intends to follow the advice of the third party, and if the employee has agreed to this kind of resolution in advance of its taking place.

More effective by far is for the supervisor to handle the situation himself. There is a slight modification at this point in the strategy used in phase four, the change being the identification of terminal outcomes. Those might include: the assumption of mutual responsibility, a transfer, termination, or redefinition of job accountabilities. Regardless, all areas of action need to be identified and considered and one finally chosen, rather than leaving the employee up in the air at the end of the encounter. Should unsatisfactory resolution or no action at all take place, the new employee will drift into the final stage of demotivation.

Phase 6 — Departure

Departure doesn't necessarily mean physical leaving; it can mean mental absence. This is dependent upon the self-motivation of the individual. If she is aware of her contributing capacity and has a strong self-concept, value system, and energy level, she will leave the organization soon after hire. Those individuals who are not prepared to face the rigors of the selection process soon after their previous experience (subconsciously) choose to become the deadwood of the department soon after they arrive in the organization. They appear not to care if the work gets done but plod along just in case someone might ask them for an accounting of their daily accomplishments. The appearance and demeanor is that of someone who has given up on the routine of work, on being accepted, on being challenged. In other words, they might appear disheveled in appearance, a bit casual in their demeanor, and a bit slow about their enthusiasm to get the department's work accomplished. In this instance, it is to the advantage of the supervisor to assist this person in determining whether she can renew the psychological contract or whether it would be more advantageous to seek employment elsewhere. If the supervisor doesn't take action, the remainder of his department will follow suit in terms of production rate, and thus the entire output will be affected.

The supervisor must have a plan for this encounter just as he had plans for the encounters in phases four and five. The supervisor needs to be firmly in command of this situation, accepting his part of the responsibility, but still decisive in the action necessary to resolve the problem. Often the best solution is to get a transfer for the employee, provided she initially had all the appearances of a winner and the organization failed to utilize those abilities to their own profit. To lose this employee is not only costly but a waste of the potential resource, and it is due to lack of appropriate nurturing by the department or the organization. With human resources growing scarcer these days, it becomes more critical to make this decision objectively; since replacement is not only difficult, but business' reputation is more public property than ever before, and future recruitment efforts must not be hindered. This is a phase where action must be taken lest the entire department continue to join the demotivated employee in her plight.

Obviously, the process and ramifications of demotivation are complex. The new employee enters an organization with a psychological contract which was formulated between the interviewer and herself, a strong contract comprised of many tacit gut-level expectations. When these expectations are negated through:

- Inconsistent behavior by those who affect success
- Lack of constructive feedback
- Lack of substantative information
- Lack of sensitivity to individual needs
- Lack of behavioral and psychological support
- Intrusion into predefined psychological and actual job space,

the employee experiences a diminishment of her motivation which results in the weakening of the whole psychological contract.

The employee, be she clerk or CEO, will pass through six phases of demotivation as the contract is negated: confusion, anger, subconscious hope, disillusionment, uncooperativeness, and departure.

Understanding the broad impact of this process and responding appropriately will positively affect the current trends in business which have escalated costs, diminished product quality and quantity, and encouraged foreign manufacturing to compete more viably with the U.S.

Bearing in mind that at this point in our socio-economic development the risks confronted by business are considerably greater and the payoffs much smaller than in past decades, it behooves us to look at the beginning of the process and examine not only products but the entire field of human resources. The negative trend does not appear to be diminishing. In the human resource area alone

- Expanded career lives are around the corner with advancing retirement age.
- Escalating minimum wages are diminishing profit margins quarter by quarter.
- The projected four-day work week will require industry to expand its payroll and training.
- Social security is being increased along with other human welfare items.
- Foreign competition is catching up technologically and has been ahead in the human resources sector for several decades.

Business cannot afford to continue on a reactive basis due to the cost factors alone. It needs to be active and responsive to the anticipated socio-economic trends. It cannot afford more EEO suits, union activity, government intervention, and employee apathy. Business needs to consider new solutions, not Band-Aids. It needs to deal with motivation and the issues which cause its diminishment. In the long run, this approach is more cost-effective and more profitable because mutual goals, both individual and organizational, are accomplished.

Such an approach does not require retraining so much as it does refocusing, which is a far easier task to accomplish. It also means that the personnel department needs to provide more functional information to top management, thereby contributing to profit and productivity, as well as to the human resource situation.

This can only be done by reconsidering the entire motivation/demotivation process from the interview through to retirement as it relates to organization goals. In this manner we can reaffirm our competitive position.

QUESTIONS

1. What factors lead to a demotivated work force?

   _____

   _____

   _____

2. If you were an employer, what would you do to motivate employees?

   _____

   _____

   _____

The Abrasive Personality at the Office

Moshe Dayan once applied for membership in a kibbutz. He was rejected — largely, he believes, because of his personality. "Emotional partnership, sociability, and absolute egalitarianism were not in keeping with my nature," Dayan says.

President Jimmy Carter describes his old mentor, Admiral Hyman Rickover, respectfully, as having absolutely no tact. "As a matter of fact," the President adds, "all the time I worked for him he never said a decent word to me. . . . If he found no fault, he simply looked, turned around and walked away. However, if I made the slightest mistake, in one of the loudest and most obnoxious voices I ever heard, he would turn around and tell the other people in the area what a horrible disgrace I was to the Navy, and that I ought to go back to the oldest and slowest and smallest submarine from which I had come."

A couple of years ago, when Henry Weigl was abruptly relieved of all his operating responsibilities as chairman of Standard Brands, *Forbes* magazine carried this account: "Weigl's abrasive, authoritarian style drove potential successors from the company, even while he was building Standard Brands in the marketplace. Says a person close to the company: 'There isn't a company in American industry with an executive turnover rate like that of Standard Brands.' Another observer states: 'Weigl had a way of publicly humiliating men at the executive level that 'no self-respecting person could stand.' "

These three examples illustrate a phenomenon that sometimes disrupts large organizations, the abrasive personality. Men and women of high achievement are often brilliant innovators who stubbornly insist on having their own way; they present special problems for bosses, subordinates, and colleagues alike. Management will frequently go to great lengths to tolerate their idiosyncrasies. In an effort to save them for their organizations, their superiors will frequently refer them to psychologists and psychiatrists or ask them to take part in relations-training programs.

The abrasive personality has a knack for jabbing others in an irritating, often painful, way; his criticisms are offered brutally and with little diplomacy. He (or she, for the abrasive personality takes the same form in both men and women) questions, analyzes, and demolishes his colleagues' positions, although his insights are often undermined by the

Source: Harry Levinson, "The Abrasive Personality at The Office," Psychology Today *(May 1978): 78–84. Reprinted with permission.*

condescending manner in which he offers them. Rarely is he able to sense other people's feelings, yet he insists that he must be "open," "truthful," and "tell it like it is."

Keenly analytical and capable of cutting to the core of a problem, the abrasive personality is impatient with those who cannot think as quickly or act as forthrightly as he can. He has difficulty delegating authority to others, who, he feels, will not work up to his standards. His capacity for analysis tends not to be matched by skill as a leader in carrying out decisions based on his insights. Despite what he says, he is usually not a good developer of people, for frequently they feel inadequate compared with him.

Although imaginative in his pursuit of bigger and broader achievement, for which he often gets many accolades, the abrasive personality may leave his colleagues with no sense of participation in a particular project. On the other hand, even with his history of spectacular achievements, his boss, fearful of giving him an inch, may tend to turn him down while the work of others, less gifted but more malleable, is accepted.

Sometimes the abrasive personality acts as if he were a privileged person with a mandate to be different and even inconsiderate of others. He takes an intense, admiring interest in himself, and others become devices for his self-aggrandizement — extensions of himself rather than independent adults with their own work styles and aspirations. He seems to expect others to accept his logic and decisions because they are his. If the abrasive personality is disappointed in those expectations, he becomes enraged.

He places great emphasis on control of himself and others — total control if possible, which does not allow him a wide range of feeling. The result of such rigid control is a sense of certainty and self-assurance. The abrasive personality is, to all appearances, emphatically right, self-confident, and assured. Unlike the "gamesman" in psychologist Michael Maccoby's best-selling book, he tends to adhere stubbornly to a position, to be unable to compromise. In fact, compromises strike him as giving in to lower standards. So he has little flexibility, and no sense of humor, for the necessary give-and-take of organizational politics, although on a one-to-one basis, he is often genial and helpful to people he is not supervising.

The parameters of the abrasive personality are thus: self-centeredness, isolation, perfectionism, condescending contempt, and attack. Although the origins of any form of behavior are complex and varied, there is enough evidence from many different sources — biographical, child studies, and clinical experience — to help us to trace in general terms what produces the abrasive personality and to suggest ways of coping with it.

It is a psychological axiom that the more extreme one's behavior is in one direction, the more likely it is that one is seeking to escape from a set of opposite feelings. In the case of the abrasive personality, we see the intense striving for perfection, even omnipotence, which reflects an underlying sense of inadequacy and, ultimately, helplessness. Because of the unconscious sense of helplessness, which stems from earliest experience as an infant, such a person develops a low self-image. He feels so small, so inadequate, and so vulnerable to destruction by a hostile environment that he strives to attain that level of perfection that will make him invulnerable.

In order to attain it, he overcontrols a situation, which, in turn, leads to overorganizing it; he copes with the imperfections of others by over-supervising them. Psychoanalyst Leon Salzman puts it this way: "The over-riding purpose of the (overcontrolling) behavior is to attempt to achieve some security and certainty for the person who feels threatened and insecure in an uncertain world. The possibility of controlling oneself and the forces outside oneself by assuming omniscience and omnipotence can give one a false sense of certainty. Therefore, the main ingredient is one of control."

If he is always pushing himself toward impossible goals and is never able to achieve them, then the abrasive personality must be constantly guilty and constantly angry with himself. That has two consequences. The greater the gap between the ego ideal and the self-image, the greater the intensity of anger with oneself. Anger with oneself is depression; attack on oneself is a product of depression. The greater the anger with oneself, the more likely one will attack oneself or drive oneself to narrow the gap, and to reduce the feelings of anger, depression, and inadequacy. However, because the given perfectionistic strivings are largely unconscious, those feelings are unlikely to be significantly reduced no matter how great the intensity of effort. Such feelings are likely to spill over onto colleagues in the form of contempt, condescension, and hostile attacks. In fact, there can be a kind of perverse pleasure in provoking others, whose rejection then becomes punishment of the unworthy self for being so inadequate.

Such extreme and continuous drivenness makes the abrasive personality vulnerable to coronaries, as is reflected in the Type A behavior described by San Francisco internists Meyer Friedman and Ray H. Rosenman. Being completely preoccupied with the ultimate attainment of their goals, driven men find it difficult to relax and enjoy the present. They are aggressively involved in a frantic, incessant struggle to achieve more and more in less and less time. Excessive competitive drive, impatience, the tendency to do two or more things at once, an obsession with numbers, the harrying sense of time urgency, the habit of talking and walking fast, and a "free-floating" hostility — these are other Type A traits that characterize the abrasive personality.

Take the case of Brian. His achievements in the development of new synthetic fibers for a multinational corporation have earned him, at 45, an international reputation in the textile industry. He is a valued employee, whose unique applications of chemical technology have allowed his company to stay on top of changing markets. But despite 10 years with the company, he has been consistently passed over for promotion to the ranks of management.

The career-development officer of his company brought the problem to me. For all of his brilliance, Brian is sarcastic and condescending with subordinates, peers, and superiors. His dealings with the executive committee have been the greatest barrier to his advancement. He is so opinionated and obstinate that they find his comments in their planning sessions disruptive; they will not consider him for promotion to any position that would involve increased contact with him.

Allen, Brian's boss for the past 14 months, is cowed by his critical outbursts and avoids confrontation by treating him with kid gloves. Recently, Brian asked to meet with Allen and demanded to know why his career was not progressing. Allen responded with an honest evaluation of just what effect his behavior was having on others in the company. Brian was stunned but genuinely interested in changing and asked for Allen's help.

There are a number of steps that must now be taken to improve Brian's situation. He has never received proper supervision and feedback on his behavior in the past, and therefore does not really know why he has been passed over for promotions. But he does feel the pain of his lack of promotability. This may provide enough motivation for him to change, even at this relatively late date in his career.

Brian must be made to understand that changing one's behavior is a long, tedious process. The executive committee has already given up on him. In time, as Brian's relations with those at his level and below become discernibly less volatile, they may become willing to re-evaluate his promotability. Allen, as Brian's immediate supervisor, has started to work closely with Brian to guide him in his day-to-day interactions with his subordinates and peers. Given Brian's age and the fact that his behavior is deep-rooted, the services of a clinical psychologist or psychiatrist might have to be used.

How does one deal with abrasive people like Brian in an organization? Obviously, the approaches of his co-workers will vary, depending upon whether he is their supervisor or a subordinate. If he's the boss, the individual will have to decide how far he or she is willing to be pushed. You may willingly endure an abrasive superior as long as you are able to learn from him (as Jimmy Carter did from Admiral Rickover). When the boss's personality is seriously impairing morale, however, you may have to explain to him tactfully the effect he is having on you and others. Try to reason with him. But if nothing works, you would do well to look for another job. Going over the boss's head usually does not help if he is valuable to the organization. If the abrasive personality is a subordinate, a wider range of strategies is possible.

Here are some recommendations, based on my experiences as a business consultant:

1. Follow the common psychological axiom that each person is always doing the best he can. Recognize the origins of such behavior—the vulnerable self-image, the hunger for affection, and the eagerness for perfection—and don't become angry with abrasive, provocative behavior. Whenever an abrasive employee disrupts the group or angers others, talk it over with him.

2. In such discussions, report your observations uncritically. Describe what you saw, especially the more subtle behavior to which people reacted automatically. Ask how he thought others felt when he said or did what you describe. How does he think they are likely to respond? Is that the result he wanted? If not, how can he act to get the response he wants?

3. Point out that you recognize that he wants to achieve and you want to help him do so, but that in order to reach his goals, he must take others into account. Note also that inevitably there will be defeats and disappointments along the way.

4. When, as is likely, his provocative behavior finally irritates you, avoid impulsive attack. Instead, report how he made you feel and how others must feel, given his hostile, deprecating, and over-controlling tactics. Let him know that you are annoyed. Also, note how frequently such behavior occurs.

5. If he challenges, philosophizes, defends, or tries to debate your observations, or accuses you of hostility toward him, don't counterattack. Merely state your observation of what he is doing or misinterpreting. Keep your eye on his goal: does he want to make it or not?

6. If your relationship with him is strong enough, you might ask why he thinks his behavior pattern persists. Why does it seem to him that he must defend or attack in situations that are not combative? Explain that being part of a critical discussion of problems is one thing, but turning it into a win-lose argument is another.

7. Note that goals are achieved step-by-step, that compromise is not necessarily second best, that the all-or-nothing principle usually results in futile disappointment, that perfection is not attainable. Expect to repeat this process again and again. But in all such criticism, always point out, at the same time, the legitimate achievements of which he can be proud.

8. Sometimes he can't hear, despite repeated comment. Perhaps he is too busy thinking up defensive arguments, or is preoccupied with his own thoughts. Then he must be confronted with the fact and cost of his arrogant, hostile, overcontrolling behavior.

9. Mere advice to relax or take a vacation will not be very helpful. Many have great stamina and indeed take exceptional pleasure in their work. Their manner of work builds certainty, security, and predictability. That is why they are so good at organization and detail. Many enjoy being "under the gun" and enjoy the pressure. To play tennis or golf or bridge is, to them, simply a different kind of work that frequently doesn't make any sense.

10. If, despite your best efforts, the abrasive personality does not respond, he needs to know in no uncertain terms that his behavior is unsatisfactory. Do not assume that he knows. He should be told repeatedly and in written form.

My experience is that most superiors, when dealing with the abrasive personality, are reluctant to reveal the effects of his behavior in performance appraisals. In one instance, I was asked to interview a problem employee; he didn't know why he had come to see me. When I told him, he was dismayed. He showed me his performance appraisal. His boss had commented highly on all of his qualities and assets, and in one sentence had stated that the employee's behavior with people was improving. Meanwhile, the boss was enraged with his behavior, which kept him from promoting his subordinate.

Perhaps the steps I have outlined have been followed to no avail. The abrasive personality clearly knows what is wrong and yet is unable to respond by changing his behavior; there is no significant improvement. The consequence is that higher management grows angry, frustrated, and disappointed. The employee feels unfairly treated—unrecognized and unappreciated. He is resentful: promotions have not come, nor have salary increases matched his demonstrated ability.

The abrasive personality should then be referred to a competent professional for psychotherapy. Nothing else will have a significant effect, and even that might not. Whether it does will depend on the severity of the problem and the skill of the therapist. The kinds of problems we are examining will not be solved in a T-group or a weekend encounter. In fact, confrontation may destroy the person because, by threatening his mode of coping with his helplessness, he runs the risk of being reduced to helplessness, for he has no other modes for dealing with those feelings. He may become subdued, but also deflated and depressed. Whatever competence and confidence he has may be undermined.

Under such circumstances, the abrasive personality, in his desperation, casts about for reasons outside himself for his problems. Alternatively, he insists he can handle them himself. He assiduously avoids professional help. The boss must be insistent about the need for behavior change and point out that he has not been able to do so by himself or with the boss's help. Professional assistance is required.

The person who is viewed by his superiors as an abrasive personality and referred to a psychologist should fully understand the two implications of such a move. The first is that the person is so competent, skilled, and capable in some dimension of his role that his superiors not only would hate to lose him but also have reason to believe that his talent can flower—that he is capable of becoming a mature executive who can assume greater responsibility. The second is that the person, at present, is incapable of getting along with other people and cannot be promoted until he changes. Both points should be made emphatically.

While the abrasive personality is involved in fascinating and sometimes exciting work, with a powerful commitment to high standards, he needs special help in order to work smoothly within an organization. Superiors need to understand and guide him if he is to use his talents and skills effectively. Assuming their efforts are successful, companies will no doubt benefit from their investment in a conscientious and sometimes brilliant performer.

QUESTIONS

1. Do you live or work with someone who has an abrasive personality? Explain.

   _____

   _____

   _____

2. What techniques do you recommend for dealing with difficult people?

   _____

   _____

   _____

On the Folly of Rewarding A, While Hoping for B

Whether dealing with monkeys, rats, or human beings, it is hardly controversial to state that most organisms seek information concerning what activities are rewarded, and then seek to do (or at least pretend to do) those things, often to the virtual exclusion of activities not rewarded. The extent to which this occurs of course will depend on the perceived attractiveness of the rewards offered, but neither operant nor expectancy theorists would quarrel with the essence of this notion.

Nevertheless, numerous examples exist of reward systems that are fouled up in that behaviors which are rewarded are those which the rewarder is trying to *discourage*, while the behavior he desires is not being rewarded at all.

In an effort to understand and explain this phenomenon, this paper presents examples from society, from organizations in general, and from profit-making firms in particular. Data from a manufacturing company and information from an insurance firm are examined to demonstrate the consequences of such reward systems for the organizations involved, and possible reasons why such reward systems continue to exist are considered.

SOCIETAL EXAMPLES

Politics

Official goals are "purposely vague and general and do not indicate . . . the host of decisions that must be made among alternative ways of achieving official goals and the priority of multiple goals . . ."(8,p.66). They usually may be relied on to offend absolutely no one, and in this sense can be considered high-acceptance, low-quality goals. An example might be "build better schools." Operative goals are higher in quality but lower in acceptance, since they specify where the money will come from, what alternative goals will be ignored, etc.

Source: Steven Kerr, "On the Folly of Rewarding A, While Hoping for B," Academy of Management Journal *18 (1975): 769–83. Reprinted with permission.*

The American citizenry supposedly wants its candidates for public office to set forth operative goals, making their proposed programs "perfectly clear," specifying sources and uses of funds, etc. However, since operative goals are lower in acceptance, and since aspirants to public office need acceptance (from at least 50.1 percent of the people), most politicians prefer to speak only of official goals, at least until after the election. They of course would agree to speak at the operative level if "punished" for not doing so. The electorate could do this by refusing to support candidates who do not speak at the operative level.

Instead, however, the American voter typically punishes (withholds support from) candidates who frankly discuss where the money will come from, rewards politicians who speaks only of official goals, but hopes that candidates (despite the reward system) will discuss the issues operatively. It is academic whether it was moral for Nixon, for example, to refuse to discuss his 1968 "secret plan" to end the Vietnam war, his 1972 operative goals concerning the lifting of price controls, the reshuffling of his cabinet, etc. The point is that the reward system made such refusal rational.

It seems worth mentioning that no manuscript can adequately define what is "moral" and what is not. However, examination of costs and benefits, combined with knowledge of what motivates a particular individual, often will suffice to determine what for him is "rational."* If the reward system is so designed that it is irrational to be moral, this does not necessarily mean that immorality will result. But is this not asking for trouble?

War

If some oversimplification may be permitted, let it be assumed that the primary goal of the organization (Pentagon, Luftwaffe, or whatever) is to win. Let it be assumed further that the primary goal of most individuals on the front lines is to get home alive. Then there appears to be an important conflict in goals—personally rational behavior by those at the bottom will endanger goal attainment by those at the top.

But not necessarily! It depends on how the reward system is set up. The Vietnam war was indeed a study of disobedience and rebellion, with terms such as "fragging" (killing one's own commanding officer) and "search and evade" becoming part of the military vocabulary. The difference in subordinates' acceptance of authority between World War II and Vietnam is reported to be considerable, and veterans of the Second World War often have been quoted as being outraged at the mutinous actions of many American soldiers in Vietnam.

Consider, however, some critical differences in the reward system in use during the two conflicts. What did the GI in World War II want?

---

*In Simon's (10, pp. 76–77) terms, a decision is "subjectively rational" if it maximizes an individual's valued outcomes so far as his knowledge permits. A decision is "personally rational" if it is oriented toward the individual's goals.

To go home. And when did he get to go home? When the war was won! If he disobeyed the orders to clean out the trenches and take the hills, the war would not be won and he would not go home. Furthermore, what were his chances of attaining his goal (getting home alive) if he obeyed the orders compared to his chances if he did not? What is being suggested is that the rational soldier in World War II, *whether patriotic or not*, probably found it expedient to obey.

Consider the reward system in use in Vietnam. What did the man at the bottom want? To go home. And when did he get to go home? When his tour of duty was over! This was the case *whether or not* the war was won. Furthermore, concerning the relative chance of getting home alive by obeying orders compared to the chance if they were disobeyed, it is worth noting that a mutineer in Vietnam was far more likely to be assigned rest and rehabilitation (on the assumption that fatigue was the cause) than he was to suffer any negative consequence.

In his description of the "zone of indifference," Barnard stated that "a person can and will accept a communication as authoritative only when . . . at the time of his decision, he believes it to be compatible with his personal interests as a whole" (1,p.165). In light of the reward system used in Vietnam, would it not have been personally irrational for some orders to have been obeyed? Was not the military implementing a system which *rewarded* disobedience, while *hoping* that soldiers (despite the reward system) would obey orders?

Medicine

Theoretically, a physician can make either of two types of error, and intuitively one seems as bad as the other. A doctor can pronounce a patient sick when he is actually well, thus causing him needless anxiety and expense, curtailment of enjoyable foods and activities, and even physical danger by subjecting him to needless medication and surgery. Alternately, a doctor can label a sick person well, and thus avoid treating what may be a serious, even fatal ailment. It might be natural to conclude that physicians seek to minimize both types of error.

Such a conclusion would be wrong.* It is estimated that numerous Americans are presently afflicted with iatrogenic (physician *caused*) illnesses (9). This occurs when the doctor is approached by someone complaining of a few stray symptoms. The doctor classifies and organizes these symptoms, gives them a name, and obligingly tells the patient what further symptoms may be expected. This information often acts as a self-fulfilling prophecy, with the result that from that day on the patient for all practical purposes is sick.

Why does this happen? Why are physicians so reluctant to sustain a type 2 error (pronouncing a sick person well) that they will tolerate many

---

*In one study (4) of 14,867 films for signs of tuberculosis, 1,216 positive readings turned out to be clinically negative; only 24 negative readings proved clinically active, a ratio of 50 to 1.

type 1 errors? Again, a look at the reward system is needed. The punishments for a type 2 error are real: guilt, embarrassment, and the threat of lawsuit and scandal. On the other hand, a type 1 error (labeling a well person sick) "is sometimes seen as sound clinical practice, indicating a healthy conservative approach to medicine" (9,p.69). Type 1 errors also are likely to generate increased income and a stream of steady customers who, being well in a limited physiological sense, will not embarrass the doctor by dying abruptly.

Fellow physicians and the general public therefore are really *rewarding* type 1 errors and at the same time *hoping* fervently that doctors will try not to make them.

GENERAL ORGANIZATIONAL EXAMPLES

Rehabilitation Centers and Orphanages

In terms of the prime beneficiary classification (2,p.42), organizations such as these are supposed to exist for the "public-in-contact," that is, clients. The orphanage therefore theoretically is interested in placing as many children as possible in good homes. However, often orphanages surround themselves with so many rules concerning adoption that it is nearly impossible to pry a child out of the place. Orphanages may deny adoption unless the applicants are a married couple, both of the same religion as the child, without history of emotional or vocational instability, with a specified minimum income and a private room for the child, etc.

If the primary goal is to place children in good homes, then the rules ought to constitute means toward that goal. Goal displacement results when these "means become ends-in-themselves that displace the original goals"(2,p.229).

To some extent these rules are required by law. But the influence of the reward system on the orphanage's management should not be ignored. Consider, for example, that the:

1. Number of children enrolled often is the most important determinant of the size of the allocated budget.

2. Number of children under the director's care also will affect the size of his staff.

3. Total organizational size will determine largely the director's prestige at the annual conventions, in the community, etc.

Therefore, to the extent that staff size, total budget, and personal prestige are valued by the orphanage's executive personnel, it becomes rational for them to make it difficult for children to be adopted. After all, who wants to be the director of the smallest orphanage in the state?

If the reward system errs in the opposite direction, paying off only for placements, extensive goal displacement again is likely to result. A common example of vocational rehabilitation in many states, for example, consists of placing someone in a job for which he has little interest and few qualifications, for two months or so, and then "rehabilitating" him again in another position. Such behavior is quite consistent with the prevailing reward system, which pays off for the number of individuals placed in any position for 60 days or more. Rehabilitation counselors also confess to competing with one another to place relatively skilled clients, sometimes ignoring persons with few skills who would be harder to place. Extensively disabled clients find that counselors often prefer to work with those whose disabilities are less severe.*

Universities

Society *hopes* that teachers will not neglect their teaching responsibilities but *rewards* them almost entirely for research and publications. This is most true at the large and prestigious universities. Clichés such as "good research and good teaching go together" notwithstanding, professors often find that they must choose between teaching and research-oriented activities when allocating their time. Rewards for good teaching usually are limited to outstanding teacher awards, which are given to only a small percentage of good teachers and which usually bestow little money and fleeting prestige. Punishments for poor teaching also are rare.

Rewards for research and publications, on the other hand, and punishments for failure to accomplish these, are commonly administered by universities at which teachers are employed. Furthermore, publication-oriented resumés usually will be well received at other universities, whereas teaching credentials, harder to document and quantify, are much less transferable. Consequently it is rational for university teachers to concentrate on research, even if to the detriment of teaching and at the expense of their students.

By the same token, it is rational for students to act based upon the goal displacement which has occurred within universities concerning what they are rewarded for. If it is assumed that a primary goal of a university is to transfer knowledge from teacher to student, then grades become identifiable as a means toward that goal, serving as motivational, control, and feedback devices to expedite the knowledge transfer. Instead, however, the grades themselves have become much more important for entrance to graduate school, successful employment, tuition refunds, parental respect, etc., than the knowledge or lack of knowledge they are supposed to signify.

It therefore should come as no surprise that information has surfaced in recent years concerning fraternity files for examinations, term-paper writing services, organized cheating at the service academies, and the like. Such activities constitute a personally rational response to a reward system which pays off for grades rather than knowledge.

---

*Personal interviews conducted during 1972–73.

BUSINESS-RELATED EXAMPLES

Ecology

Assume that the president of XYZ Corporation is confronted with the following alternatives:

1. Spend $11 million for antipollution equipment to keep from poisoning fish in the river adjacent to the plant; or

2. Do nothing, in violation of the law, and assume a one in ten chance of being caught, with a resultant $1 million fine plus the necessity of buying the equipment.

Under this not unrealistic set of choices it requires no linear program to determine that XYZ Corporation can maximize its probabilities by flouting the law. Add the fact that XYZ's president is probably being rewarded (by creditors, stockholders, and other salient parts of his task environment) according to criteria totally unrelated to the number of fish poisoned, and his probable course of action becomes clear.

Evaluation of Training

It is axiomatic that those who care about a firm's well-being should insist that the organization get fair value for its expenditures. Yet it is commonly known that firms seldom bother to evaluate a new GRID, MBO, job enrichment program, or whatever, to see if the company is getting its money's worth. Why? Certainly it is not because people have not pointed out that this situation exists; numerous practitioner-oriented articles are written each year to just this point.

The individuals (whether in personnel, manpower planning, or wherever) who normally would be responsible for conducting such evaluations are the same ones often charged with introducing the change effort in the first place. Having convinced top management to spend the money, they usually are quite animated afterwards in collecting arigorous vignettes and anecdotes about how successful the program was. The last thing many desire is a formal systematic and revealing evaluation. Although members of top management may actually *hope* for such systematic evaluation, their reward systems continue to *reward* ignorance in this area. And if the personnel department abdicates its responsibility, who is to step into the breach? The change agent himself? Hardly! He is likely to be too busy collecting anecdotal "evidence" of his own, for use with his next client.

Miscellaneous

Many additional examples could be cited of systems which in fact are rewarding behaviors other than those supposedly desired by the rewarder. A few of these are described briefly below.

Most coaches disdain to discuss individual accomplishments, preferring to speak of teamwork, proper attitude, and a one-for-all spirit. Usually, however, rewards are distributed according to individual performance. The college basketball player who feeds his teammates instead of shooting will not compile impressive scoring statistics and is less likely to be drafted by the pros. The ballplayer who hits to right field to advance the runners will win neither the batting nor home run titles, and will be offered smaller raises. It therefore is rational for players to think of themselves first, and the team second.

In business organizations where rewards are dispensed for unit performance or for individual goals achieved, without regard for overall effectiveness, similar attitudes often are observed. Under most Management by Objectives (MBO) systems, goals in areas where qualification is difficult often go unspecified. The organization therefore often is in a position where it *hopes* for employee effort in the areas of team building, interpersonal relations, creativity, etc., but it formally *rewards* none of these. In cases where promotions and raises are formally tied to MBO, the system itself contains a paradox in that it "asks employees to set challenging, risky goals, only to face smaller paychecks and possibly damaged careers if these goals are not accomplished"(5,p.40).

It is *hoped* that administrators will pay attention to long-run costs and opportunities and will institute programs which will bear fruit later on. However, many organizational reward systems pay off for short-run sales and earnings only. Under such circumstances it is personally rational for officials to sacrifice long-term growth and profit (by selling off equipment and property, or by stifling research and development) for short-term advantages. This probably is most pertinent in the public sector, with the result that many public officials are unwilling to implement programs which will not show benefits by election time.

As a final, clear-cut example of a fouled-up reward system, consider the cost-plus contract or its next of kin, the allocation of next year's budget as a direct function of this year's expenditures. It probably is conceivable that those who award such budgets and contracts really hope for economy and prudence in spending. It is obvious, however, that adopting the proverb "to him who spends shall more be given," rewards not economy, but spending itself.

TWO COMPANIES' EXPERIENCES

A Manufacturing Organization

A midwest manufacturer of industrial goods had been troubled for some time by aspects of its organizational climate it believed dysfunctional. For research purposes, interviews were conducted with many employees and a questionnaire was administered on a company-wide basis, including plants and offices in several American and Canadian locations. The company strongly encouraged employee participation in the survey, and made available time and space during the workday for completion of the instrument. All employees in attendance during the day of the survey completed the questionnaire. All instruments were collected directly by the researcher, who personally administered each session. Since no one employed by the firm handled the questionnaires, and since respondent names were not asked for, it seems likely that the pledge of anonymity given was believed.

A modified version of the Expect Approval scale (7) was included as part of the questionnaire. The instrument asked respondents to indicate the degree of approval or disapproval they could expect if they performed each of the described actions. A seven-point Likert scale was used, with 1 indicating that the action would probably bring strong disapproval and 7 signifying likely strong approval.

Although normative data for this scale from studies of other organizations are unavailable, it is possible to examine fruitfully the data obtained from this survey in several ways. First, it may be worth noting that the questionnaire data corresponded closely to information gathered through interviews. Furthermore, as can be seen from the results summarized in Table 1, sizable differences between various work units, and between employees at different job levels within the same work unit, were obtained. This suggests that response bias effects (social desirability in particular loomed as a potential concern) are not likely to be severe.

Most importantly, comparisons between scores obtained on the Expect Approval scale and a statement of problems which were the reason for the survey revealed that the same behaviors which managers in each division thought dysfunctional were those which lower level employees claimed were rewarded. As compared to job levels 1 to 8 in Division B (see Table 1), those in Division A claimed a much higher acceptance by management of "conforming" activities. Between 31 to 37 percent of Division A employees at levels 1–8 stated that going along with the majority, agreeing with the boss, and staying on everyone's good side brought approval; only once (level 5–8 responses to one of the three items) did a majority suggest that such actions would generate disapproval.

Furthermore, responses from Division A workers at levels 1–4 indicate that behaviors geared toward risk avoidance were as likely to be rewarded as to be punished. Only at job levels 9 and above was it apparent that the reward system was positively reinforcing behaviors desired by top management. Overall, the same "tendencies toward conservatism and apple-polishing at the lower levels" which divisional management had complained about during the interviews were those claimed by subordinates to be the most rational course of action in light of the existing reward system. Management apparently was not getting the behaviors it was *hoping* for, but it certainly was getting the behaviors it was perceived by subordinates to be *rewarding*.

TABLE 1

Summary of Two Divisions' Data Relevant to Conforming and Risk-Avoidance Behaviors (Extent to Which Subjects Expect Approval)

| Item | Division and Sample | Total Responses | Percentage of Workers Responding | | |
			1, 2, or 3 (Disapproval)	4	5, 6, or 7 (Approval)
Making a risky decision based on the best information available at the time, but which turns out wrong	A, levels 1–4 (lowest)	127	61	25	14
	A, levels 5–8	172	46	31	23
	A, levels 9 and above	17	41	30	30
	B, levels 1–4 (lowest)	31	58	26	16
	B, levels 5–8	19	42	42	16
	B, levels 9 and above	10	50	20	30
Setting extremely high and challenging standards and goals, and then narrowly failing to make them	A, levels 1–4	122	47	28	25
	A, levels 5–8	168	33	26	41
	A, levels 9 +	17	24	6	70
	B, levels 1–4	31	48	23	29
	B, levels 5–8	18	17	33	50
	B, levels 9 +	10	30	0	70
Setting goals which are extremely easy to make and then making them	A, levels 1–4	124	35	30	35
	A, levels 5–8	171	47	27	26
	A, levels 9 +	17	70	24	6
	B, levels 1–4	31	58	26	16
	B, levels 5–8	19	63	16	21
	B, levels 9 +	10	80	0	20
Being a "yes man" and always agreeing with the boss	A, levels 1–4	126	46	17	37
	A, levels 5–8	180	54	14	31
	A, levels 9 +	17	88	12	0
	B, levels 1–4	32	53	28	19
	B, levels 5–8	19	68	21	11
	B, levels 9 +	10	80	10	10

TABLE 1 — *continued*

Item	Division and Sample	Total Responses	Percentage of Workers Responding		
			1, 2, or 3 (Disapproval)	4	5, 6, or 7 (Approval)
Always going along with the majority	A, levels 1–4	125	40	25	35
	A, levels 5–8	173	47	21	32
	A, levels 9 +	17	70	12	18
	B, levels 1–4	31	61	23	16
	B, levels 5–8	19	68	11	21
	B, levels 9 +	10	80	10	10
Being careful to stay on the good side of everyone, so that everyone agrees that you are a great guy	A, levels 1–4	124	45	18	37
	A, levels 5–8	173	45	22	33
	A, levels 9 +	17	64	6	30
	B, levels 1–4	31	54	23	23
	B, levels 5–8	19	73	11	16
	B, levels 9 +	10	80	10	10

An Insurance Firm

The Group Health Claims Division of a large eastern insurance company provides another rich illustration of a reward system which reinforces behaviors not desired by top management.

Attempting to measure and reward accuracy in paying surgical claims, the firm systematically keeps track of the number of returned checks and letters of complaint received from policyholders. However, underpayments are likely to provoke cries of outrage from the insured, while overpayments often are accepted in courteous silence. Since it often is impossible to tell from the physician's statement which of two surgical procedures, with different allowable benefits, was performed, and since writing for clarifications will interfere with other standards used by the firm concerning "percentage of claims paid within two days of receipt," the new hire in more than one claims section is soon acquainted with the informal norm: "When in doubt, pay it out!"

The situation would be even worse were it not for the fact that other features of the firm's reward system tend to neutralize those described. For example, annual "merit" increases are given to all employees, in one of the following three amounts:

1. If the worker is "outstanding" (a select category, into which no more than two employees per section may be placed): 5 percent

2. If the worker is "above average" (normally all workers not "outstanding" are so rated): 4 percent

3. If the worker commits gross acts of negligence and irresponsibility for which he might be discharged in many other companies: 3 percent.

Now, since (*a*) the difference between the 5 percent theoretically attainable through hard work and the 4 percent attainable merely by living until the review data is small and (*b*) since insurance firms seldom dispense much of a salary increase in cash (rather, the worker's insurance benefits increase, causing him to be further overinsured), many employees are rather indifferent to the possibility of obtaining the extra one percent reward and therefore tend to ignore the norm concerning indiscriminant payments.

However, most employees are not indifferent to the rule which states that, should absences or latenesses total three or more in any six-month period, the entire 4 or 5 percent due at the next "merit" review must be forfeited. In this sense the firm may be described as *hoping* for performance, while *rewarding* attendance. What it gets, of course, is attendance. (If the absence-lateness rule appears to the reader to be stringent, it really is not. The company counts "times" rather than "days" absent, and a ten-day absence therefore counts the same as one lasting two days. A worker in danger of accumulating a third absence within six months merely has to remain ill (away from work) during his second absence until his first absence is more than six months old. The limiting factor is that at some point his salary ceases, and his sickness benefits take over. This usually is sufficient to get the younger workers to return, but for those with 20 or more years' service, the company provides sickness benefits of 90 percent of normal salary, tax-free! Therefore. . . .)

CAUSES

Extremely diverse instances of systems which reward behavior A although the rewarder apparently hopes for behavior B have been given. These are useful to illustrate the breadth and magnitude of the phenomenon, but the diversity increases the difficulty of determining commonalities and establishing causes. However, four general factors may be pertinent to an explanation of why fouled-up reward systems seem to be so prevalent.

Fascination with an "Objective" Criterion

It has been mentioned elsewhere that:

Most "objective" measures of productivity are objective only in that their subjective elements are (*a*) determined in advance, rather than coming into play at the time of the formal evaluation, and (*b*) well concealed on the rating instrument itself. Thus industrial firms seeking to devise objective rating systems first decide, in an arbitrary manner, what dimensions are to be rated, . . . usually including some items having little to do with organizational effectiveness while excluding others that do. Only then does Personnel Division churn out official-looking documents on which all dimensions chosen to be rated are assigned point values, categories, or whatever (6,p. 92).

Nonetheless, many individuals seek to establish simple, quantifiable standards against which to measure and reward performance. Such efforts may be successful in highly predictable areas within an organization, but are likely to cause goal displacement when applied anywhere else. Over-concern with attendance and lateness in the insurance firm and with number of people placed in the vocational rehabilitation division may have been largely responsible for the problems described in those organizations.

Overemphasis on Highly Visible Behaviors

Difficulties often stem from the fact that some parts of the task are highly visible while other parts are not. For example, publications are easier to demonstrate than teaching, and scoring baskets and hitting home runs are more readily observable than feeding teammates and advancing base runners. Similarly, the adverse consequences of pronouncing a sick person well are more visible than those sustained by labeling a well person sick. Team-building and creativity are other examples of behaviors which may not be rewarded simply because they are hard to observe.

Hypocrisy

In some of the instances described the rewarder may have been getting the desired behavior, notwithstanding claims that the behavior was not desired. This may be true, for example, of management's attitude toward apple polishing in the manufacturing firm (a behavior which subordinates felt was rewarded, despite management's avowed dislike of the practice). This also may explain politicians' unwillingness to revise the penalties for disobedience of ecology laws, and the failure of top management to devise reward systems which would cause systematic evaluation of training and developing programs.

Emphasis on Morality or Equity Rather than Efficiency

Some consideration of other factors prevents the establishment of a system which rewards behaviors desired by the rewarder. The felt obligation of many Americans to vote for one candidate or another, for example, may impair their ability to withhold support from politicians who refuse to discuss the issues. Similarly, the concern for spreading the risks and costs of wartime military service may outweigh the advantage to be obtained by committing personnel to combat until the war is over.

It should be noted that only with respect to the first two causes are reward systems really paying off for other than desired behaviors. In the case of the third and fourth causes the system *is* rewarding behaviors desired by the rewarder, and the systems are fouled up only from the standpoints of those who believe the rewarder's public statements (cause 3), or those who seek to maximize efficiency rather than other outcomes (cause 4).

CONCLUSIONS

Modern organization theory requires a recognition that the members of organizations and society possess divergent goals and motives. It therefore is unlikely that managers and their subordinates will seek the same outcomes. Three possible remedies for this potential problem are suggested.

Selection

It is theoretically possible for organizations to employ only those individuals whose goals and motives are wholly consonant with those of management. In such cases the same behaviors judged by subordinates to be rational would be perceived by management as desirable. State-of-the-art reviews of selection techniques, however, provide scant grounds for hope that such an approach would be successful (for example, see 12).

Training

Another theoretical alternative is for the organization to admit those employees whose goals are not consonant with those of management and then, through training, socialization, or whatever, alter employee goals to make them consonant. However, research on the effectiveness of such training programs, though limited, provides further grounds for pessimism (for example, see 3).

Altering the Reward System

What would have been the result if:

1. Nixon had been assured by his advisors that he could not win election except by discussing the issues in detail?

2. Physicians' conduct was subjected to regular examination by review boards for type 1 errors (calling healthy people ill) and to penalties (fines, censure, etc.) for errors of either type?

3. The President of XYZ Corporation had to choose between (*a*) spending $11 million for antipollution equipment, and (*b*) incurring a 50-50 chance of going to jail for five years?

Managers who complain that their workers are not motivated might do well to consider the possibility that they have installed reward systems which are paying off for behaviors other than those they are seeking. This, in part, is what happened in Vietnam, and this is what regularly frustrates societal efforts to bring about honest politicians, civic-minded managers, etc. This certainly is what happened in both the manufacturing and the insurance companies.

A first step for such managers might be to find out what behaviors currently are being rewarded. Perhaps an instrument similar to that used in the manufacturing firm could be useful for this purpose. Chances are excellent that these managers will be surprised by what they find — that their firms are not rewarding what they assume they are. In fact, such undesirable behavior by organizational members as they have observed may be explained largely by the reward systems in use.

This is not to say that all organizational behavior is determined by formal rewards and punishments. Certainly it is true that in the absence of formal reinforcement some soldiers will be patriotic, some presidents will be ecology minded, and some orphanage directors will care about children. The point, however, is that in such cases the rewarder is not *causing* the behaviors desired but is only a fortunate bystander. For an organization to *act* upon its members, the formal reward system should positively reinforce desired behaviors, not constitute an obstacle to be overcome.

It might be wise to underscore the obvious fact that there is nothing really new in what has been said. In both theory and practice these matters have been mentioned before. Thus in many states Good Samaritan laws have been installed to protect doctors who stop to assist a stricken motorist. In states without such laws it is commonplace for doctors to refuse to stop, for fear of involvement in a subsequent lawsuit. In college basketball additional penalties have been instituted against players who foul their opponents deliberately. It has long been argued by Milton Friedman and others that penalties should be altered so as to make it irrational to disobey the ecology laws, and so on.

By altering the reward system the organization escapes the necessity of selecting only desirable people or of trying to alter undesirable ones. In Skinnerian terms (as described in 11, p. 704), "As for responsibility and goodness — as commonly defined — no one . . . would want or need them. They refer to a man's behaving well despite the absence of positive reinforcement that is obviously sufficient to explain it. Where such reinforcement exists, 'no one needs goodness.' "

REFERENCE NOTES

1   Barnard, Chester I. *The Functions of the Executive*. Cambridge, Mass.: Harvard University Press, 1964.

2   Blau, Peter M., and W. Richard Scott. *Formal Organizations*. San Francisco: Chandler, 1962.

3   Fiedler, Fred E. "Predicting the Effects of Leadership Training and Experience from the Contingency Model," *Journal of Applied Psychology*, vol. 56 (1972), pp. 114–19.

4   Garland, L. H. "Studies of the Accuracy of Diagnostic Procedures," *American Journal Roentgenological Radium Therapy Nuclear Medicine*, vol. 82 (1959), pp. 25–38.

5   Kerr, Steven. "Some Modifications in MBO as an OD Strategy," *Academy of Management Proceedings*, 1973, pp. 39–42.

6   Kerr, Steven. "What Price Objectivity?" *American Sociologist*, vol. 8 (1973), pp. 92–93.

7   Litwin, G. H., and R. A. Stringer, Jr. *Motivation and Organizational Climate*, Boston: Harvard University Press, 1968.

8   Perrow, Charles. "The Analysis of Goals in Complex Organizations," in A. Etzioni, ed., *Readings on Modern Organizations*. Englewood Cliffs, N.J.: Prentice-Hall, 1969.

9   Scheff, Thomas J. "Decision Rules, Types of Error, and Their Consequences in Medical Diagnosis," in F. Massarik and P. Ratoosh, eds., *Mathematical Explorations in Behavioral Science*. Homewood, Ill.: Irwin, 1965.

10 Simon, Herbert A. *Administrative Behavior*. New York: Free Press, 1957.

11 Swanson, G.E. "Review Symposium: Beyond Freedom and Dignity," *American Journal of Sociology*, vol. 78 (1972), pp. 702–05.

12 Webster, E. *Decision Making in the Employment Interview*, Montreal: Industrial Relations Center, McGill University, 1964.

QUESTIONS

1. If you were to develop a reward system for a company or work group, what would it be?

   _____

   _____

   _____

2. What should be the role of a manager in motivating employees?

   _____

   _____

   _____

Human Relations and the Nature of Man

> "We all know how little boys love fighting. They get their heads punched. But they have the satisfaction of having punched the other fellow's head."[1]

> The principle of co-operation is the most dominant and biologically the most important.[2]

The point is constantly made that traditional organizations work on the assumption that people are essentially opposed to work and lack the capacity for self-direction and personal responsibility. Modern theories of organization take the opposite view; i.e., people do have the capacity to become psychologically involved in cooperative activity and, under certain conditions, to be virtually self-motivated and self-controlled.

Douglas McGregor, among others, has noted how these implicit assumptions about the nature of man influence organization and leadership in his now classic discussion of Theory X and Theory Y. The former assumes that man is innately lazy and unreliable, and leads to organization and control based on external or imposed authority. The latter assumes that man can be basically self-directed and creative at work if properly motivated; this assumption is said to lead toward an integrative organizational strategy.

However, neither McGregor nor other writers in this field have undertaken to reveal how deeply the roots of these assumptions about man penetrate our culture and thus how powerfully they influence human relations in our society. Not only are these assumptions important in theories of human organization, but they are also crucial in every system of thought involved with human and social control. Whether concerned with organizational strategy, the ancient social order of the Zuni, or the political theories of a Machiavelli or a Locke, one cannot escape the underlying relatedness and importance of what is assumed about man himself.

Managers need to know more about the nature, sources, and effects of one assumption or the other in order (1) to sort out and understand their own ideas about the nature of humanity, and (2) to evaluate the fundamental influence of these ideas on managerial decisions. It may be asserted that no other variable weighs more heavily on the ultimate form and quality of organizational and interpersonal relations.

The questions of the basic nature of man is, of course, as old as history and probably as old as society itself. The argument, in its many forms, stems from the ancient philosophical debate as to whether man is an end or a means. Reducing the argument to its simplest terms, and considering only the extremities of the spectrum, we treat a person as an *end* when we permit him to establish his own purposes and to choose and decide for himself. Contrariwise, we treat a person as a *means* when we limit his choices and utilize him primarily as an instrument for our own ends and purposes.

Implicit in these values are central assumptions concerning (a) whether man is "good" or "evil," (b) whether he has the ability to cooperate voluntarily or must be forced to cooperate, (c) whether he is a "pilot" capable of choosing or a "robot" imprisoned by circumstances and incapable of choice.[3] Values such as these lie at the very core of philosophies of religion, politics, education, organization, and human relations.

It is our intention in this article to describe how the choice of one or the other of these sets of values has influenced a number of systems of thought concerned with questions of human regulation and control. We do not intend to emphasize the growing body of empirical evidence which indicates that the quality of individual and group performance varies from one kind of assumption and system to the other. This area is adequately covered in the writings of such men as Chris Argyris, Rensis Likert, and, of course, McGregor. Rather, we shall explore some of the cultural roots and branches of optimistic-pessimistic assumptions about human nature in order to show that an underlying unity exists along this dimension in a variety of human-social control systems.

MAN: PESSIMISTIC VIEW

In their polar aspects, attitudes about human nature range from pessimism to optimism — from assumptions that evilness, predatory competition, and aggression on the one hand, to goodness, cooperation, and virtue on the other, constitute the central predispositions of men and, therefore, of the social order. Let us begin our discussion by examining how certain ideas about human-social control have been affected by the pessimistic or "means" view of man. This is the attitude that man is essentially evil and driven by aggressive and uncooperative motives and drives.

Fear Versus Love

As early giants in the history of Western idea makers, Niccolo Machiavelli and Thomas Hobbes — a pair of political scientists — provide us with a suitable starting point. It will be recalled that Machiavelli in *The Prince* (1515) urged that, because of man's rebellious and uncooperative behavior, he must be strictly and ruthlessly controlled by anyone who aspires to gain or maintain a position of power. A ruler, in his view, must put aside any question of morality and must achieve control at any price and by whatever means he can find:

> It is much safer to be feared than loved. . . . For it may be said of men in general that they are ungrateful, voluble, dissemblers, anxious to avoid dangers, and covetous of gain.[4]

In all fairness, however, it must be made clear that he did not advocate his "end justifies the means" philosophy to benefit the prince or the ruler but to benefit the people. He assumed that only the ruler is competent to judge what the necessary ends are and must be. In furtherance of these ends, then, the ruler must resort to means which appear ruthless and deceitful.

Hobbes in the *Leviathan* (1651) outlined a theory of social relationships which makes him a direct intellectual descendant of Machiavelli. According to Hobbes, since men covet prestige, material goods, and power and expect to attain these at their discretion, they live in perpetual fear of their neighbors:

> And therefore if any two men desire the same thing, which nevertheless they cannot both enjoy, they become enemies.[5]

Law must therefore define what is honest and virtuous. But, in order for law to be applicable, a common authority must exist to enforce it. Man recognizes this need out of fear of loss of life and property. As a consequence, he enters into a social contract in which he gives up to a central authority whatever rights he has had in nature. In this way, he brings about the creation of a commonwealth ruled by a sovereign. Each man is individually bound to this authority, or Leviathan, and the latter's powers are irrevocable. The sovereign is a despot; whatever he wills becomes the people's will. As the Leviathan, he represents the supremacy of law, absolute authority and power, and the bureaucracy of the state.

Survival of the Fittest

Both Machiavelli and Hobbes viewed human nature primarily as a product of experience. They perceived in mankind a predominance of aggressive and selfish motives as a result of socialization rather than biological inheritance, and they designed political systems in order to constrain and control human behavior and thus create order in society.

Such orderliness in nature as a whole was also evident to Charles Darwin, who, through his research into the causes of variations in species and the contribution of these variations to the survival of species in nature, became convinced that survival was assured through a process of natural selection.

Darwin thought that survival was guaranteed only to those who were the best representatives of the species and best adapted to the conditions of the environment. The survivors were those who through physical prowess and mental agility were able to win in the competition for food and mate. The suggestion here is clear, that nature is a never-ending struggle — a competition — and that a permanent state of war exists among and between all species and the natural environment.

Darwin's interpreters suggested that as with animals so with man. Herbert Spencer, who was quick to find social implications in Darwin's biological theory, argued that among men the fittest survive; indeed, they are the only ones entitled to survive. In this, the process of natural selection in man's world favors the aggressive and the strong. Man, in this scheme, is a predatory creature. Spencer's interpretations of Darwinian theory underlie much of the creed of many nineteenth century U.S. industrialists and their philosophy of the "stewardship" of the rich and the "gospel of wealth."

(It is to be noted that Darwin himself was not willing to accept Spencer's theory that the law of natural selection applied to the human race. Actually, he turned the argument around. Man's weakness, Darwin thought, becomes his greatest strength; it forces man to establish cooperative relationships with others for protection and maintenance. In addition, Darwin attributed to man a moral feeling — one of sympathy and compassion — rather than indifference toward the weak and defective. Unhappily, it has been his fate to become associated with "survival of the fittest" as a scientific theory which is applied to man as well as other natural species.)

The Invisible Hand

Often associated with Darwin as a supporter of the idea of self-regulation in human society is Adam Smith. A century earlier, he placed his special emphasis on the automaticity of economic affairs. Under his doctrine of the invisible hand, there is a just allocation of a nation's scarce resources through the price mechanism which reflects supply and demand conditions of the market. By pursuing his self-interest, each individual can further not only his own fortune but also that of society as a whole.

It is this idea of self-interest as prime mover which has led many to assume that Smith considered man to possess a basically selfish, rather than a virtuous, nature. The economic doctrine of laissez-faire which Smith originated has meant "permission to do or make what you choose"; hence, noninterference with personal indulgence. This, when combined with self-interest as motivator, would seem, ergo, to support the notion that man is by nature self-seeking, predatory, and interested only in his own good at the expense of his weaker and less fortunate fellows. For example:

> It is not from the benevolence of the butcher, the brewer, or the baker that we expect our dinner, but from their regard of their own interest. We address ourselves not to their humanity, but to their self-love, and never talk to them of our own necessities, but of their advantage.[6]

Though there is ample evidence to indicate that Smith, like Darwin, recognized that morality and government must and do govern the actions of men, he has nevertheless become, with Darwin, a symbol of individualism.

(Smith, at one time, occupied a professorial chair in moral philosophy and in *The Theory of Moral Sentiment* (1759) made it clear that he relied on natural law and, as a reflection of that, on a natural morality which prescribed three cardinal virtues: justice, prudence, and benevolence. Though he recognized some truth in the aphorism that private vices become public virtues, he clearly assumed that, as a reflection of a natural state of equality, men in pursuit of enlightened self-interest are characterized by adherence to justice—"a scrupulous refusal ever to hurt or injure anyone else, in the pursuit of one's own interest or advantage." Smith was not concerned with production and the accumulation of goods per se, but rather with the ends served thereby. In effect, the welfare of the ordinary man was on his mind to such an extent that he implicitly took the side of the underdog, which he perceived the ordinary laboring man to be.)

Sex and Aggression

Sigmund Freud, the father of psychoanalysis and the first to explore man's unconscious mind, took a clearer position on human nature than did Machiavelli, Hobbes, Darwin, or Smith. According to Freud, man is motivated by innate instincts and drives that he constantly struggles to pacify in ways which are antithetical to the norms of society. (These instincts and drives have been identified with sex and aggression but were really intended by Freud to refer to nature's and man's hankering to stay alive.) To the extent that society succeeds in curbing these animal forces, man becomes civilized and his energies can be turned toward socially acceptable goals. But, said Freud pessimistically:

> Psychoanalysis has concluded . . . that the primitive, savage, and evil impulses of mankind have not vanished in any individual, but continue their existence, although in repressed state . . . and . . . they wait for opportunities to display their activity.[7]

Freud further observed, in his *Civilization and Its Discontents* (1930), that society, itself, is perpetually threatened by the underlying hostilities which exist between human beings. Periodically, these feelings explode into open aggression which persists until the participants can once more be brought under control. However, society's attempts to neutralize destructive impulses through a "cultural superego," which defines for man what is "good" and what is "bad," create feelings of guilt. This, Freud said, is man's most urgent and important problem.[8] The anxieties generated by this constant clash between man's basic nature and the demands and needs of society increase human unhappiness and lead to mental illness. Thus, Freud seems to suggest, man is essentially doomed:

> From his [Freud's] point of view society, by its very nature, forces man to repress his inborn aggression more and more. The outlook for the future is that the more civilized he becomes, the more potentially destructive he becomes.[9]

Warrior and Weaponmaker

Recent evidence has been uncovered which seems to support the idea that man has been an aggressor and warrior since the beginning of his existence. Under the direction of L.S.B. Leakey, excavations conducted in South Africa — among what now appear to be the earliest remnants of man's ancestors — have uncovered man's earliest tools and have established that among them weapons occupied the most important place. The indications are that these were used not only for killing in the acquisition of food but also against man — for protection, in the defense of mate or of territory, and in the conduct of war. While the evidence is mixed, it has led some to theorize that a warlike, aggressive nature is a part of every man's inheritance.

As a consequence, it can be argued that Darwin's law of nature, survival of the fittest, also applies to man. Such an emphasis on aggression over a span of hundreds of thousands of years, Robert Ardrey has argued, must have had a permanent effect on his hereditary structure:

> Man is a predator with an instinct to kill and a genetic cultural affinity for the weapon.[10]

In this view the urge to aggression, the desire to dominate others, is an instinct or drive transmitted from generation to generation through the genes.

The predisposition of men toward aggression has also been noted by one of the most renowned philosophers of our own time, Henri Bergson, who wrote:

> But no matter the thing taken, the motive adduced: the origin of war is ownership, individual or collective, and since humanity is predestined to ownership by its structure, war is natural. So strong, indeed, is the war instinct, that it is the first to appear when we scratch below the surface of civilization in search of nature. We all know how little boys love fighting. They get their heads punched. But they have the satisfaction of having punched the other fellow's head.[11]

Bergson clearly joins with those who take a pessimistic view of man. By assuming that innate, predatory, and selfish instincts are first causes, he cannot conceive of a human society — with its dependence on material possessions — as capable of avoiding conflict through the processes of reason and self-control.

Manager and Managed

The underlying ideas about human nature which have been previously outlined will also be found among some thinkers whose work focuses on the relationship between the manager and the managed in business and industry. These are the writers who are generally associated with the scientific management movement and who date from about 1900.

At this time, Frederick W. Taylor, who pioneered this movement in the United States, saw a need for management to exert close control over the indifferent behavior of workmen in order to ensure their adherence to the objectives and goals of business enterprise. In spite of all the human values which have been imputed to his writings, it seem clear that Taylor and his followers made these six basic assumptions about human nature:

1. The employee is a "constant" in the production equation. The implication here is that man has a fixed nature.

2. The employee is an inert adjunct of the machine, prone to inefficiency and waste unless properly programmed.

3. The employee is by nature lazy; only managers honor the "hard work" creed of the Protestant Ethic.

4. The employee's main concern is self-interest. At work, this is always expressed in economic values.

5. Given appropriate expression, these values will make man fiercely competitive among his peers as an accumulator of financial rewards.

6. Man (at least the working man) must therefore be tightly controlled and externally motivated in order to overcome his natural desire to avoid work unless the material gains available to him are worth his effort.

In accordance with these assumptions, Taylor thought that management must assume the responsibility for specifying in detail the method to be followed by the employee in order to gain an approximation of his full output potential. In addition, a piece-rate plan would have to be included as a financial incentive to ensure maximum performance.

At about the same time, a contemporary of Taylor was developing a similar pattern of thought in Europe regarding the relationship between manager and managed. While Taylor concerned himself mainly with the shop environment, Max Weber designed the features of his ideal bureaucracy viewing the organization from the top downward.

Again, in the elements of Weber's bureaucracy—specialization of personnel, impersonality, a heirarchy of authority relationships, entry and advancement by competitive examination, written policies, rules and procedures, and others—we find the Weberian image of man as a reluctant cog in an organizational machine. Thus the great majority of employees are confined to tightly controlled and dependent relationships with their superiors.

The pervasiveness of the Taylor-Weber approach to organization and management is evident throughout industrial organization today. Management scholars such as Urwick, Mooney, and Brown, as well as important business executives like Cordiner of General Electric, Greenwalt of DuPont, and Kappel of AT&T, have generally adhered to this model of managerial control and the underlying values which emphasize the need to minimize employee resistance to work—to support the Protestant Ethic—and a consequent need for autocratic rule and the traditional bureaucratic hierarchy.

MAN: OPTIMISTIC VIEW

Now let us turn from the foregoing cynical view of the nature of man to the view which emphasizes man's strength as a potentially creative, social being. As in dealing with the opposite view discussed earlier, we shall examine how an assumption that human beings have worth and goodness influences a wide-ranging sample of systems of social control. The examples used are not intended to be other than illustrative, straddling such divergent systems of human thought as political government, psychoanalysis, sociology, and business organization.

Social Instinct and Reason

Although separated in time by sixteen centuries, Marcus Tullius Cicero and John Locke shared remarkably similar ideas about the governing of men. Cicero in *On the Commonwealth* (51 B.C.) argued that men by nature believe in goodness and well-doing, and abhor savagery and baseness. On the assumption of mutual advantage, they come together in obedience to a social instinct and where enough individuals are involved form a democratic association or commonwealth for the benefit of all. Out of this emerges a leader who governs voluntary subjects through a moral claim to their allegiance rather than through regulation based on force.

Locke, in *The Second Treatise of Government*, contended that men of reason are inherently disposed toward mutual support and cooperation:

> The state of nature has a law of nature to govern it, which obliges everyone; and reason, which is that law, teaches all mankind who will but consult it that, being all equal and independent, no one ought to harm another in his life, health, liberty, or possessions.[12]

In other words, Locke argued that man's fundamental potential is reason and *reason itself* establishes cooperation as the basis for human relationships.

Under Locke's concept of the social contract, agreement is reached between free men to entrust to the community the authority to protect the common welfare. This custodianship is continued through tacit consent and is subject to the rule of majority. For Locke, man is naturally disposed toward doing good, and government is essentially a convenience. The sovereign is assumed to will what the people will. Locke believed that man's mind at birth is a *tabula rasa*, a blank sheet of paper and, therefore, that man becomes a person through sense impressions, mediated by reason, which he derives from social experience.

Thus the human mind and character are shaped by interaction with the world; whatever man becomes is a function of reason and social interaction. The function of government, therefore, is not to create its own laws as a controlling force but to discover what natural forces bring man to a state of reason *in which he can control himself.*

Cooperation and Survival

Two men of science, W.C. Allee, a biologist, and Ashley Montagu, a cultural anthropologist, have advanced ideas from their own fields about human nature which correspond in important respects with those of Cicero and Locke. They have argued that nature, from a biological standpoint, supports the concept of survival through cooperation rather than competition.

Allee reported in his *Cooperation Among Animals* the results of a wealth of research which provides evidence that cooperative, social relationships increase the probability of survival for any single individual as well as for a species as a whole. One of his simple experiments showed that it takes proportionately less toxic colloidal silver to kill a single goldfish in an aquarium than if the aquarium holds a number of goldfish. He suggested that the ability of a group of goldfish to neutralize a poison appears to increase faster than that of a single goldfish. He concluded his discussion of complex animal life in this way:

> The conclusion seems inescapable that the more closely knit societies arose from some sort of simple aggregation . . . such an evolution could come about most readily with the existence of an underlying pervasive element of unconscious proto-cooperation, or automatic tendency toward mutual aid among animals.[13]

As Allee explored further evidences of cooperation in higher animals, he came to this conclusion:

> All through the animal kingdom — from amoeba to insects, or to man — animals show automatic unconscious proto-cooperation or even true cooperation. There is much evidence that the drift toward natural cooperation is somewhat stronger than the opposing tendency toward disoperation [among crowded animals].[14]

However, in spite of his argument that a cooperative-social instinct is readily found in nature, Allee also recognized a counterprinciple. This principle was that threat or force will be employed on the part of individuals, animal or man, to dominate others in a group in order to establish a hierarchy or pecking order. And he felt impelled to add that "much can be said for an established order of dominance and subordination."[15]

Allee pointed to evidences from the animal world which seem to reveal that any single individual thrives better where the pecking order is firmly established than where constant reorganization is in progress. He also saw evidence for this on the world scene. However, in all cases, Allee believed there will finally appear a subordinate to challenge the existing order. Thus he concluded that a pecking order brings peace and stability for the *short* run, but that an integrated unit characterized by natural cooperation promises stability for the *long* run.

Montagu agreed in all essential respects with Allee. He argued that from a biological point of view men prefer to survive through cooperation rather than competition:

> The principle of co-operation is the most dominant and biologically the most important.[16]

Montagu, of course, was particularly concerned with man rather than with the animal world. He believed that man from infancy on must rely on others for the satisfaction of his needs, and therefore affinity for interdependence is a fundamental reflection of the social state:

> All of man's natural inclinations are toward the development of goodness, toward the continuance of states of goodness and the discontinuance of unpleasant states.[17]

Thus warfare is considered by Montagu, as it was by Allee, as a human invention derived from economic or materialistic, rather than biological, considerations.

'Blank Page' Concept

On the basis of their more sanguine views of man's nature, these men, from Cicero through Montagu, have set forth behavioral concepts which support the idea of cooperation over aggression in human relationships and the need for strengthening these relationships through a constructive process of learning. Much of modern thought in psychoanalysis and psychotherapy, in sociology and social psychology, and in the field of organizational studies is also based on an optimistic view of man's nature. It resists Descartes' assumption that men are born with innate ideas and a more or less given nature.

Thus many modern behavioral scientists tend, like Locke, to think of man as entering life with a mind like a blank page on which experience is then impressed, and out of which the form and content of his personality are molded. To this way of thought, man's behavior is acquired in life and changes with experience. It is not solely predetermined by the genes, nor is it fixed and irrevocable. Out of these views have emerged new ways of perceiving man as an individual and as a member of a group.

Earlier, we outlined the pessimistic view of man on which Freud based his psychoanalytic theory. Freud's assumption about man's innate nature affected his theories in the same way as Hobbes's assumptions about man influenced his theories of government and society—man, left to his own devices, will prey on other men to satisfy his desires and must, in the interests of all, be restrained by forces in society.

The psychoanalysts who followed Freud have made distinctive contributions to modern views of the nature of man. From among them has emerged a group which broke with Freud on the issue of the basic nature of man, the so-called neo-Freudians, represented in this discussion by Harry Stack Sullivan, Erich Fromm, and Karen Horney. The neo-Freudians base their theories of human behavior on the assumption that the development of personality is influenced primarily by external societal forces and events rather than by bio-genetically determined, innate instincts or drives.

Freud, of course, assumed that man and society are basically divided—on the one hand, a set of drives in man (sex and aggression) which are at the root of man's evil and, on the other, a set of rules in the human culture which inhibit and control the individual. The neo-Freudians argue that there is no dichotomy between man and society. According to Fromm:

> 'The most beautiful as well as the most ugly inclinations of man are not a part of a fixed and biologically given human nature but result from the social process.'[18]

Necessarily then, if man is to be understood, major attention must be given to those forces in his environment which influence the molding of his personality.

J.A.C. Brown in *The Social Psychology of Industry* has described the difference between Freudian and neo-Freudian ideas about the nature of man as the difference between thinking of man as being "pushed from behind" or "drawn from in front." This, in a rough way, is the difference between psychological determinism or behaviorist psychology — with its focus on drives, instincts, or the conditioned reflex as a source of behavior — and subjectivist theories of psychology, which perceive psychic energy as being derived from personal goals and personal perceptions of reality. Sullivan's theory of personality development, like those of Fromm and Horney, belongs in this latter category.

According to Sullivan, the individual begins life with certain potentials and two basic goals: satisfaction and security. The extent to which he realizes his potential and achieves his goals depends on his experiences with other people. The pursuit of "satisfaction" has to do with satisfying physical needs like sleep, hunger, and sex.

However, the manner in which such needs are satisfied does not depend on the innate characteristics of an individual but reflects behavior patterns which are the product of interpersonal relations. It is in relation to other people that an individual seeks "security" — that is, in the avoidance of anxiety caused by feelings of disapproval or inadequacy in a social situation. Thus the matter of psychological security is culture-bound, and the form and content of the human personality is a product of specific cultural forces.

Sullivan defines the anxiety-free condition of "euphoria" as a tension-less state similar to that experienced by a new-born and sleeping child who has yet to discover that he has arrived in a threatening environment. Such as infant is at peace with the world or, in Rousseau's terms, in a state of oneness and harmony with nature. Only exposure to the anxieties which arise out of human relationships can change this profound sense of well-being into a state of tension. This state of tension then promotes education and learning through which the self-system of an individual finally emerges.

The self-system, as Sullivan defines it, represents that portion of an individual's potential which is realized, while the "true self" contains the maximum potentialities which could have, under ideal conditions of experience, been developed. Since it is an unfortunate fact of life in our culture that interpersonal experience is far from ideal, Sullivan felt that most people are "inferior caricatures of what they might have been."[19]

Cultural Determination

Fromm does not accept the "blank page" concept of Locke but, nevertheless, strongly rejects the idea that instincts are the primary source of human behavior. Fromm concedes that man comes into existence with a set of drives and instincts. However, he argues that their particular patterns of development and their manifestation in the behavior of individuals are culturally determined:

> Any given social order does not *create* these fundamental strivings but it determines which of the limited number of potential passions are to become manifest or dominant.[20]

From this, it is clear that Fromm considers that human potentialities depend to a very large extent on the *will to productiveness which society succeeds in bringing to man.* The individual is shaped by society. The environment in which the individual exists, therefore, becomes a primary factor in the way he responds to life and work.

Fromm emphasizes in his theory that man is faced with a desire to be part of nature. Animals, through their instinctual equipment, seem able to accommodate themselves to the external environment through what appears to be an automatic process and, therefore, to achieve close ties with nature. Man, in contrast, through self-awareness and reason is alienated from nature.

In fact, in industrial society he is often alienated from himself, from meaningful human relationships, and from his work. In this process man is caught in a tug-of-war between self-reliance, power, control over nature, independence, and escape from isolation, competition, hostility, and insecurity. He must find his path by relating to things and to people. Ideally, he should succeed in establishing a productive relationship in which he is able to feel and act in accordance with his potential for contributing to constructive human life.

Pilot or Robot?

As our final example of modern psychoanalytic thought, we consider Karen Horney. In her writings Horney agrees with Sullivan and Fromm in the view that Freud gave biological and genetic factors an excessive role in character formation. Taking the position that man's nature is not instinctive but learned, she was one of the first analysts to emphasize the importance of interpersonal relations in behavior development. What an individual learns — that is, how he reacts to life with others — is influenced most by the way he is treated by others.

It was Horney's view that all individuals in their natural development seek sentiments of liking and approval from others. Where interpersonal relationships do not have such support, anxiety develops and begins to interfere with the growth of a healthy personality. In such cases people respond to others in three basic ways: (1) by "moving toward people" — feeling inadequate, they become attached and dependent; (2) by "moving against people" — rejected, they become rebellious and aggressive; or

(3) by "moving away from people"—they seek comfort for rejection in symbolic substitutes and fantasy. Neurotic behavior occurs when there is conflict over which response pattern to adopt in a given situation. Various defense mechanisms help solve such conflicts but at the expense of genuineness in human relationships and of needed problem-solving behavior.

Because of her emphasis on the importance of situational factors in personality development, Horney tended to look to a person's present interpersonal involvements for the causes and solutions to neurotic problems. She did not deny that a connection exists between an individual's current responses and his early life—a connection which was so important a part of Freud's thinking—but she argued that one must look to the present situation for clues as to what triggered these responses.

Man is not, therefore, doomed by a set of prenatally determined instincts, nor are his patterns of behavior eternally established by early life experience. Horney's concept of man is cheerful and optimistic, not gloomy and pessimistic. Man is born neither a devil nor a saint; he simply reflects in his behavior the nature of relationships developed since the time of his birth with people who were important to him.

The insights into human nature which have been outlined above and which summarize the thinking of an important school of modern psychotherapy are based on the confident viewpoint that man is not doomed by a fixed and evil nature from which he cannot escape. Rather, they would seem to suggest just the opposite: man has within himself the potential to grow and develop significantly in cooperation with others. Man is a pilot, not a robot. What is needed is not a method of controlling innately selfish or even predatory drives toward war with other men, but a means of tapping man's potential for joining in productive relationships with others.

Individual or Environment?

One of the first social scientists to apply this concept of man to analysis of industrial organizations was Elton Mayo of Harvard University. Mayo's view of human nature was optimistic and anti-Freudian. To illustrate:

> The concealed assumption of the doctrine of original sin invalidates the psychoanalytic findings. The theory that life is a strenuous fight to subdue perversion, that the human mind is by nature "pathogenic" (i.e., predisposed to the pathological) is not a starting point for biological observation.[21]

In other words, the concept that life on earth is an atonement for original transgressions of God's laws, and that man is cursed with a set of evil instincts which must be curbed by society, is inadequate as a base for observing and understanding man's behavior in daily life.

Mayo argued that too much attention was being given in industrial settings to *individuals* as the source of noncooperative and unproductive relationships between the leadership of the organization and those who are employed to accomplish the work. He pointed out that developments in sociology and in social anthropology had already opened to serious question whether a merely psychological study of individuals in an organization is a logical approach to a comprehension of their behavior as workers.

On the contrary, Mayo said, such individuals constitute a group which develops responses to the total organizational environment. On the basis of this, the research interview program at the Hawthorne Works, originally consisting of isolated interviews, was restructured so that interviewers were assigned to study individuals over extended periods in relation to their jobs, the informal social organization in which they worked, and company policy.

The original isolated interviewing method was based on the premise that personal behavior or misbehavior was a result of personal rationality or irrationality; the second method assumed that the individual was only one of a number of interdependent variables relating to behavior. These other variables were part of the working environment and included such factors as leadership, working conditions, and working group membership. Science, inspired by the work of early sociologists and anthropologists, was at last beginning to show, contrary to Hobbesian theory, that man was more victim than antagonist in his environment.

Behavioral Science Man

While the initial thrust toward change in managerial philosophy and practice can be traced back to the origin of the human relations movement in the 1930's, it has continued through the present time in two somewhat divergent directions: (1) toward the fusion of the scientific organizational behavior approach with a new, more humanistic management philosophy, and (2) toward organizational reeducation and change through sensitivity or laboratory training. In both cases the importance of the roles played by behavioral and other social scientists in defining the relationship between the manager and the managed is becoming more and more evident.

While Mayo's work resulted in increasing the emphasis on human relations mainly in normative terms, much of the subsequent direction of this work is based on the research and findings of the behavioral sciences of sociology, psychology, social psychology, and cultural anthropology. Research workers such as Argyris, McGregor, and Likert have identified themselves with A.H. Maslow's theory of the need hierarchy as an aspect of human nature. Given the assumption that a satisfied need does not motivate, man is seen as satisfying in ascending order the needs of hunger in an extended sense, safety, social affection, esteem, and finally self-actualization or self-fulfillment.

The challenge for management today is seen by these authors as one of providing man at work with the opportunity to grow and mature continually into a human being who, because of a favorable working climate, is able to realize his own goals best by working for the success of the organization of which he is a member. Implicit in their assumptions is the idea that man has an essential nature which is defined by the broad spectrum of his needs, capacities, and tendencies. These needs, as expressed by Maslow, "are on their face good or neutral rather than evil."[22]

In a continuing reflection of the neo-Freudian view of man, we find McGregor stating, "If employees are lazy, indifferent, unwilling to take responsibility, intransigent, uncreative, uncooperative,"[23] this is due to the traditional bureaucratic assumptions and methods of organization and control. Argyris, in a similar vein suggests, "Mutual understanding trust, self-esteem, openness, internal commitment, fully functioning human beings who aspire to excellence . . . these values can not only be protected, but indeed increased, in an industrial setting."[24]

In the world of work, therefore, man is seen by the behavioral scientists as responding to the influences of his organizational environment. Given the opportunity, he will participate creatively in furthering the objectives of the organization. If frustrated, his behavior will characteristically revert to the basic need level of hunger; he will turn apathetic, slovenly, and totally alienated from an orientation toward work as a central life interest.

Such a basic underlying belief in man as a creative human being oriented toward constructive rather than destructive activities is even more clearly represented in the sensitivity training movement. Through this process of reeducation and skill development, Warren G. Bennis and his collaborators see the way to democratization of management — a condition which they view as essential in the face of accelerating technological change, the increasing proportion of professionals in the work force, and the consequent necessity of the organization to accept the values of science and scientific inquiry in order to survive in the future.

("Democracy" is here defined not as permissiveness or laissez-faire but as a system of values by which people in organizations are assumed to feel "internally compelled" to live. These include free communication, the consensus principle, influence based on competence rather than position, acceptance of emotion as fact, and a "basically human bias" in dealing with conflict.)[25]

In Bennis' terms, the "organization man" becomes a signpost on the road pointing the way to the kinds of flexibility and adaptability which are essential if the democratic environment to which science and scientists can flourish is to be realized. Whether one agrees or not, it is well known among men of science that personalities are only of passing interest compared to the contribution they hope to make to the accumulation of new knowledge.

WHERE DO YOU STAND?

We have confined the discussion to the pessimistic-optimistic views for the sake of simplicity and clarity, although it is, of course, a matter of common observation that all of the possible social processes are located along a continuum whose polar extremities are mutual cooperation and predatory competition.

As opposite ends of a spectrum, cooperation and competition are closely related to love and hate, friendship and enmity, harmony and discord, collaboration and opposition. They may therefore be used to describe a person's *basic* or *characteristic* propensity toward his fellowman. In terms of his attitudes toward others, every man will find himself at some point on this spectrum depending on the particular situation in which he is involved.

However, each man is drawn by the force of his own history and experience toward some primary tendency, some central quality of being, which determines the general pattern of his social behavior. Peripheral changes occur in this pattern to accommodate the demands of the various roles he plays, but there would seem to be a core pattern which represents his basic beliefs concerning the nature of man. Man is evil or man is good, depending on man's experience with mankind.

The examples from the history of human thought that we have cited illustrate this concept of the *primary tendency* in the kind of view one man takes of another. They also clearly indicate that cooperation and competition, or goodness and evilness, as human characteristics are not discrete activities or qualities but rather exist in various mixtures in human nature.

Hobbes's *primary tendency*, for example, was to view man as evil. Nevertheless, his idea of the "social contract" contains the implicit assumption of *cooperative* activity among men by which they give up their rights to a ruling Leviathan to gain protection from one another. Bergson said that war in a materialistic society is natural, but he noted that collective ownership leads to cooperation within groups to protect members from outsiders. Even Freud, who comes closest to a concept of innately evil men straining against societal constraints to satisfy their needs, conceded that man may become "good" because of his dependency on others; he will, in short, *cooperate* when he finds helping behavior in other men.

Among those whose primary tendency is to view man as good, we find similar ambivalences:

- Locke argued that reason evoked cooperation among men. However, he implied that the "social contract" exists between ruler and ruled to control man's acquired *competitive*, aggressive nature.

- The neo-Freudians believed that man's goodness or evilness was a product of experience — that is, competitive (hating) experiences lead to malfunctioning by societal standards, but cooperative (loving) experiences lead to satisfaction and to development.

The psychoanalytic assumptions and clinical findings of the neo-Freudians to the effect that man has basic worth and is capable of constructive psychic responses in an environment of understanding and encouragement have received scientific support among modern experimenters. Behavioral Science Man, whether the setting has been in the laboratory or in the field — in a business, education, or government organization — is a "good" man whose potential for productive growth and self-actualization has too often been stunted by his superiors' outmoded assumptions that he is "bad." Therefore, for their purposes, he must be manipulated like a puppet on a string.

CONCLUSION

The quality of human relations in any organization, from the political state to the business enterprise, reflects first of all its members', and particularly its leaders', views of the essential character of humanity itself. It makes a great deal of difference in systems of social control whether those involved tend to view man, in general, as good or evil. If we assume that man is good, we can believe that misbehavior is a reactive response rather than a manifestation of character. This will lead to a search for causes in his experience rather than in his nature. If we are to find a cause for behavioral failure, we are more apt to look outside the offender than inside and thus consider a whole new range of variables and contributory circumstances.

If, on the other hand, we assume that man himself is bad, a priori, then we are prone to assume that misbehavior is caused by something within him which we cannot alter directly. Accordingly, our attention will focus on limiting his freedom to choose and to act through external curbs or controls. In limiting the causes of behavior, we exclude ourselves from powerful internal sources of control. Thus the underlying human value which predominates is readily perceived in (a) the way social relationships are structured, (b) the kinds of rewards and penalties that are used, (c) the character of the communication process which links people together, and (d) the other elements of social control that characterize a relationship or an organization.

REFERENCE NOTES

1 Henri Bergson, *The Two Sources of Morality and Religion* (Garden City, New York, Doubleday & Company, Inc., Anchor Book edition, 1935), p. 284.

2 Ashley Montagu, *Man in Process* (New York, New American Library, Mentor edition, 1962), p. 50.

3 The terms "pilot" and "robot" have been borrowed from Donald H. Ford and Hugh B. Urban, *Systems of Psychotherapy* (New York, John Wiley and Sons, Inc., 1965), pp. 595 ff.

4 Niccolo Machiavelli, *The Prince and the Discourses* (New York, Random House, Modern Library edition, 1950), p. 61.

5 Thomas Hobbes, *Leviathan* (Indianapolis, The Bobbs-Merrill Company, Inc., The Library of Liberal Arts edition, 1958), p. 105.

6   Adam Smith, *An Inquiry into the Nature and Causes of the Wealth of Nations* (New York, Random House, Modern Library edition, 1937), p. 14.

7   Letter from Freud to Dr. van Eeden, quoted in Ernest Jones, *The Life and Work of Sigmund Freud*, Vol. II (New York, Basic Books, Inc., Publishers, 1957), p. 368.

8   Sigmund Freud, *Civilization and Its Discontents*, translated by James Strachey (New York, W.W. Norton & Company, Inc., 1961), p. 81.

9   Clara Thompson, *Psychoanalysis: Its Evolution and Development* (New York, Grove Press, Inc., first Evergreen edition, 1957), p. 151.

10 Robert Ardrey, *African Genesis* (New York, Deli Publishing Co., Inc., 1961), p. 166.

11 Henri Bergson, op. cit., p. 284.

12 John Locke, *The Second Treatise of Government* (New York, The Liberal Arts Press, Inc., 1952), p. 5.

13 W. C. Allee, *Cooperation Among Animals* (New York, Henry Schuman, 1951), p. 29.

14 Ibid., p. 203.

15 Ibid., p. 204.

16 Ashley Montagu, op. cit., p. 50.

17 Ibid., p. 57.

18 Erich Fromm, *Escape from Freedom* (New York, Farrar and Rinehart, Inc., 1941), p. 12.

19 J.A.C. Brown, *Freud and the Post-Freudians* (Baltimore, Penguin Books, Inc., 1961), p. 167.

20 Erich Fromm, *The Sane Society* (New York, Holt, Rinehart & Winston, Inc., 1955), p. 14.

21 Elton Mayo, *The Human Problems of an Industrial Civilization* (New York, The Viking Press, 1960), p. 152.

22 A.H. Maslow, *Motivation and Personality* (New York, Harper & Brothers, 1954), p. 340.

23 Douglas McGregor, *The Human Side of Enterprise* (New York, McGraw-Hill Book Company, Inc., 1960), p. 48.

24 Chris Argyris, *Interpersonal Competence and Organizational Effectiveness* (Homewood, Illinois, Dorsey Press, Inc., and Richard D. Irwin, Inc., 1962), p. 5.

25 See Philip E. Slater and Warren G. Bennis, "Democracy Is Inevitable," HBR March–April 1964, p. 51.

QUESTIONS

1. Is your view of human nature primarily positive or negative? Explain.

   _____

   _____

   _____

2. What experiences and factors have influenced your view of human nature? Discuss.

   _____

   _____

   _____

3. Given your view of human nature, what principles and practices do you follow in your relations with others?

   _____

   _____

   _____

What Job Attitudes Tell About Motivation

Emerson once wrote, "This time, like all times, is a good one if we but know what to do with it." With slight rephrasing, this philosophy could aptly express the typical organization's quandary with respect to the role of job attitudes: job attitudes are always present, if only we knew what they meant!

Every manager is continually being confronted with evidence that his subordinates hold a variety of attitudes toward him, toward the organization, and, especially, toward their jobs. What most managers are not sure of is how they should react to these attitudes. Should they ignore them entirely? Should they systematically try to measure them? If they decide to measure the attitudes, a whole set of other questions arises. What kinds of attitudes are important to measure? What interpretations should be put on the results of attitude studies? For example, is high job satisfaction good? Does information on job satisfaction tell anything about motivation? Finally, the organization is faced with a whole series of questions about what kinds of action, if any, it should take as a consequence of the existing attitudes. In a sense, then, management is frequently faced with the dilemma of what its own attitude should be toward employees' attitudes.

Our position on these questions can be summarized as follows: Job attitudes *are* important and merit the attention of businessmen. They are *not* important, however, in the ways that most top executives ordinarily think about them. In the succeeding pages we shall try to answer the specific questions raised above, utilizing previous evidence, some recently articulated theoretical notions, and data from our own investigations dealing with managerial job attitudes. Finally, we shall put forth some suggested guidelines for organizational action on how to utilize attitude data more effectively.

A SHORT HISTORY

Industry's flirtation with job attitudes has had an interesting history and one that sheds considerable light on the current ambiguous feelings about their importance. During the early part of this century, most business leaders doggedly avoided giving any attention at all to this aspect of employee behavior. Instead, the focus was on the principles of scientific management with their concern for maximizing operator efficiency. And since these principles were built around the "man as a machine" analogy, and since machines obviously do not have attitudes, it was logical for companies to ignore job attitudes in their search for new approaches to increased human efficiency. This neglect on the part of the owner or manager was reinforced by the activities of early personnel specialists, especially industrial psychologists. Their attention was focused on quite another area—namely, on improving the selection of employees so that only competent ones would be hired. If any attention was given to the attitudes and behavior of employees once they were on the job, it consisted almost entirely of developing certain kinds of blue-collar skill training.

Romantic Period

The lowly status of job attitudes changed rapidly and decisively in the 1930's and 1940's. During these years the topic was pursued with great ardor by businessmen, the chief reason being the dramatic impact on both business and academic circles of the findings of Elton Mayo and Fritz J. Roethlisberger in the now classic Hawthorne studies. Suddenly, it became apparent to everyone that human performance in the job situation was not solely a function of the aptitudes or skills that the employee brought to the workplace. The massive number of interviews carried out by investigators at the Hawthorne plant (some 20,000) vividly illustrated that the average worker did indeed think about his job, had various kinds of reactions to it, and, most importantly, believed his feelings affected how hard he worked. A number of managers and personnel specialists jumped to the conclusion that "if we can improve job satisfaction and morale, we can improve job performance."

Immediately, businessmen set about to take advantage of this newly found insight. Companies took action on two fronts. First, they initiated attempts to measure the state of employee feelings in order to know where to concentrate their efforts in improving employee satisfaction. Secondly, they set about to train their managers, especially first-level supervisors, to pay attention to the attitudes and feelings of their subordinates so that performance could thereby be improved. Meanwhile, personnel staff specialists began to set up studies which would demonstrate that, if companies did in fact improve morale, there would be consequent increases in performance.

Era of Disenchantment

But as often happens in the case of precipitous and intense affairs, disenchantment soon began to set in. There were those critics of the human relations movement who saw the concern with job satisfaction and morale as degenerating into a wishy-washy "make people happy" approach. For example, William Whyte in *The Organization Man* asked, "What about . . . the tyranny of the happy work team? What about the adverse effects of high morale?"[1] Similarly, Malcolm McNair, in his well-known HBR [*Harvard Business Review*] article, claimed that "devoting too much effort in business to trying to keep everybody happy results in conformity, in failure to build individuals."[2]

In effect, these critics were arguing that, even if high job satisfaction could be shown to have some relationship to employee performance, there were associated negative consequences which were being overlooked. Quite aside from the anti-human relations attacks, many companies were beginning to question whether it was worthwhile to bother with trying to improve job satisfaction. The costs involved in measuring job satisfaction, and especially in trying to increase it, often seemed to be disproportionate to the presumed gains in performance. In short, the payoff did not seem to be nearly as large as many had thought it would be.

Social scientists, especially those with an interest in seeing that attitude research was supported and encouraged by business organizations, were also slow in coming to the same realization. They finally began to suspect the validity of their hypothesis that increases in job satisfaction would result in direct improvements in performance. Two scholarly reviews of the scientific literature published in the mid-1950's appeared to demonstrate conclusively that satisfaction-performance relationships were much weaker than most people had assumed.[3] These reviews proved to have sobering effects on psychologists and others engaged in personnel research; the reviews were followed by a marked decrease in the reporting of satisfaction-performance studies in scientific journals. Having found the simple "satisfaction increases performance" hypothesis seemingly unsupported by the evidence, scholars joined managers in abandoning much of their interest in assessing employees' job satisfaction.

Mistakes in Retrospect

Several important lessons can be learned from this brief review of the rise and fall of interest in job attitude research:

- The early assumptions about the effects of high levels of job satisfaction were greatly oversimplified, if not clearly incorrect. Any view that, because a worker is satisfied, he *must* be a highly productive performer is obviously naive. The first lesson to be learned is not that job satisfaction is an inconsequential variable, but rather that its relationship to performance is more complex than previously recognized.

- Both companies and psychologists concentrated their attentions too narrowly on "satisfaction" as the only type of attitude that should be measured and dealt with. Other attitudes or views that might be held by employees were generally ignored in the attempts to see whether their liking for their jobs could be improved.

Second Look at Evidence

Before proceeding to other points, let us take another look at the accumulated evidence. While it is true that very few well-controlled investigations found highly positive relationships between satisfaction and performance, the *trend* of the relationships nevertheless seems to be in that direction. For example, one authority has reviewed some 20 studies and found that in most of the cases where data on satisfaction and performance were gathered, higher satisfaction was associated with better job performance.[4] Such consistency is highly significant in a statistical sense, and indicates that some sort of meaningful relationship probably exists between these two variables.

Also, most studies of the relationship between satisfaction and such measures of job behavior as turnover and absenteeism (but not performance) have obtained definite results in the expected direction. That is, high satisfaction is associated with low turnover and with low absenteeism.

The foregoing suggests that the demise of interest in measuring job satisfaction may be quite premature. In other words, even without any new research studies or theoretical analyses, the available data alone would appear to justify a concern with this type of attitude. Given this conclusion, the question remains: What should management do with job satisfaction information? We shall try to answer that now.

CHANGING THE FOCUS

The first step in understanding this subject is to stop putting the satisfaction cart before the performance horse, so to speak. It appears wiser to think of job satisfaction as something that is likely to result *from* performance behavior rather than as the cause of good or bad performance.

The reasoning goes like this: Satisfaction comes about when certain of our needs or desires are fulfilled. (Let us use the shorthand term "rewards" to refer to those things we receive from others or gain by our own actions that help fulfill our needs.) Thus, in an organization where we work, job satisfaction is generated when we receive rewards from our job situation. Such rewards are of many types and are provided in many ways. Some of them are intrinsic, such as when we feel a sense of accomplishment at having carried through a difficult task successfully; in such a case we can, in effect, administer the reward ourselves. Other rewards are clearly extrinsic, provided by people other than ourselves — such as when the boss gives us a promotion, or when the organization awards us a year-end bonus.

Psychologically speaking, then, the degree to which we feel satisfied should be roughly proportionate to the amount of rewards we believe we are receiving from our job environment. A crucial point in this chain of reasoning is often overlooked: the amount of rewards we receive *may* be unrelated to how well we have performed. To put it another way, high-quality performance is not the only means, nor necessarily the most important means, by which we are able to obtain rewards from our work.

Contrasting Situations

Here it will help to make the point if we consider two situations, one involving a blue-collar worker, the other a manager. The illustrations that follow are hypothetical but realistic:

Nonmanagerial worker. His base rate of pay is determined completely by a fixed schedule that provides exactly the same amount of pay for all employees holding that type of job. Short of totally unacceptable performance, his pay will not be lowered. It also is not likely to be raised easily by above-average performance. However, it *is* likely to increase as a result of seniority. The degree of his job security also is probably determined by his seniority and contract provisions, not by the day-to-day quality of his performance.

The employee's opportunities to gain considerable amounts of intrinsic rewards from performing his job duties in a superior fashion are frequently limited by the mechanical, machine-controlled nature of his work. Furthermore, his chances to assume new, more interesting duties (with higher pay) by working harder on his current job are probably sharply curtailed both in terms of the way in which the organization has arranged the work flow and by union contracts that might exist. In short, the bulk of his rewards are determined not by how good or poor his job performance is, but by factors that are largely or totally beyond his personal control.

Although our example is hypothetical, it typifies a large percentage of rank-and-file work situations in which it is nearly impossible for workers to receive varying amounts of rewards, and therefore of satisfaction, in relation to their performance. If this be the case, then the failure of most previous studies to find strong, positive relationships between satisfaction and performance is not at all surprising; it is, in fact, perfectly predictable and logical, since almost all of them were carried out at the rank-and-file level of organizations.

Manager. Rewards for this man are more nearly proportionate to the quality and quantity of his performance. Compared to the blue-collar worker's situation, at least, rewards from factors beyond the manager's control are of less importance than rewards due to his own work.

Why is this relationship likely to be found at the managerial level in a company? Because it is here, if anywhere, that the organization has the potential flexibility to give rewards commensurate with performance.

For one thing, in a given group of managers there is the opportunity to pay different salaries based on performance even though all the men are carrying out the same assigned tasks, or equivalent tasks. Other extrinsic rewards, such as status and authority, can also be dispensed in differing amounts to those working in the same kinds of jobs. Likewise, managers, as compared with nonmanagers, tend to have more flexibility in gaining intrinsic rewards from their jobs based on their efforts and performance. Their jobs usually involve considerably greater variety and hence more opportunity to achieve a sense of completion and worthwhile accomplishment.

Findings of New Study

The picture drawn from the foregoing observations can be substantiated by research data. We have recently completed a study of managers in five companies of differing types and character. A noteworthy feature of the study is that it is one of the first satisfaction-performance studies to use a sample of executives instead of nonmanagerial employees.[5] The results show:

- Managers who are ranked high by their superiors report significantly greater satisfaction than do the low-ranked managers. However, the degree of relationship between high performance and high satisfaction, though somewhat larger than in most previous studies made on nonmanagement workers, is not as large as it reasonably could be.

- The greatest differences between the high- and low-performance groups, in terms of perceived rewards, occur in those areas where personal needs are deepest and most intangible. The best performing managers do not report receiving much greater rewards in pay or security, but they do report significantly more rewards in areas concerned with opportunities to express autonomy and to obtain self-realization in the job.

The import of this is that the five organizations in our sample seem to be allowing their best management performers to gain more self-fulfillment and self-realization from work than low performers do, but they do not appear to be providing perceptibly different *extrinsic* rewards to the two groups. This was confirmed when we found that, at a given management level in any of the companies studied, pay does not show an appreciable relationship to rated job performance.

Meaning for Management

In light of the foregoing analyses and findings, the tough question for top management to face up to is this: Does the organization actively and visibly give rewards directly in proportion to the quality of job performance for all of its employees, rank-and-file as well as managers? *If* it does, and *if* employees realize this, then high satisfaction should be more closely associated with superior performance. To the extent that satisfaction and performance are positively related in a given situation, management knows that the best performers believe they are receiving the most rewards.

On the other hand, a company's failure to find job satisfaction related to job performance for a sample of its employees may mean that it is not in fact differentially rewarding its best performers. Such a failure might also suggest that employees are not working on jobs where good performance is intrinsically satisfying and interesting. Looked at in this way, the role of job satisfaction is quite different from that formerly assigned to it by the human relations advocates. Its role is not to serve as a stimulus to employees' job performance but rather as a gauge of how good a job the organization itself is doing in rewarding employees in proportion to the quality and quantity of their performance. Data on job satisfaction also suggest something about how challenging and stimulating employees feel their jobs are.

The company which takes this kind of view of job satisfaction adopts an approach which is different from the usual one. Its aim is not necessarily to increase everyone's satisfaction, and thereby to make "everyone happy," but rather to make sure that the best performing employees are the most satisfied employees. Its goal, in other words, is not to maximize satisfaction, but to maximize the *relationship* between satisfaction and performance.

ROLE OF OTHER ATTITUDES

In the past, as previously pointed out, most companies and researchers have acted as if satisfaction is the only kind of job attitude worth measuring. But it is our contention that other types of attitudes or beliefs are just as important, if not more so, in understanding and modifying employee motivation. These are attitudes that do what job satisfaction was naively assumed to do: namely, affect the amount of effort a person puts into his job.

To begin with, let us make the reasonable assumption that people want to obtain various kinds of rewards from their jobs — a certain level of pay, self-fulfillment, security, status, personal growth, and the like. Furthermore, let us assume that each person attaches different degrees of importance to these various potential rewards. We can say that people place different "values" on different rewards.

Concurrently, we can also assume that in a given job situation an employee will have notions about how likely he is to receive these rewards in return for exerting extra amounts of effort in his job. Such beliefs can be labeled "effort-reward expectations." In some cases, the individual will have low expectations that more effort on his part will provide him with increased rewards. For example, the blue-collar worker described earlier probably feels it is quite unlikely that above-average performance on his part will lead to greater security or a chance to perform a more satisfying set of tasks. On the other hand, the typical manager described might have higher expectations because he feels the organization will, to a certain degree, pay off for the effort he puts into his job.

The conceptual formulations we have discussed can be portrayed as shown in *Exhibit I.* Here performance is seen as resulting from effort. (Aptitudes and skills are regarded as constants in this formulation, as we are focusing solely on the attitude or motivational bases of performance.) Effort is seen as resulting from the interaction of reward values and effort-reward expectations in the following way: the more a reward is valued and the higher the expectation that effort will lead to this reward, the greater will be the effort exerted (and hence the better will be the performance).[6]

Putting Results to Use

The formulation diagrammed in *Exhibit I* does more than put several variables into a theoretical relationship. It tells an organization what types of attitudes should be measured and worked with if performance is to be improved through increased effort. These attitudes can be stated as questions:

1. How much does the employee value various possible rewards?

2. What are the probabilities, in his opinion, that a high degree of effort on his part will lead to the rewards he wants?

If an organization has accurate data on these two attitudes, it should be able to predict who will put forth the most effort in his job and, even more important, what might be done by the organization to increase this effort. Consider the following:

- In our study of managers, several of the questions we asked related to pay. One concerned the importance of pay to the manager; another concerned how closely he felt his pay was based on job performance factors (such as effort). The answers to these questions were then compared to superiors' ratings of the amount of effort each man put forth on his job. The results showed that the highest rated managers were those who saw their pay most closely tied to their

---

EXHIBIT I

Role of attitudes other than satisfaction in performance

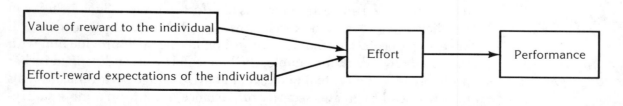

effort — that is, who had the highest effort-reward expectations. Additionally, and significantly, this relationship between expectations and rated effort was strongest for those managers *who attached the most importance to pay*.

Systematic monitoring of the effort-reward expectations held by employees will provide pertinent data on the motivation levels present in the organization. Changes in these expectations could indicate whether employee motivation has increased or decreased over a set period of time. Also, differences among parts of the organization would help pinpoint those areas where motivation is weakest.

The data on effort-reward expectations could be gathered from individuals by interview, questionnaire, and/or other appropriate methods known to personnel specialists. The data should be grouped by departments and work units for examination. In evaluating changes in employees' expectations over time, averages for the departments or units would be used.

The collection of such information may, in turn, lead to the following kinds of questions: What can companies do if they find from their attitude studies that their employees do not have high effort-reward expectations? What can they do about motivational soft spots in the organization? Where should they look in order to improve the effort-reward expectancies of employees? We shall discuss these questions in the following section.

REWARD PRACTICES

A key to the whole attitude picture for an organization revolves around its reward practices — which may or may not be similar to its reward policies. Because of this, job attitudes can be utilized as a set of indicators of an organization's ability to motivate its employees. Let us elaborate. For a company or firm to produce high levels of motivation, top management should make sure that:

1. The rewards given are those most desired in return for performing the job well.

2. Superior performers are given more extrinsic rewards (e.g., salary and bonuses) and are provided with more opportunities to gain intrinsic rewards (e.g., challenging and varied work) than inferior performers are given.

3. Most individuals in the organization *see* and *believe* that good performance leads to both extrinsic and intrinsic rewards.

Each of these steps involves careful attention to certain details, and, as we hope to show, relevant attitude data should indicate whether such attention is being given to them.

Offering What Is Desired

The first step in building effective reward practices is for the company to make sure that the rewards it is providing are ones which are widely desired. This is a seemingly simple point that is often neglected. In day-to-day operations we frequently forget that, regardless of the value the giver or observer places on a reward, its motivational influence comes about only as a result of the value the *receiver* places on it. In effect, rewards that the company considers highly positive inducements may not be so regarded by many of the persons receiving them. Yet how many times do companies check this out?

Attitude measurement provides management with a potential tool to confirm its assumptions about *what* is motivating, or will motivate, various groups and individuals in the work force. Eventually, a company may want to consider systematically selecting the kinds of employees who will value the particular rewards that it can give most readily and feasibly.

Favoring Superior Performers

Knowledge of the kinds of rewards that are most highly valued, and by whom, is only an initial step in developing psychologically meaningful reward practices. The next step involves the crucial, and sometimes difficult, process of attaching rewards to performance such that superior performers receive more than average or mediocre ones do.

Measuring differences. This involves developing methods to discriminate between good and poor performance. Of course, this is far from an easy job. Typically, in management, performance measurement involves judgments that are subjective in nature. Sometimes, it is true, objective data are available — for instance, in sales management — but often in these cases the interpretation of the "facts" is complicated because factors beyond the subordinate's control influence the final results. (An example would be where one sales manager's area has greater sales potential than another man's area.) Hence, the boss or other evaluator is often right back where he started — namely, facing the necessity of making subjective, nonprovable assessments.

Given this situation, we would like to suggest that organizations make greater use of self-ratings in measuring individual performance. This should serve to increase the accuracy of performance measurements and, perhaps even more important, their acceptance. Under such a system, the superior and subordinate would jointly establish the subordinate's performance goals for an ensuing period. The two should also agree on how progress toward these goals is to be measured and on what kinds of rewards are to be given if the goals are achieved. Finally, at the end of the period, the two men would *jointly* participate in assessing the results and determining how much progress the subordinate has made during the period. This approach does not mean that the boss gives up his role as the final arbiter; it simply provides him with other important information which he can incorporate into his decisions and which may help to increase his subordinates' confidence in them.

Providing rewards. Besides being able to distinguish among performance differences, management must be able to provide commensurate rewards. A man may know that he is regarded as one of the best employees, but this knowledge will do little to enhance his performance if his superior cannot provide him with sufficient rewards or opportunities to gain rewards. Quite often, the organization has so restricted the freedom of individual superiors to dispense rewards of any type that they are completely hamstrung in tying rewards closely to performance. The net effect is to reduce by a considerable amount the possibilities of motivating employees.

However, granted that the boss has the power to provide appropriate rewards, will he go ahead and actually give them out? The process frequently breaks down at this point. For instance, the boss may hesitate to act because of the threat of competition from below or because of the possible complaints he will receive from those who do not get what they desire. The main role that higher management can play in dealing with these types of situations is to endeavor to provide concrete rewards to superiors who do not shrink from evaluating and rewarding outstanding subordinate performance. It has been well established by research that the right types of reward policies higher up the line can have positive impacts on those practiced lower down in the organization.

Maintaining Credibility

A good performance reward system must have credibility. Oftentimes it seems that management will pay a great deal of attention to setting up elaborate compensation schemes and then will proceed to nullify its efforts by actions designed to disguise the whole procedure.

For one thing, as we have already mentioned, many organizations miss the opportunity to increase managers' trust and confidence in the evaluation procedure by neglecting to secure judgments from all relevant sources. Usually only the immediate superior or a group of superiors evaluates a manager's performance. While this is traditional, it may not be adequate for the organization's needs in the future. As the requirements for sophisticated technical expertise increase throughout wide areas of management, many subordinates may come to expect that the boss's perspective is not necessarily the only one that should be used in performance evaluation.

Subordinate ratings, which we advocated earlier for purposes of making valid measurements, could be particularly useful in developing credibility. By taking them into account, management could determine in advance the motivational impact of giving rewards to particular individuals. It would then be better able to dispense rewards in such a way that the system would be respected and trusted by most members of the organization.

Is secrecy necessary? Another practice which serves to weaken credibility in the reward process is secrecy. Companies often go to great lengths to maintain a shroud of secrecy surrounding their reward practices, especially as they relate to managers' pay. It is next to impossible for the typical manager to know to what degree the organization is actually giving larger monetary rewards in proportion to above-average performance. Even worse, the top-notch performer who *is* getting paid substantially more than his peers may not be aware of just how much more he is receiving.

While there may be some valid reasons for retaining secrecy in the managerial salary system, one of them certainly cannot be that it promotes credibility in the reward process. If anything, secrecy about who gets what in terms of salary and bonuses works to reduce credibility in the whole program, and to this extent weakens the motivational possibilities of linking higher pay to better performance.

Our viewpoint here is not that pay secrecy be summarily chucked out the corporate window and replaced by a policy of publicizing what everyone is being paid. Rather, we are advocating that companies take a serious look at the disadvantages described and consider whether they are outweighed by the presumed advantages of secrecy. At the very least, it would seem that companies might undertake some small-scale and relatively controlled experiments to test executives' assumptions about secrecy. In such experimentation, attitude measurement — both of satisfactions and of effort-reward expectations — could be usefully employed to calculate the impact of the changes.

If a company's reward practices are considered valid by those affected, this should serve to reduce a boss's reluctance to evaluate subordinates candidly, since resentments from those receiving low evaluations will be minimized. The boss is most vulnerable to complaints from below when the whole reward process — not just his own evaluations — is regarded skeptically and suspiciously.

CONCLUSION

Having reviewed the basic components in the chain of steps linking rewards to performance in the eyes of the members of an organization, we can summarize the effects of inadequate reward practices — that is, practices severing or reducing the link between rewards and performance. The effects are portrayed in *Exhibit II*. When the *satisfaction* of a number of individuals is measured and compared with their *performance* ratings, a weak or low association of satisfaction with performance will be found. At the same time, many individuals will have weak beliefs that increased *effort* on their part will result in increased *rewards* (and, hence, satisfaction). Such perceptions, if they are held, are likely to reduce the motivations of people to try to improve their performance.

Evidence that satisfaction is not related to performance should be regarded as a signal for management to investigate effort-reward expectations.

EXHIBIT II

Consequences of inadequate reward practices

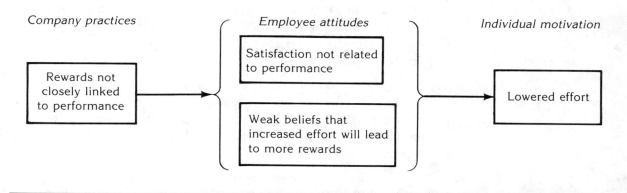

Company practices   *Employee attitudes*   *Individual motivation*

| Rewards not closely linked to performance | Satisfaction not related to performance / Weak beliefs that increased effort will lead to more rewards | Lowered effort |

Evidence that these expectations are weak indicates a need for some of the actions and procedures described earlier in this article.

Program of Action

To sum up, we recommend the following steps to top management:

1. Try to assess the satisfaction level of managers, supervisors, and, if desired, other employees.

2. Compare individual satisfaction levels with individual performance assessments, in order to determine the extent to which satisfaction is related to performance.

3. From a motivational point of view, there is no particular utility in trying to increase the satisfaction of all employees in the organization. There *is*, on the other hand, considerable utility in trying to increase the strength of the *relationship* between satisfaction and performance.

4. In addition to measuring the relationship between satisfaction and performance, attempt to measure systematically other types of attitudes — expecially, attitudes about what people want from their jobs and whether they hold strong effort-reward expectancies.

5. If such effort-reward expectancies are found to be weak or low, a company should undertake an examination of its reward practices (as opposed to its reward policies), looking particularly hard at how individuals *perceive* these practices.

6. If changes in reward practices are made, assessment of their impact should be carried out by planned *continuous* monitoring of

satisfaction-performance relationships and of effort-reward expectancies.

Even if present practices already appear good as indicated by current attitude data, continuous assessment at appropriate intervals — intervals far enough apart not to be annoying to individuals but close enough to provide valid comparisons of results so that trends can be assessed — would seem to be of great value to the organization.

7. With respect to new employees, their attitudes could be monitored frequently — perhaps even weekly — during the first few months they are with the organization. This information would be useful in detecting potential turnover in advance, thus providing time for corrective action.

All men seek one goal: success or happiness. The only way to achieve true success is to express yourself completely in service to society. First, have a definite, clear, practical ideal — a goal, an objective. Second, have the necessary means to achieve your ends — wisdom, money, materials, and methods. Third, adjust your means to that end.

Aristotle, 384–322 B.C.

REFERENCE NOTES

1 New York, Simon & Schuster, 1956, p. 401.

2 "What Price Human Relations?" HBR March–April 1957, p. 20.

3 See Arthur H. Brayfield and Walter H. Crockett, "Employee Attitudes and Employee Performance," *Psychological Bulletin*, September 1955; and *Frederick Herzberg*, et al, *Job Attitudes: Review of Research and Opinion* (Pittsburgh, Psychological Service of Pittsburgh, 1957).

4 See Victor H. Vroom, *Work and Motivation* (New York, John Wiley & Sons, Inc., 1964), Chapter 6.

5 For a detailed report of the findings, see our book, *Managerial Attitudes and Performance* (Homewood, Illinois, Richard D. Irwin, Inc., 1968).

6 For a similar approach to work motivation, see Victor H. Vroom, op. cit.

QUESTIONS

1. What is the relationship between job attitude and job performance? Cite personal examples to support your opinion.

   _____

   _____

   _____

2. What reward system would you use to increase job performance?

   _____

   _____

   _____

CASES

Bruce, the Behavior Mod Landlord

Bruce Charter, a tennis professional teaching at the Seaview Swim and Tennis Club, reached a major business decision. He would invest the $14,000 he inherited from his father in real estate. After combing the real estate pages of the local newspapers and speaking to real estate agents for a three-month period, Bruce decided what kind of property to purchase. With the assistance of Carol Travis, his agent, Bruce took possession of a six-family, 70-year-old frame building in a low to moderate income section of the city.

Margot, Bruce's girlfriend, had some reservations about this business venture. She explained it this way:

"Bruce, friends of mine have gone into the real estate business and most of them have wound up broke. They tell me the whole thing can be a nightmare. If you don't get the right kind of tenants, they can wreck the place.

"Another problem I've heard about is collecting rent. Poor people just don't send you the rent the first of the month, right on time as though they were worrying about getting a bad credit rating. You'll probably be spending many of your evenings knocking on doors trying to collect rent money that has already been spent in the neighborhood bars."

"Margot, I'm well aware of the stories about how landlords have failed in their real estate ventures," said Bruce. "But, I'm going to take a scientific approach to dealing with tenants. I do the same things with my students on the tennis court. I was never a famous tennis player myself, but I'm very knowledgeable about teaching people the right responses. My study of the psychology of learning has made me realize that tennis coaching closely follows the principles of behavior modification."

"In what way?" asked Margot.

"I may be oversimplifying, but it works something like this," replied Bruce. "In coaching a person about tennis, we give him or her reinforcement almost every time the right response is made. Either we say 'nice shot' or the ball goes over the net in the right way, which is a reward in itself. The more I analyze Skinner's theories and apply them to tennis, the stronger the association I see between reinforcement theory and tennis.

"When a person is an absolute beginner, he is also subject to direct application of some of Skinner's ideas. For instance, we use successive

Source: Reprinted with persmission. Andrew J. DuBrin, Casebook of Organizational Behavior, *copyright © 1977, Pergamon Press.*

approximations. Let's say a man age 40 has decided to take up tennis. We start him off with the simplest task imaginable. We throw him a ball from a few feet away and have him tap it back to us—just to get the feel of the ball on the racket. It works, the guy smiles, he's reinforced for doing something that approximates a tennis stroke. He gets a little reinforcement at every step. Usually, he learns how to stroke a tennis ball by the end of the season."

"What about punishment?" asked Margot. "Isn't that ever used in Skinner's framework?"

"As you know, behavior modification emphasizes praise and reward more than punishment, but punishment of a mild sort is sometimes used. One of my colleagues, Don, screams at people in a good-natured way when they do something awful like standing facing the net when they hit a ground stroke. Of course, seeing a ball go over the fence or dribble off the racket is punishment in itself."

"Bruce, I like your ideas, and I wish you the best of luck," said Margot. "But you're forgetting one major thing. People who take up tennis do so voluntarily. They want to learn. Some of the characters who rent apartments in a building like the one you've bought have no interest in paying the rent, protecting their credit ratings, or in pleasing you. They have no pride. Their values are warped."

"Margot, there is where you are wrong. In Skinner's system, you don't have to worry about values like pride and good citizenship. You just manipulate the environment so you get the right response from people."

"Bruce, your analysis sounds terrific. I can't argue with logic like that, but let's see what happens after you own the building for a while. I hope you do become the first Skinnerian real estate tycoon, but I'm skeptical."

Thirteen months later, Bruce Charter gave a verbal report of his experiences at applying reinforcement theory to real estate management. Margot, intrigued with her boyfriend's behavioral science experiment, suggested the case writer interview him. A full disclosure of the highlights of his experiences follows, at least to the extent that Bruce was able to present an accurate picture of the events that took place.

"After over one year of running the building, I would have to say that I'm mildly encouraged. The events that have taken place during the last year are so complex that I can't give you a categorical 'Yes, it was a success,' or 'No, it was a failure,' response. It's necessary to sort out my observations into different categories. Running a building involves much more than collecting rents and making minor repairs. It's like running an enterprise all by yourself.

"Who your tenants are is one very important consideration. I would assume that if you rent to people who are willing to pay $475 a month for housing, you have a different set of problems than if you deal with tenants on public assistance who are paying an average of about $155 per month rent. Welfare pays the rent for all my tenants, but Welfare sends them the money. They in turn cash the check or mail it directly to me if their welfare payment is the same as the rent.

"I'll begin my explanation of trying to use reinforcement theory at Watkins Street by telling you about the lawn mowing situation. Although the building is hardly a showplace, it does have a front lawn and some grass in the back yard. When I took over the building the lawn and yard were a mess. I made the classical mistake that a lot of people in the real estate business make — I tried to appeal to the pride of my tenants. I told them that they would have a much more attractive place to live in if they took it upon themselves to clean up the yard and mow the lawn. A few of them nodded in agreement, but they didn't seem committed to sprucing up the outside of the house. When no results were forthcoming from the simple approach of appealing to their pride, I made an attempt to change the natural barriers that were preventing my tenants from having a neat and trim yard.

"I invested about $100 in new garbage cans, a set of clippers, and a push lawn mower. I left the mower with the woman who lived in one of the downstairs front apartments. My assumption was that anyone who wanted to take his or her turn mowing could use the mower without having to drag it up and down stairs. Two weeks after I bought the garden equipment and the garbage cans, I made an on-site inspection of the building. The lawn and yard were in passable condition, but only one garbage can out of six was in the yard. At least some progress was being made. I had successfully arranged conditions so that tenants who wished to could do a better job of keeping the outside of the house in good shape.

"I praised the tenants for the appearance of the lawn and asked their opinion about what could be done to keep garbage cans in the yard. One tenant suggested that we use chains and a lock to keep the cans secured every day but on garbage collection day. I took care of that condition for about $12. One night Margot and I were coming home from a downtown movie. I drove by the property and saw that the yard was fairly clean and that the garbage cans were intact. The next day I wrote post cards to each of the six tenants telling them how pleased I was with the appearance of the yard. According to behaviorism, you have to tie the reward (my post card) pretty close to the response that is to be rewarded.

"After about two months of ownership of the property it dawned on me that it paid to take periodic trips to the building. Sometimes I would duck down there in the morning before I went to the club. One purpose of these trips was to give the tenants an on-the-spot reaction to the appearance of the place. It seemed a quick transfusion of praise was enough to keep everything in passable shape for a couple of weeks. Of course, I served another function at the same time, so we cannot say that what I was doing was 100 percent behavior mod. I would spend a few minutes chatting with the tenants and listening to the problems they were having with each other or with the plumbing and/or heating. It would be reasonable to assume that the tenants like the fact that I took a sincere interest in their problems.

"I developed a simple method of dispensing praise or disapproval. I would tell each tenant something like this, 'The porch is real clean. It looks great. But the grass has a lot of dog droppings. What seems to be the problem?' If I bought some paint for a tenant and she did a good job painting a room with it, I would buy her a few more cans of paint (if she wanted them). My approach was taking time and it seemed somewhat childlike. But, it was working.

"By now you must be wondering why I was turning over the supplies to the women, and also dispensing rewards to them, rather than also working with the male tenants. My reasoning is simple. In these families the women call the shots. They obtain the apartment; they pay the rent; they call when there are any problems associated with the apartment— plumbing, heating, or screaming neighbors.

"Even if you were the best applied behavioral scientist in the world, and even if you had the most sincere, trustworthy tenants imaginable, you still are left with the mechanical problems in keeping an old building running. For instance, it's inevitable that a hot water heater will blow every once in a while, or that a faucet will stop functioning, or that a furnace will shut off at three in the morning and not return to normal functioning. You also have to cope with suppliers of plumbing and heating services.

"I try a little behavior mod in this area, too. The first people I dealt with were Conkey Heating and Plumbing, an outfit recommended to me by my real estate agent. My first hot water heater cost me $225 installed. I kind of gulped, but paid the bill without voicing a complaint. Next, I called them to replace a faucet. That bill was about $85. Again I paid the bill without complaining. The next time I had a problem, though, I switched suppliers. I told the man in charge of Culver Plumbing and Heating that I was giving them a try because the people I had been using seemed to be high priced and their work wasn't anything exceptional. Culver installed their first hot water heater for me. I paid their bill of $175 in 48 hours.

"I wrote a note on the invoice, 'Thanks for your prompt and efficient work. I appreciated your fair price. Keep up the good work.' Two weeks later another faucet went out. They replaced it for $50. Again I paid the bill promptly and wrote a note of appreciation. I intend to keep up this approach of dispensing praise and paying bills promptly. Maybe that's the kind of reward suppliers need to keep their prices down.

"Rent collection, obviously, is the mainstay of the property owner's business. If you can't collect almost all of the rent due, you go under faster than a restaurant that's been declared unsafe by the Board of Health. Another consideration is that you can't spend too much time and effort collecting rent. If I have to give up a tennis lesson here and there to chase rent, owning real estate becomes very unprofitable. Also, if I have to worry about rent while I'm supposed to be coaching somebody, real estate has become a detriment to my regular work.

"My first step in collecting rent was to promise each tenant that she would be eligible for a prize if she was paid to date at the end of a six-month period. Four of the tenants qualified for the gifts—a choice of clock radio, lamp, or hanging plant. All chose the clock radios which I purchased through a friend for $13 each. One of the other professionals at the club told me that he thought offering people prizes for paying rent on time would be demeaning their character. My experience was that each of my tenants thought I was a nice guy for doing it and gladly accepted the radios. If their feelings were hurt, they sure are good actresses.

"In over a one-year period I have only hand collected rent about three times. I insist that the tenants mail the rent directly to me. When a rent check comes promptly, let's say within the first four days of the month, I call the tenant to say 'Thanks for the rent. It's very helpful to me to receive the rent on time.' I don't make the phone calls all the time; behaviorists would call this intermittent reinforcement.

"There are times when rent collection does not proceed swiftly or smoothly. I did have to ease one tenant out — my only bad experience. She finally left without my having to start formal eviction procedures, which has to be a landlord's last resort. It can easily cost up to $500 in legal fees, plus you don't get any rent for a minimum of two months. Nobody will send you rent if she knows about the eviction.

"When a tenant is more than 10 days late with the rent, I telephone her a few times to describe the gravity of the situation. When tenants are behind on their rent, they may not answer the phone or one of their children may answer and tell you 'She isn't home.' People are hard to locate when they fall behind on the rent. So I try my stern letter — a form of punishment to be used only in emergencies. My recent collection letter goes something like this:

> Dear Mrs. Gray:
>   You are now 15 days late in your rent. That means the bank will fine me for being late. When the tenants don't pay the rent, the cost of running this building goes up. That will mean higher rents for everybody.
>   If you do not pay your rent on time you will have to leave my building. I like you and your family and I want you to stay as long as you pay the rent.
>   Call me right away. This situation is very important.
>
> Sincerely,
>
> Bruce Charter
> Landlord
> 244-4048

"There are times when I have to use unusual rewards to get a tenant back on track with respect to paying the rent. Audrey Thompson, a woman in her fifties, is a hardworking person. She's on public assistance, but she also takes care of elderly people in their homes as well as raising her own three children. If she were a better organized person, she might not be in her present predicament. Her disorganization shows up in the fact that she is chronically late with her rent, despite her good intentions. It would be hard for me to live with myself if I evicted this woman and her family.

"Two months ago, Mrs. Thompson had slipped behind in her payments so that she owed me the December and her current rent — over $300. She kept telling me that she would be caught up soon, but she could never quite get up that past due rent from the month of December. I decided to offer her a substantial reward if she would get caught up with her rent. I told her that if she paid up the rent I would give her a sofa in good condition. (I was contemplating purchasing a new sofa, so I could easily afford to give her my present living room sofa.) Mrs. Thompson made arrangements with her minister who owned a car to drive her to my apartment to pick up the sofa. She arrived 24 hours late, but she did bring $300 in small bills with her. She thanked me profusely for the sofa and for having been so patient.

"When I told Margot about the incident, she said, 'Good play, Bruce, but what do you do next month when you don't have another sofa to give to Mrs. Thompson? How will you collect your rent then?' I hope that Margot isn't missing the point of what I'm doing."

QUESTIONS

1. What explanation can you offer other than reinforcement theory for the good results that Bruce Charter seems to be obtaining?

   _____

   _____

   _____

2. To what extent do you think Bruce is "manipulating people"?

   _____

   _____

   _____

3. What other approaches to motivating the tenants to pay rent and keep the grounds clean would you recommend that Bruce try?

   _____

   _____

   _____

The EZ Cleaners' Bonus Plan

When Bill Madison first took over as president of his family's chain of dry cleaning stores, he was full of energy and fresh ideas. One of his main ideas was to reward employees for loyalty and hard work. The timing was right, because EZ Cleaners was having a record year in sales and profits.

Madison was hesitant to raise base wages because he thought he might be unable to sustain the new rates, especially if new competitors moved into EZ Cleaners' market area. Yet he did want to reward employees for their services and to encourage them to continue their efforts.

Madison settled on a Christmas bonus plan. As he said when he announced the plan, "There's nothing like money to motivate people." His bonus plan was as follows:

Wages	Bonus
Less than $8,000	$800
$8,001–$9,000	$900
$9,001–$10,000	$1,000
More than $10,000	10% of wages

The Christmas bonuses were very popular with the employees. Everyone remarked how good it was to work for a company that cared for its people. Madison was pleased to hear from his store managers and department heads that the employees appreciated the bonus and that overall job performance was up.

During the next year, EZ Cleaners faced stiffer competition from other cleaning stores. In fact, a national firm entered the EZ market area. Sales went down; profits went down; and, as a result, bonuses were decreased as follows:

Wages	Bonus
Less than $8,000	$400
$8,001–$9,000	$450
$9,001–$10,000	$500
More than $10,000	5% of wages

This time, Madison heard few comments from supervisors about employee appreciation and increased productivity. In fact, he heard complaints. In talking with the supervisors, he learned that many employees were counting on last year's bonus, if not more, and had already spent the old figure for Christmas gifts and bills. The supervisors reported that employees were not working as hard as they were prior to the first year's bonus.

Madison's reaction was surprise, then anger, then resentment. He said: "It's not fair. They never received any bonus before. This was all new money to them, over and above base wages." Then, as if to himself, "I guess it shows how unappreciative and greedy people can be."

QUESTIONS

1. Do you believe in bonuses as incentives for employee performance?

   _____

   _____

   _____

2. What formula or policy would you recommend for disbursing incentive income to employees?

   _____

   _____

   _____

3. If you were Bill Madison, what would you do?

   _____

   _____

   _____

Making Eight Is a Hassle

"My case is hardly unique," commented Jack Whitney. "But perhaps in telling it other people like myself will avoid the same trap. We've all heard this story many times, but it bears repeating. Engineers and the companies that employ them seem to need constant reminders about this problem.

"When I was released from the service, I was looking forward to finally getting a chance to be a real engineer. I guess you could have said I was gung-ho. You see, I had spent a total of six years in college earning a master's degree in electrical engineering. Starting my engineering career had to be postponed for almost five years after graduation while I repaid Uncle Sam for financing my education, but now I was ready to go.

"I took a job with a large shipyard in Virginia that had several contracts to build Navy warships. I had almost four years of sea duty as a missile fire control and systems officer and felt I could apply my education and experience to building those ships and their missile systems. It was a rude shock to me when I was assigned to antisubmarine systems about which I knew very little. It was worse to realize a few weeks later that I wasn't expected to know or, for that matter, to do very much. I read more than one novel and many magazines just to have something to fill the hours. I was not alone in my frustration either. Numerous other engineers referred to their time-filling activities as 'making eight'. To compound the aggravation, we were occasionally required to put in overtime because 'the project is behind'. Talk about waste, a master's degree in automatic control systems engineering, four years of experience on the Navy's newest missile system, and I was reduced to checking plans from some jerk in Washington who probably had never seen the inside of a college or a ship.

"It really got to me. I was coming home from work frustrated and discouraged. I've never been particularly easy to get along with, but my wife said I was becoming even more of a grouch. I had to do something!

"More education wasn't the answer. An engineer friend in the same company took a year's leave of absence without pay, went back to the University of Virginia, and earned a master's in electronics. When he came back to work, he got his old desk, his old job, and his old salary. We held another going-away party for him two months later.

Source: Reprinted with permission. Gerald Soltas, in Andrew J. DuBrin, Casebook of Organizational Behavior, *copyright © 1977, Pergamon Press.*

"About the time I had been with the yard a year, I started sending out my resume and talking to employment agencies. In 1970–71, however, things were not exactly rosy for engineers. Once, out of 75 resumes I mailed, I received not one reply. Not so much as a 'thanks, but no thanks' letter. Just nothing. I even tried to get back into the Navy. You can imagine how desperate I was becoming. Then, to make matters worse, I was pulled from my projects on antisubmarine warfare and placed in a submarine development group. Just so you won't get the wrong idea, I was doing excellent work according to my supervisors and had already been promoted, at very little increase in salary, incidentally, to Senior Design Engineer, a move which usually took six to eight years for an engineer just out of college.

"In the submarine development group, I was further from my missile background and was only pretending to be an engineer. I was assigned to write various chapters in a training and maintenance manual dealing with systems which had already been designed and constructed. I specifically remember the first chapter I wrote was on the ship's entertainment system. Talk about useless!

"That was the last straw! I doubled and redoubled my job hunting efforts. Finally, one of the companies I had interviewed in college eight years before responded with what seemed to be a perfect opportunity at a decent increase in pay, at least enough to cover the cost of living difference between here and Virginia. At this point, however, pay was secondary in my mind. I was going to seed in that job and would have taken almost anything that offered the chance of a challenge.

"I have been at my new job almost two years now and it is everything I had hoped for. I have more projects now than I have time for. The challenge is stimulating; I have to dig and push, but I get more done, enjoy it more, and come home refreshed instead of depressed. Don't get me wrong, I still have problems and there are days when almost nothing goes right, but I have never once wished I had my old job back."

QUESTIONS

1. Discuss the relationship between job satisfaction and employee motivation.

_____

_____

_____

2. How much blame should Jack Whitney accept for this situation? What is the responsibility of the employee for taking initiative to work out solutions to morale problems?

_____

_____

_____

3. What policies and practices should management follow to prevent cases such as Jack Whitney's?

_____

_____

_____

The Satisfied Sales Representative

The Shifting Sands Mutual Insurance Company is a medium sized concern situated in Portsmouth, Virginia. Carl Carson, a manager for the Shifting Sands Company, is currently in charge of ten insurance sales representatives whose principal responsibility is to sell all lines of property and casualty insurance to individuals and to business firms.

The sales representatives are paid a guaranteed salary of $800 per month, which is a draw on (is deducted from) future commission sales, and a flat percentage of all new and renewable insurance premiums.

Sammy Sereno, one of the ten sales representatives directly responsible to Carson, has been with Shifting Sands Mutual Insurance for slightly more than fifteen years. During his first ten years, Sereno was highly ambitious and energetic and built up a substantial volume of business, most of which has been renewed automatically each year. Last year, Sereno devoted much of his time to his favorite hobbies, sailing and skin diving, and as a result produced very little new business for the firm. In spite of his current, relatively leisurely life, his net personal income after taxes last year was $31,000. Sereno is married but has no children. He and his wife are seriously considering the adoption of a Vietnamese orphan.

Last week while analyzing the previous year's production figures, Carson noticed that Sereno ranked number ten among the sales representatives in the production of new business. Because of his large volume of renewable sales, however, Sereno ranked third in total earnings.

One of Carson's primary responsibilities is to motivate his representatives into continually acquiring new business, since renewable accounts often do not stay with the company because of the dissolution of customers' businesses, the death of customers, or the accounts moving out of the Portsmouth area and obtaining their insurance elsewhere.

Source: P. 129 *from* The Human Side of Organizations, *1st edition and 2nd edition, by Stan Kossen. Copyright © 1975, 1978 by Stanley Kossen. Reprinted by permission of Harper and Row, Publishers, Inc.*

QUESTIONS

1. Assuming that you are Carson, how would you attempt to motivate Sereno?

   _____

   _____

   _____

2. What would you do if Sereno said to you, "I am tired of busting my back canvassing my territory for new business"?

   _____

   _____

   _____

You Need Connections to Be Obnoxious

Falcon Aircraft of Memphis, Tennessee, has shown a record of steady growth since the sale of its first private airplane to a business corporation in 1962. Falcon manufactures and sells a line of small aircraft to businesses who (a) believe that ownership of private planes is economical when all costs (including cost of executive time) are analyzed, and/or (b) value the status associated with the ownership of aircraft. In recent years, five different sports and entertainment figures have purchased personal jets, suggesting an expansion area for Falcon.

Steve Christie, President, and Allan Garfinkel, Vice President of Marketing, look forward with optimism to the future of the executive aircraft business. Among the reasons they cite as harbingers of good times is the trend toward larger and larger commercial aircraft. Although the larger airplanes have more luxury appointments, many executives resent being packed in with 200 or 300 other passengers. Steve Christie calls these new oversize commercial transporters, "subways in the skies." Another factor underlying the anticipated expansion of sales is the cost factor of not using private aircraft. An innovative cost analysis prepared by the Falcon financial analyst has demonstrated that the true cost of purchasing a Falcon Jet is quite often much less than that incurred by using commercial airlines. The analyst's figures include such costs as depreciation and the fact that one key sales person can cover much more territory in less time using personal air transportation. A national advertising campaign of this nature produced better than expected results in terms of inquiries and actual sales.

An international sales meeting (eight United States and two European sales representatives) was called in the context of prosperous business conditions. A feeling of camaraderie pervaded the group as the executive team and the sales reps met in a posh Pocono Mountain resort. Steve Christie keynoted the meeting with an after-dinner talk titled "Good Times Ahead for Falcon." Ten o'clock the next morning the non-inspirational or business side of the international meeting was underway. Allan Garfinkel conducted this meeting, accompanied by his administrative assistant, Ginger Baston. Dressed in casual attire, and equipped with red vinyl loose-leaf

Source: Reprinted with permission. Andrew J. DuBrin, Casebook of Organizational Behavior, *copyright © 1977, Pergamon Press.*

binders embossed in gold with "Falcon," the sales force listened with anticipation to Allan Garfinkel's presentation, "A New Marketing Outlook for Falcon." Smiling, he began:

"Gentlemen, gentlemen, and my trusted aide Ginger, thanks so much for all flying here to the beautiful Poconos. I see that a couple of you have bloodshot eyes. Perhaps, against company advice, you arrived here by commercial airlines or the Greyhound bus. That only proves that even a Falcon representative can at times be a slow learner." (After a mixture of laughs and boos had subsided, Allan continued.)

"My marketing knowledge tells me the best time to make changes, to strengthen something that already works is when times are good. And friends, times are good right now. But if we don't make a few modifications in our business approach right now, maybe times won't always be so good. I'm here to talk about positive, constructive changes which can keep Falcon in orbit. Nothing would be more discouraging to me than to see Falcon go into a tailspin after the enviable record we have established so far. I see three areas in which we need either to make some changes in our way of doing business, or to be mindful of some strategic mistakes we might be making.

"I note with some concern that we have been falling behind schedule in getting our sales-by-objectives program off the ground. As we explained in our last meeting, from now on we would sell by objectives. Everything we do must fit into some overall company objective. We are a modern organization that must utilize modern management techniques. I see a hesitancy on some of your parts to suggest some objectives that we can use as a starting point. I detect an almost superficial amount of attention being paid to this program. Yet a sales force without specific objectives could become a ship without a rudder."

Pete Zigafoo, the Western Regional Manager (all sales representatives at Falcon are called Regional Managers), raised his hand and began to speak without an acknowledgment from Garfinkel: "Allan Baby, who are you kidding? Objectives are for neophyte salesmen. We know why we are all here. My job is to peddle airplanes. Does a surgeon need objectives to tell him to remove a hurting appendix? Does a big-league baseball player need an objective to tell him to raise his batting average? We have enough paper work around here already without the addition of a sales-by-objectives packet. Are we here to sell airplanes or to fill out forms?"

Allan replied weakly, "I didn't solicit your opinion, but thanks for your candor. However, please, let us not dismiss the value of an important new management system because one seasoned campaigner has been achieving decent results by an intuitive approach. I know Ziggy quite well. He sells by objectives, but he writes his objectives down on the back of an envelope or sometimes on his cuffs. His wife wrote me a nasty letter complaining that objectives written in ball point pen don't come off white-on-white cuffs!

"My second concern is that some of us — and I'm not naming names — are forgetting that the role of a sales representative is undergoing a transition — even in the executive aircraft business. The sales representative of today is a true business or technical consultant to his or her customers. When you are talking to a prospective purchaser of an executive jet, you are often talking to a person with sophisticated knowledge of aircraft. You have to have some updated answers. You have to be able to converse intelligently with an engineer the customer might bring in as a consultant on the purchase of the airplane.

"And not only do you have to speak intelligently about the technical properties of the aircraft, you have to do head-on battle with the cost accountants. You have to be able to rigorously defend the position taken by our financial people about the cost effectiveness of our product.

"I know you have all done a good job in the past. Yet there is a need for continuous updating of your knowledge in both aircraft technology and financial analysis. Self-improvement of this nature can be incorporated into your sales-by-objectives program. I am not here to point a finger at anybody, but I have a record of an instance where we lost out on a sale because the Regional Manager did not have the right information at his fingertips. He could not talk the language of the aeronautical engineer who consulted on the purchase of that piece of equipment. We lost that sale to a competitor.

"In another instance the customer decided to continue using commercial scheduled flights because one of our Regional Managers could not handle the pointed questions asked by one of the prospect's accountants. In both instances an updating of knowledge most likely would have resulted in consummation of the sale by the Regional Manager. I recognize that everybody who sells for Falcon is a licensed pilot. However, being a pilot is not enough. Your base of knowledge about aircraft and financial analysis must continue to expand."

"Hold on, Allan," interrupted Pete Zigafoo, "you're hitting at one of my pet peeves. A lot of salesmanship is going down the drain these days because the salesman forgets his true function. A good salesman exercises personal influence. People still buy airplanes from you because they like you. If you can't make that company president a fan of yours, he'll take our ideas and buy from a competitor. If you try to dazzle the customer with technical information, he may get suspicious. If a customer needs some more technical information, I have the guy speak to somebody in Memphis.

"But, Allan, don't feel alone in your mistakes. A lot of marketing managers these days have forgotten what good old-fashioned selling is all about. Whether it's vacuum cleaners or $250,000 jets, you have to be a likeable peddler."

"Ziggy, you might be talking about a style that is comfortable for you, but the idea of a technical consultant replacing personal salesmanship will work for most people in today's business. I'm not denying that you are successful, yet, we must adopt a sales strategy that will work best for most people in the long range. I hope that the rest of you in this room can see my point of view.

"A third topic I want to talk about for now deals with a rather indelicate issue. We all want to increase sales, and we all recognize that lavish entertaining is part of this business. Prospective customers expect to be whisked around the country for a demonstration ride, and perhaps have a fine meal at an exotic restaurant. Nevertheless, we have to be careful about what kind of token of appreciation we give them. Certainly, sending someone a gift pen set with the inscription 'Falcon Jet' is not out of line. Nor is flying someone to the World Series and giving him box seats at our expense. Recently, information came back to me that one of us seated in this room — and he shall be nameless — was attempting to influence sales by furnishing a prospective customer with call girl privileges at our expense."

"Hold on, Mr. Garfinkel," said Pete Zigafoo in a strident tone. "You wouldn't want to take some of the fun out of buying a $250,000 piece of equipment, would you? One customer I'm familiar with is a very lonely man with a very unfriendly wife. When he makes a big purchase he expects a little entertainment on the side. If you enforce a policy of not charging call girls to entertainment expense, some Regional Managers will simply have to charge that kind of entertainment to our miscellaneous category. Allen, I think you should learn to overlook a few things. Get my point?"

"Pete, I get your point, but it will not influence my judgment about what is sound business practice versus what is a low-level way of making a sale. I want everybody in this room to be proud of the methods he used to obtain a contract for Falcon Aircraft."

Two months after the national meeting, Dick Clapham, Eastern Regional Manager and youngest member of the sales team, was paid a visit by Allan Garfinkel. The purpose of Garfinkel's trip was to critically review Clapham's performance. Among Garfinkel's points of contention was that Clapham had made almost no progress in implementing his sales-by-objectives program. Neither had he taken steps to upgrade his knowledge of aircraft technology or financial analysis. Garfinkel addressed him sternly, "Dick, didn't you get the point of our national meeting? It's been several months since the meeting and you have done nothing along the lines that I recommend about upgrading yourself. I would even say you are ignoring the objectives program."

Dick Clapham replied, "Come off it, Allan. I got the impression that you don't take this program seriously. You're probably doing it just to look good in the eyes of Steve Christie."

"You're absolutely wrong," countered Garfinkel. "I'm dead serious about every thing I said at that meeting. That's why I'm here visiting with you to get things straightened around. Right now you are on a collision course with failure. Even some of your entertaining expenses are getting out of line in relation to your sales volume."

"Come off it, Allan. Look at the way Ziggy toyed with your plans at the national meeting. It looked to all of us as though he wasn't taking you very seriously."

"Dick, what I'm going to tell you next is just between you and me. If you repeat this conversation, I will deny that I ever said it. Old Pete

Zigafoo has much more power in this company than you would realize. His situation and yours are not comparable. We can bend the rules a little bit for him for a couple of reasons. One, he has a tremendous hold over a number of major customers who update their equipment every couple of years. He sells more Falcon Aircraft than any other three Regional Managers combined. Two, he has a very close tie-in with the President. The story I have heard is that Ziggy lent Steve Christie $35,000 in cash to help him get into this business.

"What I'm telling you, Dick, is that you don't have the connections of a Pete Zigafoo. And only people with connections can afford to be obnoxious."

QUESTIONS

1. Do you know a person who is successful but obnoxious?

   _____

   _____

   _____

2. How do you deal with people who are obnoxious? What techniques work for you?

   _____

   _____

   _____

APPLICATIONS

Values Auction

Introduction

The following exercise demonstrates that what you want in life (your values) and why you want it (your needs), as well as how you go about satisfying these wants and needs (with whom, when, and where), are the result of interaction between you and your world. The directions are as follows:

1. Gather in a group of 8–20 people for the purpose of having an auction for the 20 values listed on the "values worksheet."

2. One person should be chosen to be the auctioneer.

3. Each participant in the auction should receive ten tokens (ten pennies, matchsticks, or slips of paper). Only these tokens will be accepted as payment for any value purchased.

4. If your bid is highest, you will own the value.

5. You may pool resources with others in order to purchase a particularly high-priced value. This means that two, three, or more people may extend a bid for any one value. If they win, they must share it. You are allowed to participate in (and win) such a pool only one time.

6. The auctioneer's task is to collect the highest number of tokens possible in the course of the auction.

7. Take five to ten minutes so that each participant may budget the desired amount to bid for preferred values. Notice that these amounts may change during the course of the auction. Use the values worksheet.

8. Begin the auction.

9. At the conclusion of the values auction, discuss the following questions:

   a. How did experiences during the imprinting, identification, and socialization periods of life influence your choice of values in this exercise?

Source: Mary Gray, Northern Kentucky University. Based on "University 101 – A Freshman Orientation Course," Jerry Jewler and Mary Stuart Hunter, University of South Carolina, 1986.

b. What cultural forces—media, family, institutions, etc.—cause you to value what you do?

c. Have you ever had a significant emotional experience that has caused you to put special emphasis on one or more of these values?

d. What motivation level does your choice of values reflect?

e. What motivation level were you attempting to satisfy as you related with others during the exercise?

f. Are you living in accord with your motivation levels and cultural values? (Does your job, community, and personal life meet your needs and satisfy your values?)

g. What were the cooperation and trust levels among the participants during the values auction—high, middle, or low?

h. Were you able to spend all of your tokens in this exercise?

VALUES WORKSHEET

	The Amount I Budgeted	The Highest Amount I Bid	The Winning Bid
1. All the food and drink you want without getting fat			
2. Freedom to be and do what you want in life			
3. A chance to direct the destiny of a nation			
4. The love and admiration of good friends			
5. Travel and tickets to any cultural or athletic event as often as you wish			
6. Complete self-confidence with a positive outlook on life			
7. A happy, healthy family			
8. Recognition as the most desirable person in the world			
9. A long life free of illness			
10. A complete library with all the time you need to enjoy it			
11. A deep and satisfying religious faith			

12. A lifetime of financial security and material wealth   _____   _____   _____

13. A lovely home in a beautiful setting   _____   _____   _____

14. A world without prejudice and cruelty   _____   _____   _____

15. A world without sickness and poverty   _____   _____   _____

16. International fame and renown for your achievements   _____   _____   _____

17. An understanding of the meaning of life   _____   _____   _____

18. As much sexual pleasure as you want with anyone, anytime   _____   _____   _____

19. The highest success in your chosen profession or vocation   _____   _____   _____

20. A deep and satisfying love with someone   _____   _____   _____

Significant People and Critical Events

Introduction

The following exercise deals with significant people and critical events in your life.

The Significant Other Tree

In the blank space below, draw a "significant other tree." On the roots, trunk, and leaves, place the names of those individuals who have helped to shape your life.

Source: *Mary Gray, Northern Kentucky University, 1982.*

Answer the following questions:

1. Who have been positive forces in your life?

   _____

   _____

   _____

2. Who have been negative forces in your life?

   _____

   _____

   _____

3. Who has influenced you most to this point in your life?

   _____

   _____

   _____

4. Whom have you influenced most to this point in your life?

   _____

   _____

   _____

5. Have you been a positive force, and for whom?

   _____

   _____

   _____

7. What is your opinion of your "significant other tree"?

   _____

   _____

   _____

   _____

The Critical Events Line

On the figure below, put the calendar year of your birth in the box marked "Beginning." Put the calendar year you expect to die in the box marked "Ending." Place an X on the line at the point that represents your age today.

```
┌─────┐                                        ┌─────┐
│     │                                        │     │
│     │────────────────(Time Line)─────────────│     │
│     │                                        │     │
└─────┘                                        └─────┘
Beginning                                       Ending
```

Above the time line, indicate the positive events that have been especially critical to this point in your life and the positive events you expect to experience from this point on in your life. Below the time line, indicate the negative events that have been critical in the past and the negative events you expect to face in the future.

Answer the following questions:

1. Have the events you listed been predominantly good or bad?

   _____

   _____

   _____

2. Have these events been triggered primarily by you or by others?

   _____

   _____

   _____

3. Do you feel satisfied with your life up to this point in time?

   _____

   _____

   _____

4. Do you feel satisfied with the events listed for the future?

   _____

   _____

   _____

5. What is your opinion of your critical events line?

   _____

   _____

   _____

   _____

   _____

Money as a Motivator

Introduction

To understand the importance of the administration of compensation and the role that money plays in motivation, read the following situation and then complete the required actions.

You are the manager of a computer programming department for a medium-sized aerospace firm. You have only 10% ($16,400) of your current total salary pool ($164,000) to give as raises for next year. You have three female and five male subordinates. Four of your eight subordinates are senior people with five or more years of experience, and four are junior people with three or fewer years of experience. Trying to allocate the raise money presents a lot of problems. You are afraid that you might lose some of the people if you don't give them a big enough raise. And you do not want to demotivate anybody by not providing rewards. You also have two minorities, a Spanish female and a black male. Minorities could get more in the job market than whites, so perhaps you should give them more . . . or maybe you should give more just to women. After all, women are more in demand in these positions than men. You also have considered the possibility that there are already some inequities. You think, "Well, all of this unorganized thinking is getting me nowhere; I'll make a list of the people and the relevant factors":

Christina Colby. Age twenty-eight. Systems Analyst. Six years with the company. Married. Husband has a good job. Two kids, both preschoolers. Better than average performance appraisal — a 92% score. Not likely to leave the company. We fit her hours around her family needs. *Current salary: $28,000.*

Frances Sanchez. Age twenty-two. Junior Programmer. One year with the company. Single. Supports her mother and lives with her. Attending school at night to finish her degree. Average performance appraisal — an 80% score. Lots of potential, but does not seem to like her work. Might leave. We let her leave work a little early to get to school on time. *Current salary: $21,500.*

Betty Lou Morrison. Age twenty-three. Programmer. Two years with the company. Married, but marriage is shaky. No kids. She and her husband spend money like it's going out of style. Superior performance

Source: *James M. Higgins*, A Manual of Student Activities in Human Relations: Cases, Exercises, and Readings *(New York: Random House, Inc., 1982)*, 36–37. *Reprinted with permission.*

appraisal — a 96% score, but not much potential for advancement into management, and no expressed interest in a systems position. Very likely to leave if raise is not big enough. *Current salary: $22,500.*

Whatley Waltersheid. Age thirty-one. Senior Systems Analyst. Eight years with the company. Married. Wife works as a legal secretary, makes good money. Three kids. No personal problems. Better than average performance appraisal — a 91% score. Will probably get my job when and if I move up. Not likely to leave. *Current salary: $32,000.*

Budd Kescenza. Age twenty-seven. Systems Analyst. Five years with the company. Single. Spends his money quickly; also moonlights. Likes to party. Better than average performance appraisal — a 90% score. Doesn't seem to like it here. Likely to leave if pay raise not sufficient. *Current salary: $30,000.*

Jeffrey Nord. Age twenty-five. Programmer. Five years with the company. Single. Shy, very immature, and not aggressive. Wonder how he ever got to be a programmer. Below-average performance appraisal, but had been average up to this time. Counseled with him, but so far little change in behavior. Might be on drugs. Wouldn't care if he did leave. *Current salary: $25,000.*

Michael Washington. Age twenty-one. Junior Programmer. One year with the company. Black. Single. Very studious, goes to night school. Better than average performance appraisal — a 91% score. Could leave and probably would if offered a big raise somewhere else. Needs money. *Current salary: $22,500.*

Pete Peterson. Age twenty-two. Junior Programmer. Nine months with the company. Married. Two little kids, wife quit work because third child is on the way. A little better than average performance appraisal — an 85% score. A hard worker, also moonlights. Would definitely leave the company if he doesn't get a good raise. *Current salary: $21,500.*

How much of a raise would you give each of the above and why?

1. Christina Colby:

   _____

   _____

   _____

2. Frances Sanchez:

   _____

   _____

   _____

3. Betty Lou Morrison:

   _____

   _____

   _____

4. Whatley Waltersheid:

_____

_____

_____

5. Budd Kescenza:

_____

_____

_____

6. Jeffrey Nord:

_____

_____

_____

7. Michael Washington:

_____

_____

_____

8. Pete Peterson:

_____

_____

_____

Personal and Interpersonal Growth

Introduction

There are seven points to remember about personal and interpersonal growth:

1. Growth is improvement in attitudes and behaviors that are related to self-concept.

2. Growth is not always possible in all areas of life. Heredity or strong environmental forces may prevent even desirable changes.

3. Habits, attitudes, and opinions may deter growth because they reduce receptiveness to alternative ways of thinking and acting.

4. Defensive behavior may interfere with growth by distorting reality.

5. Growth is accelerated by openness, receptivity to new experience, curiosity, eagerness to learn, and lack of fear.

6. Because of the complexity of who we are, the varying degrees of self-understanding, and the difference in levels and kinds of aspirations we have, each person is unique in the need for, and experience of, growth.

7. Generally, we have more ability and potential for personal and interpersonal growth than we realize.

The following is a two-part inventory designed to help you maximize personal and interpersonal growth. The inventory may be used alone, with another person, or in a group. This is an instrument for learning and is not a test.

Directions

Read each item and place a "P" on the scale at the position that best describes your opinion of yourself at present. You may see yourself as encompassing a segment of the scale. If so, draw a circle around that part

Source: *Jacque Huber, Southwestern Ohio Steel Company, 1976. Based on the work of Michael G. Blansfield and Gordon L. Lippitt.*

of the scale and label the whole area "P." Do the same for each item indicating your goals for the future. Mark this point with an "F" (P = present, F = future). After completing all of the items, go back and put a check next to the three or four that you would most like to improve. Next, depending on the situation, you may want to have another person evaluate you on the "opinion of others" scale, and then discuss both evaluations.

Example

ABILITY TO LISTEN IN AN UNDERSTANDING WAY

						(P)		(F)		
0	1	2	3	4	5	6	7	8	9	(personal opinion)

Very low   Very high

0	1	2	3	4	5	6	7	8	9	(opinion of others)

Part I

Personal Growth Items

1. SELF-UNDERSTANDING

0	1	2	3	4	5	6	7	8	9	(personal opinion)

There are things about   I know myself completely.
myself I do not understand.

0	1	2	3	4	5	6	7	8	9	(opinion of others)

2. SELF-CONCEPT

0	1	2	3	4	5	6	7	8	9	(personal opinion)

There are many things I do   I like myself the way I am.
not like about myself.

0	1	2	3	4	5	6	7	8	9	(opinion of others)

3. SELF-CONFIDENCE

0	1	2	3	4	5	6	7	8	9	(personal opinion)

I lack self-confidence.   I am not afraid of failure.

0	1	2	3	4	5	6	7	8	9	(opinion of others)

4. PEACE OF MIND

| 0 | 1 | 2 | 3 | 4 | 5 | 6 | 7 | 8 | 9 | (personal opinion) |

I am restless and dissatisfied.   I am at peace with myself and the world.

| 0 | 1 | 2 | 3 | 4 | 5 | 6 | 7 | 8 | 9 | (opinion of others) |

5. OUTLOOK ON LIFE

| 0 | 1 | 2 | 3 | 4 | 5 | 6 | 7 | 8 | 9 | (personal opinion) |

I am pessimistic.   I am optimistic.

| 0 | 1 | 2 | 3 | 4 | 5 | 6 | 7 | 8 | 9 | (opinion of others) |

6. INDEPENDENT THINKING

| 0 | 1 | 2 | 3 | 4 | 5 | 6 | 7 | 8 | 9 | (personal opinion) |

I let others think for me.   I always think for myself.

| 0 | 1 | 2 | 3 | 4 | 5 | 6 | 7 | 8 | 9 | (opinion of others) |

7. INTEREST IN LEARNING

| 0 | 1 | 2 | 3 | 4 | 5 | 6 | 7 | 8 | 9 | (personal opinion) |

I have learned enough.   I want to learn new things.

| 0 | 1 | 2 | 3 | 4 | 5 | 6 | 7 | 8 | 9 | (opinion of others) |

8. HUMOR

| 0 | 1 | 2 | 3 | 4 | 5 | 6 | 7 | 8 | 9 | (personal opinion) |

I rarely laugh.   I often laugh.

| 0 | 1 | 2 | 3 | 4 | 5 | 6 | 7 | 8 | 9 | (opinion of others) |

9. SENSE OF ETHICS

| 0 | 1 | 2 | 3 | 4 | 5 | 6 | 7 | 8 | 9 | (personal opinion) |

I have trouble understanding or doing what is right.   I have a definite sense of ethics by which I live.

| 0 | 1 | 2 | 3 | 4 | 5 | 6 | 7 | 8 | 9 | (opinion of others) |

10. PERSONAL MOTIVATION

| 0 | 1 | 2 | 3 | 4 | 5 | 6 | 7 | 8 | 9 | (personal opinion) |

I have trouble motivating myself. I am a highly motivated person.

| 0 | 1 | 2 | 3 | 4 | 5 | 6 | 7 | 8 | 9 | (opinion of others) |

11. AWARENESS

| 0 | 1 | 2 | 3 | 4 | 5 | 6 | 7 | 8 | 9 | (personal opinion) |

I often miss what is going on. I am always sensitive to what is happening around me.

| 0 | 1 | 2 | 3 | 4 | 5 | 6 | 7 | 8 | 9 | (opinion of others) |

12. PROBLEM-SOLVING ABILITY

| 0 | 1 | 2 | 3 | 4 | 5 | 6 | 7 | 8 | 9 | (personal opinion) |

I am not good at solving problems. I am good at solving almost any problem.

| 0 | 1 | 2 | 3 | 4 | 5 | 6 | 7 | 8 | 9 | (opinion of others) |

13. PHYSICAL HEALTH

| 0 | 1 | 2 | 3 | 4 | 5 | 6 | 7 | 8 | 9 | (personal opinion) |

I tire easily or I am often ill. I am strong and healthy.

| 0 | 1 | 2 | 3 | 4 | 5 | 6 | 7 | 8 | 9 | (opinion of others) |

14. VANITY

| 0 | 1 | 2 | 3 | 4 | 5 | 6 | 7 | 8 | 9 | (personal opinion) |

I think too highly of myself. I am realistic in my self-evaluation.

| 0 | 1 | 2 | 3 | 4 | 5 | 6 | 7 | 8 | 9 | (opinion of others) |

Part II

Interpersonal Growth Items

1. KNOWLEDGE OF HUMAN BEHAVIOR

| 0 | 1 | 2 | 3 | 4 | 5 | 6 | 7 | 8 | 9 | (personal opinion) |

I have difficulty understand-ing people.   I understand why people do what they do.

| 0 | 1 | 2 | 3 | 4 | 5 | 6 | 7 | 8 | 9 | (opinion of others) |

2. KINDNESS

| 0 | 1 | 2 | 3 | 4 | 5 | 6 | 7 | 8 | 9 | (personal opinion) |

I am not always kind.   I am always kind.

| 0 | 1 | 2 | 3 | 4 | 5 | 6 | 7 | 8 | 9 | (opinion of others) |

3. SHARING

| 0 | 1 | 2 | 3 | 4 | 5 | 6 | 7 | 8 | 9 | (personal opinion) |

I am selfish.   I am generous.

| 0 | 1 | 2 | 3 | 4 | 5 | 6 | 7 | 8 | 9 | (opinion of others) |

4. TOLERANCE

| 0 | 1 | 2 | 3 | 4 | 5 | 6 | 7 | 8 | 9 | (personal opinion) |

My level of tolerance harms my dealings with people.   My level of tolerance helps me deal with people.

| 0 | 1 | 2 | 3 | 4 | 5 | 6 | 7 | 8 | 9 | (opinion of others) |

5. HELPFULNESS

| 0 | 1 | 2 | 3 | 4 | 5 | 6 | 7 | 8 | 9 | (personal opinion) |

I let others take care of themselves.   I lend a helping hand.

| 0 | 1 | 2 | 3 | 4 | 5 | 6 | 7 | 8 | 9 | (opinion of others) |

6. TRUSTWORTHINESS

| 0 | 1 | 2 | 3 | 4 | 5 | 6 | 7 | 8 | 9 | (personal opinion) |

I am not dependable.　　　　　　　I am dependable.

| 0 | 1 | 2 | 3 | 4 | 5 | 6 | 7 | 8 | 9 | (opinion of others) |

7. CONCERN FOR OTHERS

| 0 | 1 | 2 | 3 | 4 | 5 | 6 | 7 | 8 | 9 | (personal opinion) |

I have trouble controlling
jealousy.

I am happy for the good
fortune of others.

| 0 | 1 | 2 | 3 | 4 | 5 | 6 | 7 | 8 | 9 | (opinion of others) |

8. SENSITIVITY

| 0 | 1 | 2 | 3 | 4 | 5 | 6 | 7 | 8 | 9 | (personal opinion) |

I am insensitive to the
feelings of others.

I am sensitive to the feelings
of others.

| 0 | 1 | 2 | 3 | 4 | 5 | 6 | 7 | 8 | 9 | (opinion of others) |

9. GIVING FRIENDSHIP

| 0 | 1 | 2 | 3 | 4 | 5 | 6 | 7 | 8 | 9 | (personal opinion) |

I am aloof.　　　　　　　　I am affectionate.

| 0 | 1 | 2 | 3 | 4 | 5 | 6 | 7 | 8 | 9 | (opinion of others) |

10. ACCEPTING AFFECTION

| 0 | 1 | 2 | 3 | 4 | 5 | 6 | 7 | 8 | 9 | (personal opinion) |

Receiving affection makes
me uneasy.

I value all the affection I
can get.

| 0 | 1 | 2 | 3 | 4 | 5 | 6 | 7 | 8 | 9 | (opinion of others) |

11. EXPRESSING ANGER

| 0 | 1 | 2 | 3 | 4 | 5 | 6 | 7 | 8 | 9 | (personal opinion) |

When I am angry, I usually
worsen the situation.

I express anger in a con-
structive way.

12. RECEIVING HOSTILITY

```
0   1   2   3   4   5   6   7   8   9        (personal opinion)
```
It immobilizes me.   I can think clearly.

```
0   1   2   3   4   5   6   7   8   9        (opinion of others)
```

13. CLARITY IN EXPRESSING THOUGHTS

```
0   1   2   3   4   5   6   7   8   9        (personal opinion)
```
I am vague and have   I am clear and communicate
trouble saying what I want   what I want to say.
to say.

```
0   1   2   3   4   5   6   7   8   9        (opinion of others)
```

14. ABILITY TO LISTEN IN AN UNDERSTANDING WAY

```
0   1   2   3   4   5   6   7   8   9        (personal opinion)
```
My mind wanders when   I am a good listener.
others are talking.

```
0   1   2   3   4   5   6   7   8   9        (opinion of others)
```

15. REACTION TO COMMENTS ABOUT MY BEHAVIOR

```
0   1   2   3   4   5   6   7   8   9        (personal opinion)
```
What other people think   I consider other people's
upsets me.   opinions without letting
                               them upset me.

```
0   1   2   3   4   5   6   7   8   9        (opinion of others)
```

Scoring and Discussion

Add up your total score for all personal and interpersonal growth items. You should know that a score of 200 or above shows generally high personal and interpersonal effectiveness. As you reflect on those items you chose as targets for growth, you should consider the factors that support the achievement of your goals and those that may block achievement. List these in the following spaces.

Factors That Support You
In Your Growth Goals

Factors in self: _____

_____

_____

Factors in others: _____

_____

_____

Factors in the work situation: _____

_____

_____

Factors That May Block You
In Your Growth Goals

Factors in self: _____

_____

_____

Factors in others: _____

_____

_____

Factors in the work situation: _____

_____

_____

Consider what you can do to reduce the blocking forces in your life and to encourage the supporting forces. Establish a plan to improve, and set realistic behavior and time targets. Implement your improvement plan, and record results. Reinforce the progress you make through meaningful intrinsic and extrinsic rewards. These steps will allow you to realize your potential for personal and interpersonal growth.

APPENDIX A

Background Information, Teaching Suggestions, and Testing and Grading

The Human Side of Work is a series of desk books for managers, handbooks for practitioners, and workbooks for students. These are applied books that combine behavior theory with business practice. Each book teaches central concepts and skills in an important area of the world of work. The set of eight books includes stress management, communication skills, employee motivation, leadership principles, quality of work life, managing for excellence, employee participation, and the role of ethics.

Each book combines theory with practice, gives commonsense answers to real-life problems, and is easy to read and fun to use. The series may be used as a set or as stand-alone books. The subject areas are made more forceful and the impact greater by the self-evaluation questionnaires and practical exercises that are used for personal development.

AUDIENCE

The Human Side of Work is written for two audiences. One audience includes managers and professionals interested in personal and professional development on their own or within the context of a management development program. Another audience includes students in human relations, organization behavior, and other management-related courses.

The material is appropriate for use at the four-year college and university level as well as in community colleges, proprietary schools, extension programs, and management training seminars.

CONTENT AND STYLE

The difference between most organization behavior texts and *The Human Side of Work* can be compared to the difference between a lecture and a seminar. Although both are good educational vehicles, the lecture is better for conveying large amounts of information, while the seminar is better for developing skills. The good lecture is interesting and builds knowledge; the good seminar is stimulating and builds competency. *The Human Side of Work* emphasizes the interactive, seminar approach to learning.

The writing style is personal and conversational, with minimal professional jargon. True-life examples clarify points under consideration. Concepts are supported by stories and anecdotes, which are more meaningful and easy to remember than facts, figures, and lists. Each book includes learning activities to bridge the gap between classroom theory and on-the-job practice.

The Human Side of Work is more than a series of textbooks. These are "learning" books that actively involve the reader in the learning process. Our goal has been to include material that is interesting to read, relates to the reader's own concerns, and is practical to use. The following captures the spirit of our effort:

I Taught Them All

I have taught in high school for ten years. During that time, I have given assignments, among others, to a murderer, an evangelist, a pugilist, a thief, and an imbecile.

The murderer was a quiet little boy who sat on the front seat and regarded me with pale blue eyes; the evangelist, easily the most popular boy in school, had the lead in the junior class play; the pugilist lounged by the window and let loose at intervals with a raucous laugh that startled even the geraniums; the thief was a gay-hearted Lothario with a song on his lips; and the imbecile, a soft-eyed little animal seeking the shadows.

The murderer awaits death in the state penitentiary; the evangelist has lain a year in the village churchyard; the pugilist lost an eye in a brawl in Hong Kong; the thief, by standing on tiptoe, can see the windows of my room from the county jail; and the once gentle-eyed little moron beats his head against a padded wall in the state asylum.

All of these young men once sat in my room, sat and looked at me gravely across worn brown desks. I must have been a great help to those pupils — I taught them the rhyming scheme of the Elizabethan sonnet and how to diagram a complex sentence.

Naomi John White

The focus of *The Human Side of Work* is self-discovery and personal development as the reader "learns by doing." The material covered is authoritative and up to date, reflecting current theory and practices. The level of material is appropriate for all levels of expertise (new and experienced managers) and all levels of education (undergraduate and graduate).

TESTING AND REVIEW PROCESS

The Human Side of Work has been tested and refined in our classes at Northern Kentucky University. The information and activities have been used with hundreds of organizations and thousands of employees in business, industry, and government. Users include American Telephone and Telegraph Co., International Business Machines Corp., John Hancock, Marriott Corporation, Sun Oil, and Ford Motor Co. in the private sector and the Department of Transportation, the Environmental Protection Agency, the Internal Revenue Service, the National Institutes of

Health, and state governments in the public sector.

The following are sample evaluations:

> Good for student participation. My students like the exercises and learning instruments, and the fact each is a stand-alone book that is bite-size. Their reaction: "Everyone should read them!"
>
> *Joseph F. Ohren, Eastern Michigan University*

> A comprehensive series dealing with employee development and job performance. Information is presented in an interesting and easy-to-use style. Case studies and readings help teach the topics, and applications make the material more meaningful. It is an excellent guide for the practicing manager. Ideal as desk books.
>
> *David Duncan, IBM*

> I am a non-traditional student. As one who has worked for over twenty years, I thoroughly enjoyed the material. An understanding of the world of work is presented in a way that is usable at any level of an organization. The books present a common sense approach to management.
>
> *Naomi Miller, Northern Kentucky University*

> Best I've seen on the people side of work. Helps the person. Helps the company. Good for personal and management development. Popular with participants from all backgrounds.
>
> *Charles Apple, University of Michigan*

> This is an easy-to-read, comprehensive series in organization behavior. It puts theory into relevant, usable terminology. Methods for identifying and solving human relations problems are pinpointed. It sets the stage for understanding how people, environment and situations interact in an organization.
>
> *David Sprouse, AT&T*

TEACHING FORMATS

The Human Side of Work is versatile and can be used in many formats:

- for seminars and training programs
- as classroom texts
- as supplemental information and activities

The following is a discussion of each option.

Seminars and Training Programs

Books used for seminars and training programs should be selected to meet the objectives and needs of the participants — communication, stress, leadership, etc. Material can be mixed and matched for training programs in personal development, professional development, management development, and team building. Material in each book is appropriate for a variety of time periods: one-half day (3 to 4 hours), one full day (6 to 8 hours), and two full days (12 to 16 hours).

The books provide excellent learning activities and questionnaires to encourage participation and personalize the subject. Books then serve as "take-home" material for further reading and personal development. In this format, study quizzes are rarely used for grading, and homework assignments are seldom given. See the following table for appropriate audiences, program focus, and recommended books when using *The Human Side of Work* for seminars and training programs.

Classroom Texts

The series is appropriate for use as texts in college courses in human relations, organization behavior, and organizational psychology. The following is a sample lesson plan using the set for a one-semester course:

Week	Focus on the Person	
1	Stress	Part One, Part Two
2	Stress	Part Three, Part Four
3	Communication	Part One, Part Two
4	Communication	Part Three, Part Four
5	Human Behavior	Part One, Part Two
6	Human Behavior	Part Three
7	Ethics	Part One, Part Two
8	Ethics	Part Three, Part Four

	Focus on the Organization	
9	Morale	Part One, Part Two
10	Morale	Part Three
11	Leadership	Part One, Part Two
12	Leadership	Part Three, Part Four

USING THE HUMAN SIDE OF WORK FOR SEMINARS AND TRAINING PROGRAMS

Appropriate Audiences	Program Focus	Recommended Books
Personal and professional development	Focus on the individual	* Stress Without Distress: Rx for Burnout * Communication: The Miracle of Dialogue * Human Behavior: Why People Do What They Do * Ethics at Work: Fire in a Dark World * Morale: Quality of Work Life (optional) * Performance: Managing for Excellence (optional)
New and experienced managers	Focus on management	* Morale: Quality of Work Life * Leadership: Nine Keys to Success * Performance: Managing for Excellence * Groupstrength: Quality Circles at Work * Stress Without Distress: Rx for Burnout (optional) * Communication: The Miracle of Dialogue (optional) * Human Behavior: Why People Do What They Do (optional) * Ethics at Work: Fire in a Dark World (optional)
Employee development and team building	Focus on the organization	* Communication: The Miracle of Dialogue * Morale: Quality of Work Life * Groupstrength: Quality Circles at Work * Stress Without Distress: Rx for Burnout (optional) * Human Behavior: Why People Do What They Do (optional) * Performance: Managing for Excellence (optional)

Popular seminar and program titles with corresponding books are as follows:

Managing Change: Personal and Professional Coping Skills	* Stress Without Distress: Rx for Burnout
Communication: One to One; One to Many	* Communication: The Miracle of Dialogue
Human Relations and the Nature of Man	* Human Behavior: Why People Do What They Do
Business Ethics and Corporate Culture	* Ethics at Work: Fire in a Dark World
Quality of Work Life	* Morale: Quality of Work Life
The Human Side of Management	* Leadership: Nine Keys to Success
Managing for Productivity: People Building Skills	* Performance: Managing for Excellence
Employee Involvement: If Japan Can Do It, Why Can't We?	* Groupstrength: Quality Circles at Work

13	Performance	Part One, Part Two
14	Performance	Part Three
15	Groupstrength	Part One, Part Two
16	Groupstrength	Part Three

Related Activities and Homework Assignments

Week	Suggested Readings, Cases and Applications
1	*Anatomy of an Illness as Perceived by the Patient* (reading) *The Price of Success* (case)
2	*Death of a Salesman* (reading) *Scientific Relaxation* (application)
3	*Barriers and Gateways to Communications* (reading) *The Power of Vocabulary* (application)
4	*The Dyadic Encounter* (application) *Attitudes toward Women Working* (application)
5	*The Human Side of Enterprise* (reading) *Significant People and Critical Events* (application)
6	*Values Auction* (application) *Personal and Interpersonal Growth* (application)
7	*If Hitler Asked You to Electrocute a Stranger, Would You?* (reading) *How Could the Jonestown Holocaust Have Occurred?* (reading)
8	*Values Flag* (application) *The Kidney Machine* (application)
9	*Work* (reading) *The Joe Bailey Problem* (application)
10	*The Coffee Break* (case) *In Search of Excellence* (application)
11	*What Happened When I Gave Up the Good Life and Became President* (case) *Black, Blue, and White* (case)
12	*The Forklift Fiasco* (case) *Train the Trainers* (application)
13	*Games Mother Never Taught You* (reading) *How Will You Spend Your Life?* (application)

14	*How to Manage Your Time: Everybody's No. 1 Problem* (reading)
	Chrysler's Turnaround Strategy (case)
15	*Groupthink* (reading)
	The Dean Practices Participative Management (case)
16	*Decisions, Decisions, Decisions* (reading)
	The Bottleneck (application)

This format for a one-semester course uses selected readings, cases, and applications from all eight books. For a two-semester course, additional readings, cases, and applications are provided.

Another popular format is to use fewer books in a one-semester course, and to use these more thoroughly. The books can be selected by the instructor or the class. For example, stress, communication, morale, and leadership may be best suited for a given group.

Testing and Grading

When using *The Human Side of Work* as classroom texts, study quizzes in each book can be used to evaluate content knowledge. Although quiz scores can be used to assign formal grades, students learn best when they are also asked to apply the concepts in some personal way. Examples include a term journal, a related research paper, a small-group project, a field assignment, and/or a self-improvement project.

Grades can be assigned on the basis of test scores and term project(s). Projects can be evaluated according to the three C's: clarity, comprehensiveness, and correctness. Half the course grade could be based on study quiz scores, and the other half on the term project(s).

Supplemental Information and Activities

The books in *The Human Side of Work* can provide supplemental information and activities for various college courses. State-of-the-art questionnaires and user-friendly exercises add variety and increase student involvement. Books matched with appropriate college courses are as follows:

Recommended Books	College Courses
Stress Without Distress: Rx for Burnout	Personal Development
	Personal Health
	Human Relations
	Organization Behavior
	Organizational Psychology
	Supervisory Development

Communication: The Miracle of Dialogue	Personal Development Communications Human Relations Organization Behavior Organizational Psychology Supervisory Development
Human Behavior: Why People Do What They Do	Personal Development Human Relations Organization Behavior Organizational Psychology Supervisory Development
Ethics at Work: Fire in a Dark World	Personal Development Business Ethics Human Relations Organization Behavior Organizational Psychology Supervisory Development
Morale: Quality of Work Life	Personnel/Human Resources Human Relations Organization Behavior Organizational Psychology Supervisory Development
Leadership: Nine Keys to Success	Management Principles Human Relations Organization Behavior Organizational Psychology Supervisory Development
Performance: Managing for Excellence	Management Principles Human Relations Organization Behavior Organizational Psychology Supervisory Development
Groupstrength: Quality Circles at Work	Personnel/Human Resources Human Relations Organization Behavior Organizational Psychology Supervisory Development

When used as supplemental material, books are rarely tested for grades. The emphasis is on using the questionnaires, exercises, cases, and applications to increase interest and participation and to personalize the subject.

APPENDIX B

Additional References

ADDITIONAL REFERENCES

The following books are recommended for further reading in the areas of motivation, values, and personality. Each is included because of its significance in the field, support to this text, and value for further personal development.

Bloom, Benjamin S., et al., eds. *Taxonomy of Educational Objectives Handbook. Vol. I: Cognitive Domain.* New York: McKay, 1956.

Coleman, James C. *Abnormal Psychology and Modern Life.* 5th ed. Glenview, Ill.: Scott, Foresman & Company, 1976.

Coleman, James C. *Contemporary Psychology and Effective Behavior.* Glenview, Ill.: Scott, Foresman & Company, 1978.

Coon, Dennis L. *Introduction to Psychology: Exploration and Application.* 4th ed. St. Paul, Minn.: West Publishing Co., Inc., 1986.

Kesey, Ken. *One Flew Over the Cuckoo's Nest.* New York: The Viking Press, 1973.

Levinson, Daniel J. *The Seasons of a Man's Life.* New York: Alfred A. Knopf, Inc., 1978.

Maslow, A.H. *Motivation and Personality.* New York: Harper & Row, Publishers, Inc., 1970.

Maslow, A.H. *The Farther Reaches of Human Nature.* New York: The Viking Press, 1971.

Massey, Morris E. *The People Puzzle.* Reston, Va.: Reston Publishing Co., 1979.

McGregor, Douglas. *The Human Side of Enterprise.* New York: McGraw-Hill, Inc., 1960.

Menninger, Karl. *Human Mind.* Rev. ed. New York: Alfred A. Knopf, Inc., 1945.

Menninger, Karl. *Man Against Himself.* New York: Harcourt Brace Jovanovich, Inc., 1956.

Raven, Bertram H., and Jeffery Z. Rubin. *People in Groups.* Toronto, Canada: John Wiley & Sons, Inc., 1976.

Rogers, Carl R. *On Becoming a Person: A Therapist's View of Psychotherapy.* Boston: Houghton Mifflin Company, 1961.

Rubin, Zick, and Elton B. McNeil. *Psychology: Being Human*, 4th ed. New York: Harper & Row, Publishers, Inc., 1985.

Sheehy, Gail. *Passages*. New York: E.P. Dutton, Inc., 1976.

Skinner, B.F. *Walden Two*. New York: Macmillan, Inc., 1971.

Spranger, Eduard. *Types of Men: The Psychology and Ethics of Personality*. New York: Johnson Reprint, 1966.

Steiner, Gary A., and B. Berelson. *Human Behavior: An Inventory of Scientific Findings*. New York: Harcourt, Brace & World, 1964.

Thomas, Lewis. *Lives of a Cell: Notes of a Biology Watcher*. New York: The Viking Press, 1974.

White, Robert W. *Lives in Progress: A Study of the Natural Growth of Personality*. New York: The Dryden Press, 1952.

Yankelovich, Daniel. *The New Morality*. New York: McGraw-Hill, Inc., 1974.

APPENDIX C
Suggested Films

The following films are excellent learning aids. These are supplementary media that can enrich a class or training program. They are ideal for small-group discussion, panel debates, and question-and-answer periods. Topics are listed in the order in which they appear in the text.

THE HIDDEN UNIVERSE: THE BRAIN
(CRM. Part I, 23 min.; Part II, 25 min.)

This film provides an overview of brain function; includes operating room scenes, "split brain" research, implants, and brain malfunctions. Award winner.

CRM Educational Films
Del Mar, California 92014

LEARNING
(CRM, 30 min.)

This entertaining, excellent film explores a variety of learning phenomena.

CRM Educational Films
Del Mar, California 92014

MASLOW'S HIERARCHY OF NEEDS
(Salenger, 16 min.)

What motivates people? What makes them do the things they do? This film presents Maslow's "hierarchy of needs" theory and indicates its relevance to supervisors and managers.

Salenger Educational Media
1635 12th Street
Santa Monica, California 90404

MASLOW AND SELF-ACTUALIZATION
(Psychological Films. Parts I and II, 30 min. each)

Maslow discusses themes of honesty and awareness in Part I and freedom and trust in Part II.

Psychological Films
205 West 20th Street
Santa Ana, California 92706

THE SELF-MOTIVATED ACHIEVER
(BNA, 28 min.)

David C. McClelland, authority on the "achievement motive," believes that although most people have some degree of achievement motivation, not more than 10% of the U.S. population is highly motivated. A dramatized sequence contrasts a highly successful salesman with a less successful one, pointing out the qualities of the self-motivated achiever. A second dramatic vignette illustrates the problem of a sales manager who must select between a self-motivated achiever and a less successful salesman to succeed him as manager.

BNA Films
5615 Fishers Lane
Rockville, Maryland 20852

MOTIVATION THROUGH JOB ENRICHMENT
(BNA, 28 min.)

Frederick Herzberg discusses his "motivation hygiene" theory, offering management a new strategy to increase employee productivity. The "hygiene" factors — good pay, security, friendly supervision — do not necessarily overcome apathy and minimum effort. At best, they only keep employees from complaining — they do not make them want to work more efficiently. Job enrichment — the enlargement of a job's responsibility, scope, and challenge — is an impressive, tested technique that can aid materially in "turning people on," in building true motivation.

BNA Films
5615 Fishers Lane
Rockville, Maryland 20852

EYE OF THE BEHOLDER
(USC, 29 min.)

This is a classic in the area of psychology, showing that the truth is often "in the eye of the beholder." Perennially popular.

University of South Carolina Film Library
Constructional Service Center
Columbia, South Carolina 29208

WHAT YOU ARE IS WHERE YOU WERE WHEN
(CBS/Fox Video, 90 min.)

Morris Massey's unique theory of human behavior. How values, prejudices, and ways of reacting to change are "programmed" into different age groups. Massey explains the programming periods people go through from an early age and the influences that guide adult behavior. He points out that only a "significant emotional event" will alter basic values. Our nation's attitudes and outlook for the future are determined by the values of the existing population. Understanding how people deal with differences allows us to form more effective relationships. Award-winning film. Highest rating.

CBS/Fox Video
Management Products
23705 Industrial Park Drive
Farmington Hills, Michigan 48024

THE HUMANISTIC REVOLUTION: PIONEERS IN PERSPECTIVE
(Psychological Films, 32 min.)

This film begins with an interview with Abraham Maslow on self-actualization. Interviews then follow with other pioneers in the field: Gardner Murphy, Carl Rogers, Rollo May, Paul Tillich, Fritz Perls, Viktor Frankl, and Alan Watts.

Psychological Films
105 West 20th Street
Santa Ana, California 92706

FREUD: THE HIDDEN NATURE OF MAN
(University of Illinois, 29 min.)

Freud's theories are discussed and placed in perspective, and his biography is presented.

University of Illinois
Visual Aids Service
Division of University Extension
Champaign, Illinois 61820

DEPRESSION: A STUDY OF ABNORMAL BEHAVIOR
(CRM, 26 min.)

Depression, the primary subject matter of the film, is offered as a model to aid in the understanding of all abnormal behavior. This orientation permits some discussion of how to define abnormality and also how various theories view depression as a specific example of abnormal function.

CRM Educational Films
Del Mar, California 92014

PROFESSOR ERIK ERIKSON
(AIM. Parts I and II, 50 min. each)

In Part I, Erikson discusses his eight-stage theory of psychosocial development. In Part II, he discusses such concepts as ego, identity crisis, libido theory, and existentialism.

Associated Instructional Materials (AIM)
600 Madison Avenue
New York, New York 10022

ROCK-A-BYE BABY
(Time-Life, 30 min.)

Shows the work of Spitz and others on the effects of early deprivation on infant development. Award winner.

Time-Life Films
43 West 16th Street
New York, New York 10011

ADOLESCENCE: THE WINDS OF CHANGE
(Harper & Row, 30 min.)

The physical, sexual, and cognitive changes in adolescence are discussed, as are the effects of parental attitudes and the pressures of our rapidly changing world.

Harper & Row Media
Order Fulfillment/Customer Service
2350 Virginia Avenue
Hagerstown, Maryland 21740

MEN'S LIVES
(New Day Films, 43 min.)

An excellent film about growing up male in America. Topics include sex role development, aggression, and occupational adjustment. Award winner.

New Day Films
P.O. Box 315
Franklin Lakes, New Jersey 07417

GROWING UP FEMALE: AS SIX
BECOME ONE
(New Day Films, 50 min.)

Focuses on the socialization processes that influence six women and girls, aged four to thirty-five.

New Day Films
P.O. Box 315
Franklin Lakes, New Jersey 07417

I'M A FOOL
(Perspective, 38 min.)

A young man's job, his relationships with his co-workers, and his desire to impress those around him mark his passage to adulthood. In this film, Ron Howard plays Andy, a "swipe" doing manual labor on the Ohio racetrack circuit in the early 1900's. When Andy meets a beautiful young woman at the track, he tries to impress her by exaggerating his position in life. When the girl reveals her fondness of him, Andy is trapped — afraid to win her with the truth. Award winner. Highest rating.

Perspective Films
108 Wilmot Road
Deerfield, Illinois 60015

STICKY MY FINGERS, FLEET MY FEET
(Time-Life, 35 min.)

Examines with pathos and humor one of the classic American stereotypes: the middle-aged male who clings to a youthful standard of physical prowess and he-man virility. In this case, the man's grip is slippery indeed. He is Norman, a fortyish executive (played by Gene Williams, whose New Yorker story was the basis of the film). Addicted to Sunday orgies of touch football, he is drawn to New York's Central Park like a Moslem to Mecca to engage in ritual combat with his huffing, puffing, flabby contemporaries. But their dreams of glory turn to dust when they patronizingly permit a 15-year-old boy to join their sport. His flashing performance leaves them dazed and a little older, wiser, and sadder. Recommended film.

Time-Life Films
43 West 16th Street
New York, New York 10011

AGING
(CRM, 22 min.)

Gerontologists generally agree that two major patterns of aging exist: the activity pattern and the disengagement pattern. There are a number of subdivisions and variations within these two large groups, and people's individual differences must be taken into consideration.

CRM Educational Films
Del Mar, California 92014

PEEGE
(FI, 28 min.)

A young man home for Christmas accompanies his family to visit his dying grandmother in a nursing home. Peege (the grandmother's nickname) has gone blind and has lost some mental acuity. The visit is awkward because no one in the family knows how to deal with the non-responsive shell that once was a vibrant woman.

When the visitors find an excuse to leave, the young man remains with his grandmother for a few minutes. He tries to trigger a response by whispering into Peege's ear some of his early memories of her. His efforts succeed, and he is able to communicate despite the barrier of disease and age. When he leaves, she is alone again . . . but reassured, perhaps, that someone still cares.

Focus International, Inc.
333 West 52nd Street
New York, New York 10019

ON DEATH AND DYING
(Films Incorporated, 58 min.)

Elisabeth Kubler-Ross discusses her experiences in working with terminally ill patients and outlines the stages of adjustment to impending death.

Films Incorporated
737 Green Bay Road
Wilmette, Illinois 68091

HARD CHOICES: DEATH, DYING, AND GRIEVING
(PBS, 30 min.)

This is a thought-provoking look at the issues and controversies surrounding death today. It is an objective and authoritative treatment of the subject. Award winning. Recommended.

PBS Video
475 L'Enfant Plaza, S.W.
Washington, D.C. 20024

APPENDIX D
Study Quiz Answers

STUDY QUIZ ANSWERS

Part One	Part Two	Part Three
1. a	1. a	1. a
2. b	2. d	2. b
3. d	3. a	3. a
4. b	4. c	4. b
5. a	5. b	5. b
6. b	6. a	6. a
7. c	7. a	7. a
8. d	8. a	8. b
9. d	9. d	9. b
10. b	10. a	10. c
11. a	11. b	11. d
12. a	12. d	12. b
13. c		13. c
14. d		14. b
15. a		15. c
16. a		16. a
17. b		17. d
18. a		18. d
19. a		19. a
20. c		20. c
		21. a
		22. d
		23. e
		24. c
		25. a
		26. b
		27. c
		28. a
		29. a
		30. c
		31. b
		32. d
		33. a

APPENDIX E

The Relationship of the Quiz Questions and the Discussion and Activities to the Part Objectives

The following chart shows the relationship of the quiz questions and the discussion and activities to the part objectives:

PART ONE

Objective Number	Quiz (Q), Discussion and Activities (D & A)
1	Q: 1, 7, 8 D & A: 1
2	Q: 2, 3, 4, 9, 10, 11, 12, 13, 18, 20 D & A: 2
3	Q: 5, 19 D & A: 4, 5
4	Q: 6, 14, 15, 16, 17 D & A: 3
5	Q: 14, 15, 16, 17 D & A: 3
6	Q: 2 D & A: 2, 3

PART TWO

Objective Number	Quiz (Q), Discussion and Activities (D & A)
1	Q: 4, 11, 12 D & A: 1, 5, 10
2	Q: 12 D & A: 2, 4, 7, 8
3	Q: 2, 5, 9 D & A: 2
4	Q: 1, 8 D & A: 3, 6
5	Q: 3, 12 D & A: 5, 7, 8

6	Q: 6, 10 D & A: 4, 7
7	Q: 10 D & A: 4, 7
8	Q: 6, 10 D & A: 4, 7
9	Q: 7, 8 D & A: 6
10	Q: 11 D & A: 5, 9

PART THREE

Objective Number	Quiz (Q), Discussion and Activities (D & A)
1	Q: 16, 19, 21, 30 D & A: 1, 8
2	Q: 17 D & A: 2, 9, 10
3	Q: 14, 20 D & A: 3, 11
4	Q: 15, 18, 21 D & A: 8
5	Q: 9, 25, 26, 27, 28 D & A: 7
6	Q: 29 D & A: 4, 12
7	Q: 4, 6, 10, 11, 12, 13, 22, 23 D & A: 5
8	Q: 4, 6, 10, 11, 12, 13, 22, 23 D & A: 5, 13
9	Q: 5, 33 D & A: 13
10	Q: 1, 2, 3, 7, 8, 29, 32 D & A: 6, 11, 14
11	Q: 1, 2, 3, 7, 8, 24, 32 D & A: 6, 14